"The Sixteenth Rail is a compelling r
ous crimes of the last century. Ada
forensics with a gripping tale of a U!
knowledge of wood to finger the su
crimes by the dozen every night, here is a true tale of a real, mild-
mannered guy and his amazing knowledge of all things wood. It is a
great story about the unpredictable relevancy of obscure knowledge."

—Kirk Johnson, Sant Director, Smithsonian
National Museum of Natural History

"Industry rightfully spends millions of dollars to stimulate innova-
tion. They should spend some of those millions distributing this
book. The modest Arthur Koehler was perhaps the greatest detective innovator of the 20th Century."

—Colorado Governor John Hickenlooper

"This exceptionally well written book is a must for anyone interested
in the Lindbergh Kidnapping and the history of forensic science.
Adam Schrager has done a masterful job by providing new information in what is perhaps the greatest forensic case in history."

—Paul Dowling, Creator and Executive Producer of *Forensic Files*

"A well-researched, well-written account of Arthur Koehler, the
wood expert who has been called "the father of forensics" and his
exacting study of the ladder in the Lindbergh baby kidnapping. *The
Sixteenth Rail* explains how forensic science began expansion into
new scientific realms beyond fingerprints and bullet markings. A
thoroughly engaging account of the times and the trial."

—Dr. Shirley Graham, Curator at the Missouri Botanical Garden

"A dedicated government employee of the U.S. Forest Service's Forest Products Laboratory, Arthur Koehler, uses keen forensic skills
with wood to help solve one of the 20th Century's greatest crimes.
The author masterfully depicts how Koehler, who knew that the
wood from trees never really dies, deploys the tenacity of a great
detective to make the ladder used in the kidnap of Charles Lindbergh's son eventually point to Bruno Hauptmann. The reader is
continually captivated by the incredible force and unflinching will
Arthur Koehler brings to his scientific craft to coax compelling

clues from the 'rails and styles' to help solve one of America's most horrific crimes."

"I have never read a book so well researched or with as much depth into the forensic issues of a criminal case. The background on Arthur Koehler, "Slim" Lindbergh, and the other characters made it such an enjoyable read - which is not typically the case when science is such a large factor in a book. For those of us who have a keen, or even passing, interest in criminal justice cases and particularly forensic science, *The Sixteenth Rail* is a must read. Arthur Koehler is now on my list of American heroes. I will want to get my hands on more copies to gift my fellow Police friends."

"*The Sixteenth Rail* is a riveting chronicle of the investigation and trial that dominated American public life for over two years in the early 1930s -- and the "xylotomist" ("expert on the identification of wood") at the center of that case, Arthur Koehler. In my 12 years as a federal prosecutor, I never encountered a witness remotely like Koehler; he combines unquestioned expertise, precision, and drama. Adam Schrager weaves a compelling tale of forensic science, criminal law, and American history. This incredible true story reads like a novel."

"As Arthur Koehler's granddaughter I grew up hearing his story and knew how it ended. Yet I raced through Mr. Schrager's suspenseful and perceptive book, eager to see how it all unfolded: the farm boy turned world-renowned forensic scientist, his meticulous investigations, and the dramatic courtroom testimony. Schrager's portrait feels true to the intelligent, conscientious, outdoors-loving man I knew-- and I even learned some surprising things about my own grandfather!"

The Sixteenth Rail

Rail

The Evidence,
the Scientist, and
the Lindbergh
Kidnapping

Adam J. Schrager

FULCRUM
GOLDEN, COLORADO

Library of Congress Cataloging-in-Publication Data
Schrager, Adam.
  Sixteenth rail : the evidence, the scientist, and the Lindbergh kidnapping / Adam Schrager.
    pages cm
  ISBN 978-1-55591-716-6
1. Lindbergh, Charles Augustus, 1930-1932--Kidnapping, 1932. 2. Koehler, Arthur. 3. Kidnapping--New Jersey--Hopewell. 4. Criminal investigation--United States--History--20th century. 5. Forensic sciences--United States--History--20th century. I. Title.
  HV6603.L5S37 2013
  364.15'4092--dc23
                      2013003985

Printed in the United States of America
0 9 8 7 6 5 4 3 2 1

Design by Jack Lenzo

Fulcrum Publishing
4690 Table Mountain Dr., Ste. 100
Golden, CO 80403
800-992-2908 • 303-277-1623
www.fulcrumbooks.com

To Harper, Clark, and Payton
The journey is the reward.

Contents

Prologue

My three older sisters, Julie, Sarina, and Abbey, would assert the roots of this project date back to my "G-man" fixation during the summer of 1977.

We were driving to the West Coast from the Chicago area, and my reading material for the trip included FBI tales of heroism and ingenuity. My fascination with crime fighting and J. Edgar Hoover was matched only by my love of the Chicago Cubs and outfielder José Cardenal.

Roughly six years earlier, a man known as D. B. Cooper hijacked a Northwest Orient Boeing 727 plane and parachuted out somewhere between Seattle and Portland with a $200,000 ransom. He was described as roughly six feet tall, in his mid-forties, and was last seen wearing a dark suit with a white shirt and black tie.

For the three weeks of our trip, every day—multiple times per hour, at times—this seven-year-old aspiring special agent implored his parents and sisters to call the police anytime we saw a man in a dark suit. The fact that in the five-plus years since the crime he had likely changed outfits at least once was clearly lost on me.

Because my sisters weren't interested in solving crimes, I occupied myself on that trip out west by reading. I distinctly remember learning about the kidnapping of Charles A. Lindbergh Jr. and how the subsequent investigation including forensic science sparked a modernizing of the FBI.

So some thirty-five years later, when a colleague of mine at Wisconsin Public Television mentioned to me that the ladder used in the Lindbergh kidnapping was here in Madison, at the US Forest Products Laboratory, I immediately picked up the phone to learn more.

It turned out the ladder at FPL was only a replica, but the story of Arthur Koehler, who once studied parts of the original ladder there and became, in the words of journalists, "the Sherlock Holmes of our era," was new to me.

In fact, Koehler knew far more about botany than Sherlock Holmes did, as I learned from Holmes expert Resa Haile in Janesville, Wisconsin. She provided me with detailed information about how the world's most famous detective fared in the world of botany. This project would not have gotten off the ground without the help of Rebecca Wallace and Julie Blankenburg at the Forest Products Lab. I greatly appreciate their efforts to find all things Koehler-related in the files there. Their colleague, Dr. Rick Green, challenged me from the get-go to ask questions, dig deeper, and probe further. I hope the efforts displayed here meet his high standards of approval.

Former FPL employees Dr. Regis Miller, Robert Kurtenacker, and Diana Smith were also extremely helpful. The personnel files of the lab employees at the center of this case were provided by Ashley Mattingly, an archivist with the National Archives and Records Administration. Family members, including John Marshall Cuno and Yvonna Cuno, supplemented those findings with personal details.

My family is a great support system, serving as early readers and as constant listeners throughout the process. My parents, Joyce and Leonard Schrager; my in-laws, Geneva and Bill Jokerst; and my aunt, June Sochen, a former college history professor and author, deserve particular thanks.

Honestly, there was a time, with three kids under six, that I didn't think I would finish this project. That's only because I did not want to miss a moment with my constant sources of joy, our three children, Harper, Clark and Payton. Realistically, though, without the help of my wife and best friend, Cathy, this book would not be a reality. What can you say to the person who makes you better? "Thank you" simply doesn't seem like enough.

My friends Rob Witwer, Will Steinberg, Bob Delaporte, Phil Yau, Josh Mitzen, Rebecca Fitzgerald, Tony Barkow, Adam Benson, Jim Wilson, Christy Tetzler, Eli Stokols, and Eleanor Atkeson have listened to me drone on about this story for a while, as have numerous colleagues, particularly Ryan Ward and Bruce Johnson.

The executive producer of my unit, Christine Sloan-Miller, whose father worked to preserve Wisconsin's great outdoors during his career with the Department of Natural Resources, recognized the value of this story and allowed me to pursue it in my free time. I thank her for that.

My former Colorado colleague Dan Weaver provided some background on his home state of South Carolina. Another former colleague, Nicole Vap, helped me track down an interview subject in Australia.

When it came to researching the criminal case against Bruno Hauptmann, Michael Melsky, Dr. Lloyd Gardner, Jim Fisher, Kelvin Keraga, and Kevin Klein provided invaluable insights. One of the nation's preeminent archivists, Fred MacDonald, sent me video of the crime scene, of the courthouse in Flemington, New Jersey, and more, bringing the years 1932 to 1935 to life for me.

My neighbor here in Madison, Elizabeth Kingston, opened up her house, where Arthur Koehler used to live, and let me hang out in what was Koehler's study one afternoon to see what vibes I might be able to feel.

The soundtrack I listened to while writing was once again supplied by the KBCO Studio C Channel. I may have moved out of Colorado, but it's nice to know there's a still a great song available to me at any time online. Jennifer Ryan, Melanie Roth, and Jack Lenzo at Fulcrum Publishing, also located in Colorado, have been a joy to work with.

Unlike many authors today, I am fortunate to be able to contact my publisher directly. Sam Scinta approved this project on one of the many calls he's received from me that start with me saying, "I've got an idea." His confidence in me supersedes my own, and I am forever indebted to him for that faith.

On Sam's request and with Terry Frei's strongest of recommendations in mind, I met Kate Thompson for coffee and a conversation about this project before she ever laid eyes on anything I'd written. She has since hooked me on the Avett Brothers and endowed me with a better appreciation of the *Chicago Manual of Style,* even if I do find that guidebook archaic and unwieldy. I've always believed the best editors make writers and authors out of storytellers. I knew going into this that Arthur Koehler's story was a fantastic one, and if it's told well in the subsequent pages, a great deal of credit goes to Kate.

There is no one who studies the Lindbergh case without paying homage to Mark Falzini, the archivist at the New Jersey State Police Museum. He oversees the 250,000-plus documents, exhibits, and artifacts associated with the case, and he's forgotten far more about this case than I will ever know. I cannot say enough about how much help he provided me, but more importantly, in Mark I've found a new friend who's generous with his time, intelligent, funny, a terrific author himself, and a heckuva bagpiper in his free time.

Finally, there could be no book about Arthur Koehler without the aid of his son, George Koehler. He and his wife, Margie, could not have been more gracious, opening up their home and their private records to me in the process. As the caretakers of Arthur's letters to his wife and to his brothers and parents for decades, they have shared more than I could have imagined. I truly hope I have treated their family story with the respect it deserves. They have my sincere gratitude and admiration.

It's a long way from a family driving trip to a biography about the father of forensic botany. But as Arthur Koehler would often say, "Go as far as you can see, and then see how far you can go."

Introduction

To Arthur Koehler, no detail was too small. He lived in a world of microscopes and ultraviolet rays, centimeters and millimeters.

And on September 20, 1934, while he focused through his silver-framed hexagonal glasses, he found the column inches of his paper woefully lacking.

"Ding bust it," he murmured with a furrowed brow as he scoured the three-cent extra edition of the *Wisconsin State Journal*. It was as close to an expletive as the nondemonstrative scientist would utter.

Koehler's official title was xylotomist, US Forest Service, Forest Products Laboratory, Madison, Wisconsin. He was the federal government's first-ever xylotomist, translated from Greek as a "cutter of wood." For all intents and purposes, he was the country's preeminent expert on wood identification. He studied under his microscope up to three thousand slivers of wood annually for the government, labeling and chronicling his findings.

Xylotomy was so unknown, the Associated Press sarcastically reported in 1912, that the US Civil Service Commission was spending all of its time "explaining the meaning of the term" after it posted the position Koehler eventually obtained. But Koehler had known what it meant, had met the qualifications of a mastery of both systematic and structural botany, and for the last two decades had served as the only xylotomist in the country, at the world's foremost laboratory on the topic, where he oversaw the Section of Silvicultural Relations.

The Wisconsin native wrote the book on wood, literally. *The Properties and Uses of Wood* had come out in 1924, published by

New York house McGraw-Hill and distributed worldwide through its London office. "We are prone to think of timber in its various forms as a gradually passing material of construction and manufacture," he wrote.

> On every hand we see evidences of steel, stone or concrete being used in place of wood. However, the fact remains that the annual consumption of timber in this country has decreased very little during the last two decades. . . .
>
> This book deals with facts about the characteristics and properties of wood which can be applied by the forester in selecting the more useful kinds of timber to grow, and by the lumberman, manufacturer, dealer and consumer in promoting the more efficient utilization of forest products.

As he sat in his living room that Thursday night, still dressed in his work clothes of a gray suit, white shirt, and blue tie, he studied the paper as intently as he would a piece of black locust from the spire of an eighteenth-century Pennsylvania church or a Sitka spruce used to make a famous violin or a thousand-year-old sample of cypress found during the excavation of a Washington, DC, hotel sent to his Wisconsin laboratory for identification.

"Lindbergh Kidnapping Suspect Arrested, $35,000 of Ransom Money Recovered," blared the newspaper headline. "EXTRA! Alien Nabbed in Effort to Pass $10 Bill."

Like millions worldwide, Koehler found the kidnapping of Charles A. Lindbergh Jr. riveting. It was, after all, the violation of "America's best-loved couple" and the country's most famous child. One Movietone newsreel announcer had soberly called the search for the culprit or culprits in the spring of 1932 "the greatest manhunt in history." Another called it "the most atrocious crime in America's history."

When Lindbergh Sr. became the first person to successfully fly across the Atlantic Ocean, he had earned more than the $25,000 prize. No one in the world—no government leader, no religious figure, no athlete—was as famous as Lindbergh. His presence anywhere drew thousands of spectators, dignitaries, and common

The three sections of the ladder left at the Lindbergh estate. It was used to climb into the 2nd floor nursery of the home to abduct "the world's baby," Charles A. Lindbergh Jr. (Courtesy: Dr. Regis Miller/Forest Products Laboratory)

folks alike. His every move was chronicled, his every expression analyzed, his every word parsed and reported.

But unlike most of those following the news story, Koehler's fascination with Charles and Anne Lindbergh's situation was rooted not in their fame but in the instrument used to carry out the crime. The three-section telescopic ladder used in the kidnapping was made of wood, Koehler's real passion.

Aside from a chisel, a wooden dowel, and a ransom note, the ladder was the only physical evidence left at the scene of the crime. Ransom money had been delivered, but the crime remained unsolved. The public was angry, especially after the baby was found dead in a shallow grave not far from the Lindbergh estate a couple of months after his disappearance. "There can be no immunity now," moviegoers in the summer of 1932 heard on the newsreel before their picture started. "It is up to America to find the perpetrator of this crime or it is to be America's shame forever."

Frustration didn't begin to describe the mood of authorities working on the case. The investigation continued with an abundance of law enforcement resources, despite it being the middle of the Depression. But for nearly a year, detectives had been stymied. Leads had dried up. The ransom money had disappeared. Witnesses had clammed up. Suspects' alibis had panned out.

"If the kidnaper came into this room and told me he had kidnaped the baby, I'd have no case against him," Colonel H. Norman Schwarzkopf, the superintendent of the New Jersey State Police, told the United Press in the summer of 1932. "There are no fingerprints, nothing that would directly connect an individual with the crime. When we get our break, we'll depend on circumstantial evidence.

"We have scores of circumstances which we will seek to fit with the circumstances in the life of the man we find with the ransom money. If they dove-tail even 60%, we'll send that man to the chair."

Investigators knew the crime scene ladder provided an opportunity, but they didn't know how. Forensic science was in its infancy, and forensic botany wasn't even a sparkle in any detective's eye. They had brought Koehler in to pursue any leads the ladder might generate.

And so, roughly a year after the crime, Koehler began his scientific detective work on the case. He traveled to New Jersey to take a detailed inventory of the ladder. He numbered the rails and rungs 1 through 17. He inspected each thoroughly. He took pictures. He cut slivers from the ladder and analyzed them under his microscope.

"The ladder was homemade," he would later write, "which meant that it contained individual characteristics. It was not one out of a thousand or ten thousand, all superficially alike; it was the only one like it and could be expected to reveal some of the peculiarities and associations of the man who made it."

The ladder's rungs showed no signs of wear, indicating the wood had never been used elsewhere. Five of the six rails were like that as well, unused before the ladder. But one rail, Rail 16, was different.

The wood used in Rail 16 had four nail holes previously hammered into it that had no apparent connection with the ladder, so Koehler figured it had been used somewhere else before. Because it had no rust and no finish, he surmised it had been nailed down inside a barn, a garage, or an attic. Further, the rail's two edges had been treated with a rather dull hand plane, leaving distinctive marks similar to marks on the ladder's rungs. The longer the crime went unsolved, the more unlikely it was to find the plane in the same condition it had been in when it was used in the construction of the kidnap ladder.

Koehler had walked the streets of the Bronx, trying to glean what he could from simply looking at the outside of buildings, barns, and garages in the neighborhoods of some of the case's key witnesses.

Other clues had led to the canvassing of more than 1,500 lumber mills on the East Coast. Koehler had traced two bottom rails of the ladder to a lumber mill in South Carolina. Planed with a defective knife, the wood carried a different kind of fingerprint, man-made and equally telling. Discovering where that wood had been shipped had become his next quest.

But searches of backyards, henhouses, outhouses, garages, and lumber yards throughout the New York/New Jersey area had led nowhere. Finally in the Bronx he had found a match: wood at a lumber yard with the same planer marks as those found on the ladder. He had been so close to finding the man who had made the ladder, only to find out that the yard didn't have sales records because they no longer let customers buy on credit.

Now, as he sat in his favorite chair next to the brick fireplace on this September evening, his role in the investigation of the century had stalled. No New Jersey State Police detective was calling the Koehler family phone at Badger 7269 for his advice. Colonel Schwarzkopf had not called or wired him at the lab.

Yet he still felt sure he could help.

He turned back to his evening paper. There was more about detectives raiding the suspect's house and finding some of the ransom money Lindbergh had paid more than two years earlier.

And then Koehler felt a jolt, a sense of adrenaline rushing through his body, as he read what followed.

"[Authorities] said the investigation of the suspect had not been completed. He is a carpenter, unemployed at the present."

A carpenter.

And no wonder he was unemployed, Koehler thought.

He had told authorities from the get-go that the ladder showed poor design and workmanship and that he did not believe its maker to be a "high-grade" carpenter.

He closed his gray-blue eyes and lifted his muscular arms to rub the bald top of his head. Koehler had always loved wood, from when he was a little boy and called his father's tool box a "toodle box." His mother often had to call him several times for dinner because he was so engrossed in making something in his father's shop.

When people knocked on wood for good luck, Koehler actually knew why. He could explain the superstition dating back to ancient times, when trees were held as deities of the forest and simply tapping on them invoked the aid of those higher powers to ward off evils.

Koehler knew that every tree in the world was distinct, just like every person. As he liked to say, "A tree never lies."

And so the revelation came.

He raised his nearly five-foot-nine frame into an upright posture, pulled out his notebook, and began to write to his best contact at the New Jersey State Police, Captain J. J. Lamb, the man leading the Lindbergh baby kidnapping investigation. He wanted to remind Lamb of the report he had submitted on the ladder a year and a half earlier.

Dear Captain Lamb:

Congratulations on success so far.

In my work I have not said much about rail 16. That is the one that has the cut nail holes in it and has both edges dressed by a hand plane as if cut down from a wider board, perhaps matched or shiplapped. I have not tried to trace it on account of its apparently old origin.

That board may have been taken from a local structure accessible to the maker of the ladder, possibly because something may have gone wrong with a piece of 1x4 that originally had been secured for the purpose. I suggest that a search be made for such lumber on the premises of any suspect, so as to secure additional circumstantial evidence. The planer marks on the rail and on similar lumber should be a highly reliable check.

Then, of course, there may be chances of finding lumber as in the other rails or rungs, or even the dowel, around the premises; or the plane, saw, and ¾-inch auger, which you undoubtedly have considered.

Very sincerely yours,

Arthur Koehler, In Charge, Section of Silvicultural Relations

He decided he would send the letter from the lab first thing the next morning, and so he turned off the first-floor lights at 1819 Adams Street and headed up to bed. Koehler had overseen the design and construction of this house on Madison's near west side, the first for him and his family, and of course it was outfitted entirely with wood floors. As Koehler climbed the steps to his second floor bedroom, he continued to think about what he'd just read—or more tellingly, what he hadn't read—about the case. Not surprisingly, the steps creaked and moaned as he climbed.

Wood could talk, after all.

By the time he reached the top, he was convinced he could make Rail 16 and the rest of the ladder tell their secrets.

1

James Tarr surprisingly didn't feel a chill as he hiked to the end of his grandparents' driveway to pick up the mail. The mercury hovered at 37 degrees, balmy for two days after Christmas 1922 in central Wisconsin.

Twenty-year-old James looked around at the eighty acres Grandpa James Chapman had cultivated into a prosperous farm, with crops and dairying, having a good herd of graded cattle with a pure-bred Holstein sire at the head. Just a couple years earlier, Chapman had built a modern barn with a basement.

James's mom, Lorena, had grown up here, an only child, nurtured and loved by her parents, James and Clementine. They shared their affection with young James and his siblings, Manning and Sadie, and on their grandparents' farm the children were experiencing much of the life their mom had known as a child. Grandpa James had one of those great bushy mustaches that tickled when he gave kisses and held leftovers from an earlier meal.

Grandpa James and Grandma Clementine were popular in their neighborhood, and James was well-respected in Wood County. He served as chairman of the county board and as a member of the county drainage board. Various businesses sought his involvement as an investor, a consultant, anything to be able to associate with him.

So it wasn't a surprise to find some straggler Christmas cards in the mailbox that day. It was the foot-long gray package that intrigued the boy, especially since it had no return address and listed his grandparents' address as "Marshfild, Wisconsin," instead of the accurate name, Cameron Township, which is located just a few miles south of Marshfield.

James kicked the slushy snow as he returned up the driveway. He stomped out his shoes before going back into the house and handing the package to his grandparents, who were in their dining room. As his grandma held the Christmas cards, his grandfather sat down with the package on his knees and took out his pocket knife to cut the wrapping paper lengthwise.

Clementine leaned over his shoulder and he cut through the twine. She never got to see what was inside the package.

Moments later, Tarr stumbled to the phone and called a family friend, Ole Gilberts, at the Klondyke General Store, a mile away from the home.

"For God's sake, come up here!" he shouted into the phone.

Gilberts rushed to help the Chapmans. He later told authorities that when he got to the farmhouse, he found James Chapman lying unconscious near the dining room, with his left hand blown off and a bleeding leg. Clementine was face down in a pool of blood, dying from massive chest and stomach wounds and significant internal bleeding. Tarr suffered only minor physical injuries.

The dining room walls and ceiling looked like Swiss cheese studded with metal fragments. A six-inch iron pipe, stuffed with explosive picric acid, a dynamite substitute, was lodged in the Chapmans' floor. Picric acid, usually used to clear land, left the odor of antiseptic soap. Those first on the scene after the blast swore they could smell it.

In this case, it had been used to make a bomb. The pipe had been encased in a block of wood, and the twine around the package had served as the trigger.

Authorities, including Wood County Sheriff Walter Mueller, wondered whether the motive was political, perhaps retaliation for a vote Chapman had cast that a neighbor didn't like. But James Chapman had served his county for nearly two decades, and he had taken many controversial votes during his time in office. Recently, he had voted to authorize money to crack down on moonshiners and bootleggers to implement Prohibition, ratified in the form of the 18th Amendment to the US Constitution a couple of years earlier. Or maybe it had something to do with a ditch the county drainage board and Chapman had supported that headed through the southern part of the county. Many farmers didn't like it because it traversed their properties. Just a couple of months earlier, a suspicious fire had destroyed the barn of one of Chapman's fellow drainage commissioners. A few months before that, the equipment set to dig the ditch had been blown up with dynamite.

Forty-four-year-old John Magnuson, a native of Sweden, had fought for the British in the Boer War in Africa before owning a garage in Chicago and then moving north to eighty acres in Wood County. To authorities he was the most outspoken opponent of the drainage ditch. Witnesses said he had threatened violence against those who supported the ditch. Chapman later told investigators looking into the explosion at his house that Magnuson had threatened a lawsuit to stop the drainage ditch. If the best Chicago lawyer couldn't stop the project, Magnuson said his guns would.

While the general public was fixated on the crime that killed Clementine Chapman, authorities were fixated on Magnuson. He would be arrested and charged with first-degree murder.

Just two days after the explosion at the Chapman home, the nearby *Wisconsin Rapids Daily Tribune* reported on its front page that "Marshfield has been transformed from a peaceful city to one of hubbub due to the influx of the government operatives and to the large press gallery which has assembled there. It is regarded by the press to be one of the biggest stories of the year and over a dozen of special correspondents were sent to the scene immediately by press associations and metropolitan newspapers."

Prosecutors knew that the case, albeit "premeditated . . . to effect the death of a human being with malice aforethought," would be circumstantial in nature. For example, no one had seen Magnuson make the bomb. No one had seen him put it in the mail along Rural Route 5, which was nowhere near his property. No fingerprints were found on the bomb materials left behind by the explosion.

The prosecution gathered handwriting experts from New York, Milwaukee, and Chicago. They brought in an engineering professor from the University of Wisconsin–Madison to testify that steel from a gas engine on Magnuson's farm matched the steel in the bomb trigger. A UW chemistry professor matched the bomb's metal with metal found at Magnuson's.

And to Judge Byron B. Park's Branch 2 courtroom, prosecutors brought a thirty-seven-year-old xylotomist, an expert in wood identification, to weigh in on the fifty-one wood shavings and chips found under the lathe in Magnuson's workshop. The balding judge in his three-piece suit looked over his wire-rim glasses at a type of forensic science expert witness he'd never seen in his courtroom before.

Ever meticulous, Arthur Koehler had analyzed all fifty-one samples under his microscope. Now he told Stan Peters, the foreman of the jury, and his fellow Wood County citizens that forty-six of the samples were white oak. One was hemlock, and one was ash.

And three of the chips and shavings investigators had brought to Koehler's Madison laboratory were white elm, the same wood from which the bomb casing had been constructed. According to Koehler, those wood chips displayed the "beautiful chevron-like distribution of pore structure on the cut surface." The newspaper headline called Koehler's testimony a "Blow to Bomb Defense" and "the most important" of the expert testimony delivered in court.

Despite the defense attorney lamenting that the case against his client was solely circumstantial in nature, and despite Magnuson protesting to the court, "Time will prove my innocence," the Swede was convicted of murder.

For Koehler, wood identification, while new to a courtroom in 1923, was standard practice.

Arthur Koehler was born in 1885 on a farm south of Mishicot, which was about eight miles north of Manitowoc, nestled nicely along Lake Michigan and at the mouth of the Manitowoc River. President Andrew Jackson had authorized land sales for the region in 1835, and Koehler's parents, Louis and Ottilie, took advantage four decades later, purchasing eighty acres for $1,800.

Louis bought the first combined reaper and mower in the area, cutting not only his own grain, but that of his neighbors as well. He also bought the first gas engine in the neighborhood and used it to saw wood at one dollar an hour.

The Koehlers had five cows, two horses, a wagon, a sled, and a sow at the beginning. Shortly after moving in, Louis planted one hundred apple trees for use at home and for sale. He put in berry bushes as well: blackberries, strawberries, and black, red,

Arthur Koehler was born in 1885 in this farm house near Manitowoc, Wisconsin. He was the sixth of nine children born to Louis and Ottilie Koehler. Four of those children would die before the age of 10. (Courtesy: George E. Koehler)

brown, and yellow raspberries. They grew oats, rye, and peas. The cows provided milk and butter for every meal, with "a considerable quantity" of butter to be sold at market as well, along with eggs from the Koehlers' chickens.

But the Koehler family derived most of its income from bees. The hive located on the farm when the Koehlers bought it died that first winter, as did replacement hives he bought the following winter. Louis got a number of books on the subject and built a bee cellar to protect them from inclement weather, and by 1906 his apiary would number 250 hives. It was profitable as early as 1891, when Louis sold more than 10,000 pounds of honey at 18 cents per pound from 130 hives.

Louis's interests didn't stop at farming and bees. He gave eulogies for community members when the minister wasn't available. He extracted teeth. One time he sewed up a young man cut by an axe using nothing more than an ordinary needle and thread.

But his passion was carpentry. The year Arthur was born, 1885, Louis built Ottilie a brick kitchen and turned the old frame kitchen into his carpentry shop. Once he built a coffin and lay down in it to give Ottilie a start and him a laugh.

The matriarch of the Koehler family was too busy for such shenanigans. "Ottilie milked the cows, raised chickens, knit socks, wove cloth and made clothing for the children," Ben Koehler, Arthur's brother, would later write. Ben's wife, Edith, said of her mother-in-law, "I never saw anyone with more patience. . . . I feel that she was the most unselfish woman I ever met. I had great respect for her. I never heard her say anything against anyone. She was a truly Christian woman."

She needed to be, with the losses she and Louis experienced. Both of their first two children, William and Martha, died before their first birthdays. Their third child, Amanda, was very healthy, but at just over a year old, she choked on a plum pit and died of suffocation.

Hugo, born in 1881, would be the first of the Koehler children to make it to his second birthday. Lydia was next, born in 1882. Arthur Koehler was the sixth child born to Louis and Ottilie, arriving in 1885. Three more boys, Ben, Walter, and Alfred, would come over the next eleven years.

Tragedy would strike again when Arthur was seven, as Lydia and Ben suffered from a severe case of diphtheria in 1892. Ben would recover, but Lydia died two weeks shy of her tenth birthday.

"One hour before she left us she prayed to God to leave her with her papa and mamma and her brothers," Louis wrote in the *American Bee Journal.* "Still the Great Shepherd took her away from us to a better land, where the storms of this life will never reach her any more, and where all diseases are unknown—to a home in Heaven. What a joyful thought."

Arthur grew up happy, spending hours upon hours in his father's workshop. He made miniature threshing machines during bean harvesting time, crafting teeth for the cylinder out of cut shingle nails with their heads flattened on an anvil. These activities weren't without episode, either, with a narrow cutter head once cutting a triangular hole in his fingernail. It happened in the dead of winter, and Arthur later reported that "the cold seemed to increase the pain which was excruciating."

Despite growing up on a farm, he always "preferred winter work in the woods to summer jobs. A particularly repulsive job in the fields was to shock bundles of rye or barley on a hot summer's day with the barbed 'beards' of the grain finding their way inside my shirt." In winter, however, he found "there was something fascinating about the cold stillness of the forest; or, if the wind was blowing, to hear it moan in the pine tops overhead."

The only rule his father had for him in the shop was that he was not allowed to use the saw or hammer on Sundays, as it might be disrespectful to the neighbors. The Koehlers weren't particularly religious, although Louis did say grace in German before every meal.

In fact, Arthur and his brothers spoke German when their parents were included in the conversation and English to each other. The five boys were close, literally and figuratively, three of them at one time sleeping in an attic room usually used for storage. Walter remembered once being upstairs with Hugo and Arthur in the middle of the winter and having to "shake the snow off his underwear before dressing."

They weren't the type of family to play games together or dance around the phonograph. When Arthur's parents had spare time, they chose to read. His father liked his children to keep quiet after dinner so he could read the paper undisturbed.

Arthur's affection for learning was apparent at an early age. He began attending school at age three and went fulltime after he turned four. He finished eighth grade at age twelve and then moved in with Hugo and their maternal grandmother in Manitowoc so he could attend the high school, which was nearly ten miles from the farm. He worked as a school janitor and in various stores to help support himself.

He graduated high school at age sixteen with a focus in English and a thesis on Arctic exploration. His commencement program mistakenly listed him as "Arthur G. Koehler," the only time he would have a middle initial until getting involved in the Lindbergh case more than three decades later.

In his junior year, Arthur began chronicling literally every expense he incurred, a practice he would follow for the next sixty-three years. On the first page of his first financial ledger, he wrote: "Though money talks, As we've heard tell, To most of us it says—'Farewell.'"

The very first cash received came in a $5.00 payment for his janitorial services and an additional $1.10 from "Grandma." He already had seventeen cents in savings for an opening balance of $6.17 for the month of June 1900. On the spending side, on June 2 he spent seventeen cents on a "Fishing outfit" and another six cents on laundry. He balanced his new ledger just two days later—his birthday, June 4. He accounted for every penny, including numerous five-cent payments for ice cream, cookies, and banjo strings.

In his senior year, he spent and earned more, including spending eighteen cents for each book of the Leather Stocking Tales series by James Fennimore Cooper. For his graduation from high school, he spent five cents on firecrackers, fifty cents to attend the banquet, and five cents for a banana. He left high school and headed back to the family farm with $13.67 in his pocket.

To say Arthur Koehler lacked direction after high school would be accurate. He bounced around in Manitowoc, working for a bookstore, a wholesale fruit dealer, and at the general store, and then moved back home from 1903 to the fall of the following year. He was nineteen years old, with no job and no career. But he had developed a passion for photography that would stay with him for the rest of his life. As an early Christmas present to himself in 1903, he spent $5.14 for a "camera outfit," including developing paper, chemicals, a tripod screw, and exposure tables.

That fall, he moved to Milwaukee to work for a wholesale candy dealer who offered room and board as part of the compensation. Arthur delivered the candy and took care of the horses that got him to where he needed to go.

His older brother, Hugo, got him a grocery clerk job in Ohio in the fall of 1905. He was earning ten dollars every two weeks with room and board covered. He closed the year and his first ledger with a balance of $108.80.

The second edition begins with three quotes, including from the business magazine *Collier*: "As a man spends his money, so is he."

Another business magazine made an even greater impact on Arthur. *Success* was founded by Orison Swett Marden, who encouraged readers that "all who have accomplished great things have had a great aim, have fixed their gaze on a goal which was high, one which sometimes seemed impossible." Marden was America's first true self-help guru. Like Arthur, he had been born on a farm with modest means, but unlike Arthur, Marden had gone to college and graduate school before embarking on his career. To Marden, education was vital to success.

The monthly publication he founded in 1897 had half a million subscribers just a decade later, meaning it likely was read by roughly three million people. To Arthur, it certainly was worth the ten cents per issue. He had read it off and on during his time in Milwaukee, but the move to Ohio seemed to fuel his own desire to succeed, and he bought the magazine every month. He liked it so much, he ended up working to sell subscriptions.

If the publication inspired Arthur to go to college, his preferred area of study percolated after he spent the 1907 New Year's back at the family farm. His trip to Ohio took him through Chicago's Union Depot, created in 1874 by five separate railroads. The station opened to Canal Street and stretched from Madison to Adams Streets. Commercial vendors lined the building that served as the main passenger thoroughfare to the city. In addition to buying the January edition of *Success* from an area merchant, Arthur braved Chicago's westerly winds and relatively mild 40-degree temperatures to spend two dollars on a book called *Our Native Trees*.

His brother Ben said Arthur started thinking about a career in forestry right after high school, after he heard a speaker discuss the topic. But it wasn't until he picked up the seminal book in the field by naturalist Harriet L. Keeler that the idea took shape.

The book came out in 1900 to rave reviews. *The New York Times* called it "well-written and thoroughly interesting." Keeler wrote eloquently about trees from the Atlantic Ocean to the Rocky Mountains and from Canada to the southern states.

Arthur wanted to learn more and would enroll at Lawrence University in Appleton, Wisconsin, in the fall of 1907 at age twenty-two. On his first day in botany class, he was paired up with Ethelyn Smith to go to the home of a woman who raised petunias and bring back a flat for the rest of the students.

His third financial ledger tells the tale of a blossoming romance with the young woman, three years his junior, from Evansville, just south of the Wisconsin state capital of Madison. He took Ethelyn to a "Magic Show" for a dollar, bought her ice cream and candy for a nickel each, and treated her to meals and to the theatre for two dollars.

The Lawrence yearbook, the *Ariel*, mentions their relationship, proclaiming during their freshman year spring break that "Koehler wanders about Botany lab, but all in vain: Miss Smith has left for home." The next year, the yearbook postulated, "Did you ever see Koehler without Miss Smith on Sunday evenings?"

He put his passion for photography to work capturing his newest passion. She was tall, standing above most other women on campus and even an inch or two above his five-foot- nine frame. The camera liked her, as did the photographer behind it. She exuded warmth and an openness emblematic of a woman happy to dote on those she encountered.

When he wasn't focusing his lens on Ethelyn, Arthur focused on mathematics, averaging 93 over six different courses. Despite being brought up in a home where his parents spoke the language, he scored

Arthur Koehler worked at a grocery store in Ohio and sold subscriptions to a leading business magazine before going to college. Here he is at age 23 before his sophomore year at Lawrence University in Appleton, Wisconsin. He would finish his degree at the University of Michigan in Ann Arbor. (Courtesy: George E. Koehler)

only a 90 in third-year German. His lowest grade was in freshman elocution, a 78, which he raised to a 90 in his sophomore year.

His income came primarily from a serving job in the Ormsby Hall dining room, supplemented by selling his photos, which his younger brother Ben would point out proved to be "quite profitable work."

Arthur knew all along he couldn't study forestry at Lawrence, so in the fall of 1909, after a five-day "vacation" to see Ethelyn in Madison and Evansville and one more trip to Appleton, he crossed Lake Michigan on the ferry boat and began his junior year at the University of Michigan in Ann Arbor.

He took his first job in the field, working in the Botany Department for $7.20 per month. He supplemented that by working as a commercial photographer, taking group and individual pictures, as well as waiting tables. He continued to see Ethelyn despite the distance between them.

He bought more publications related to forestry, including a booklet called *Timber* published by the US Department of Agriculture. Arthur started his senior year in Ann Arbor with a balance of $601.17 in his ledger. He sold his waiter's coat and apron for fifty cents because he was hired on campus as an assistant instructor in tree identification, a job he later said "helped very much in fixing in my mind how the different species of trees can be distinguished and in permanently increasing my interest in life outdoors."

His interest in Ethelyn remained a constant as well, and the Lawrence yearbook staff continued its chronicling of the now long-distance relationship, writing, "What would happen if Ethelyn Smith failed to hear from Ann Arbor?"

That would not be an issue. The Christmas before their last semester in college, they met in Milwaukee and got engaged. Arthur graduated and left the university on June 21, traveling back to Evansville to see Ethelyn before going to work for the summer for the Wisconsin Forestry Department near Trout Lake, in the northern part of the state. He apparently did so more for the experience than the wages, since his ledger records little income—or expenses, for that matter—during that summer job.

Arthur returned to Ann Arbor that fall to start postgraduate

Arthur was partnered with Ethelyn Smith on their first day of Botany class at Lawrence. They would be married roughly five years later in 1912. (Courtesy: George E. Koehler)

work in forestry while still earning twenty dollars a month from the university for teaching undergraduates in that field. Only a month later, after paying fifty cents to watch his Michigan Wolverines wallop Ohio State 19–0 behind All-American Stanfield Wells, Arthur left campus for Washington DC, and a job with the US Forest Service as an "assistant in the study of the cellular structure of wood."

His first check came on November 16, a whopping $41.00. He'd receive another $42.33 from the "U.S.," according to his ledger, for a total of $83.33 per month. The goal was to save money. Ethelyn was doing the same, teaching high school math in a small town in western Wisconsin.

Over Christmas 1912, he took an unpaid vacation to head home for nearly two weeks. During that time, he separated from his fiancée long enough to take the federal Civil Service exam. He needed a 70 to pass, which would make him eligible for promotion opportunities. He scored 87.60 on the practical questions, 85 on the thesis, and 92 on the education, training, and experience component. It was another step, like those he had read about so often in *Success*, toward bettering himself and creating a better future for himself and Ethelyn.

The couple planned to be married in October, but in August Arthur got sick, threatening the event. Purchases mentioned in his journal—a nasal atomizer, syringe, and two medications—suggest he thought he had a cold, but four days later he paid $1.50 for a "Taxi to Hospital." A full seven weeks passed before the next expense was recorded. The cold was in reality typhoid fever and required a long stay at Providence hospital at a cost of $100.75. Further costs incurred included $70 to a Dr. Yates.

Before the medical bills came in, he had nearly doubled his savings, from $461.77 when he left Ann Arbor to $899.25 by October 1. That's when he left for Wisconsin, "to recuperate and also to get married," as Ben would later write. Two days before the October 16 wedding, Arthur started spending some of that money on things he needed for the event, including twenty-five cents for a haircut (basically a trim around the sides, as he was already bald on top of his head) and ten cents for a shave. The biggest expenses would be four dollars for shoes and four dollars for a ring.

The early-morning ceremony would be on Ethelyn's twenty-fourth birthday at the farm where she grew up. Her new husband was twenty-seven.

Arthur got married with $627.80 on hand, finishing the last open space on his third financial ledger. The fourth, a large, gray, cloth-bound book, began with a five-dollar payment to Reverend Charles E. Coon, a Methodist pastor, for officiating the wedding, two train tickets to Manitowoc for $6.58, and the beginning of their trip back to Washington, where they would start their new lives together.

They would rent for their first couple of months there before a disagreeable landlady hastened their plans to buy a home in December 1912. They put $300 down on a three-bedroom, two-bathroom $1,300 house at 167 Uhland Terrace, in the northeast quadrant of the city. It was off of North Capitol Street, about three miles from the Department of Agriculture headquarters on Independence Avenue.

By that time, Ethelyn was pregnant and they were enjoying what Washington had to offer. Ethelyn wrote home that "it is so beautiful here . . . the most beautiful city I ever saw or imagined." They saw *Ben Hur* at the theatre, went to movies, even attended the inauguration of Woodrow Wilson in January 1913.

Kathryn Marie Koehler was born on August 20, 1913, in Madison, where Ethelyn had spent the last few months of her pregnancy at her parents' newly built home on the city's near west side. The Smiths had sold their farm and moved to the city to live near Ethelyn's Aunt Cora, her mother's sister.

Arthur returned to Washington a few days after Kathryn's birth, and mother and daughter would join him in late September. Despite the family's enjoyment of where they lived, they were planning a move roughly a year later, as Arthur had applied for and was accepted as a xylotomist with the US Forest Service in Wisconsin. The job would pay $1,000 per year and would take them back to Madison.

Family lore has Ethelyn's father lying awake all night as he contemplated how the new home he was building for his retirement could be expanded to accommodate an additional family of three. Arthur and Ethelyn put their Uhland Terrace home up for sale. Before they sold it to G. L. Keenan, who provided a down payment of $100, the total family savings was only $67.99.

The Koehlers left for Madison on January 14, 1914, for Arthur's position, which was at a new facility called the Forest Products Laboratory. It was an assignment his Washington colleagues didn't understand. They openly pitied him for being sent to "Indian Country."

In reality, Arthur Koehler and his family were being sent home. And they couldn't have been happier about it.

2

Since its founding in 1905, the US Forest Service had preached the need to study, research, and preserve the nation's wood supply. After all, in the story of creation the word *knowledge* is symbolized by a tree. In 1902, President Theodore Roosevelt spoke to the Society of American Foresters at a private home in Washington about the country's direction with regard to its most important natural resource at the time:

> You can never afford to forget for one moment what is the object of our forest policy. That object is not to preserve the forests because they are beautiful, though that is good in itself, nor because they are refuges for the wild creatures of the wilderness, though that, too, is good in itself; but the primary object of our forest policy, as of the land part of the United States, is the making of prosperous homes. It is part of the traditional policy of home making of our country.
>
> Every other consideration comes as secondary. The whole effort of the Government in dealing with the forests must be directed to this end, keeping in view the fact that it is not only necessary to start the homes as prosperous, but to keep them so. That is why the forests have got to be kept. You can start a prosperous home by destroying the forests, but you can not keep it prosperous that way. Forestry is the preservation of forests by wise use.

So in 1909, US Forest Service Chief Gifford Pinchot sought the cooperation of a university willing to provide space and equipment to create the world's first research facility dealing solely with wood. The University of Wisconsin in Madison was selected over a number of universities that "showed a keen interest" and who made "very generous offers." The university promised to build, heat, light, and power the new laboratory at an initial cost of $50,000.

The facility opened on October 1, 1909, in a temporary headquarters in a house at 1610 Adams Street, a couple of miles west of the State Capitol and a few blocks away from the campus. When the new building on campus formally opened in June 1910, a couple of months after the staff of forty-five had officially moved in, its focus centered on four specific research areas: wood preservation, timber tests, wood chemistry, and wood technology. The facility would shortly thereafter add units dealing with engineering, pathology, wood distillation, and pulp and paper.

The Forest Products Lab's early work focused on building relationships with the principal forest products industries, laying out its general plans for research, and gathering as much data as possible on the fundamentals and properties of wood. Then the lab, which did not seek dramatic increases in appropriations, began to slowly grow its staff and its capabilities.

It was to this wood mecca that Arthur Koehler arrived in January 1914. His job functions were specifically described as the "Determination and description of species, Instruction of industrial representatives and Relation of structure to properties."

He worked in the Wood Anatomy unit for Eloise Gerry, the first female scientist in the US Forest Service. Gerry arrived the day after the facility's formal opening with bachelor's and master's degrees from Harvard University's Radcliffe College to prepare microscope slides and photomicrographs for wood anatomical study. Her thesis had focused on the bars or folds of cellulose found in the genera of living conifers. As she later noted, "I must admit the Forest Service did not want a woman, but as it happened there wasn't any man willing to come and do the work."

FPL didn't have much of a wood collection when it opened, and Gerry had to borrow a microtome from one of her former professors at Harvard to help begin the process of wood anatomy research. She solicited samples from expositions and fairs throughout the United States. Those initial samples were usually one-meter logs cut and finished to show their bark, end grain, and longitudinal grain. Pieces were cut off for closer study and added to the collection, while the rest of the logs were used to decorate the halls of FPL.

What the lab did have right off the bat was supplied by Harry Tiemann, who was in charge of the Timber Tests unit. He was a kiln drying specialist who had worked at Yale University before moving to Forest Service headquarters in Washington, DC. When Koehler arrived at the lab, he supplemented what Gerry had accumulated by bringing Tiemann's collection, stored in beautiful walnut cabinets, from Forest Service headquarters.

By the time the United States was fighting World War I, FPL was making its knowledge and facilities available to the War Department and other areas of the government that needed help; Eloise Gerry had moved to Columbia, Mississippi, to help the navy by applying her knowledge to the research of the wood in its ships; and Koehler was basically in charge of the Wood Anatomy unit.

Three thousand pieces of wood came to the Forest Products Lab for identification in September 1918, the most in its short history. The government wanted to make sure the wooden parts of war equipment came from the best possible lumber, and thus knowing the origin of the material coming to the laboratory was vitally important to winning in Europe.

In 1920, Arthur became the head of a new FPL division, Wood Technology, formed due to the growing belief by Forest Service management that there should be a closer relationship between the living forests and products made from wood. The lab's wood collection was still small, only a few thousand samples, the majority of which were native to the United States. Only a small percentage was tropical.

It was as the head of Wood Technology that Arthur was now being called as an expert witness. Besides his testimony in the murder trial against John Magnuson, he found himself testifying in civil cases as well, including an insurance trial where he was asked his opinion on whether a tree in question had been hit by an automobile sixteen months prior. He appeared as a witness on behalf of the Federal Trade Commission when it was trying to stop the Indiana Quartered Oak Company from selling material identified as Swietenia, or "true mahogany," when in reality it was Shorea, or "Philippine mahogany." The resulting cease-and-desist order against the company was later upheld by the 2nd Circuit Court of Appeals and the US Supreme Court.

Koehler wasn't necessarily a fan of the courtroom or, more specifically, of being a witness. "A wittness [sic]," he wrote his brothers, "has got to be one sided or he won't be asked to testify, and he can't say any more than he is asked. There is no chance for a wittness [sic] to get up and give an impartial discussion or opinion of the case."

He wrote his first book, *The Properties and Uses of Wood*, released in 1924, in part to "increase interest in wood by more widely disseminating information about it." But more fundamentally, his work was important because "better selection of [wood] materials and improved manufacturing processes also mean the production of more satisfactory products. This is of direct benefit to the consumer and eventually results to the advantage of the manufacturer.

"The builder who sees to it that his lumber is carefully selected and properly seasoned, and that untreated and non-durable wood is not used in situations which favor decay, is building not only for the advantage of his client but also for the good of his own reputation and the permanency of his own interests."

Two years later, in 1926, he wrote *The Kiln Drying of Lumber*, also published by McGraw-Hill. Shortly thereafter, his FPL department was expanded to become the Division on Silvicultural Relations, "to tie in more closely with the work in the field," and he was promoted to run it. He kept even busier by teaching courses in forest products at the University of Wisconsin and giving speeches like The Unusual Uses of Wood, which he delivered to the three hundred people attending a January 1927 meeting of the American Institute of Electrical Engineers.

"Unusual uses of wood often bring to light qualities that might not be suspected when one sees the wood used in carload lots," he said in that speech to the electrical engineers in Pittsfield, Massachusetts. "For example, spruce lumber is used for siding, sheathing, rough construction and a score of other common-place purposes;

but it issued for airplanes, ladders, masts and the like, that bring out the value of its combination of light weight with rigidity and a considerable degree of toughness—a combination not found in many species of lumber." The local newspaper, the *Berkshire County Eagle,* called the speech "very interesting."

Koehler's professional life was thriving. So, too, was his personal life.

The Koehlers had moved to Madison and into a five-room upstairs apartment located within the bungalow-style home of Ethelyn's parents. Her father had added a second story to his home to accommodate the new family. The city, in the south-central part of Wisconsin, had become the state capital shortly after its founding in 1836. Three lakes are found within its city limits. The university opened in 1849; less than a decade later, Horace Greeley would declare Madison to be "the most magnificent site of any inland town." By the time the Koehlers arrived, more than thirty thousand people lived in Madison and the State Capitol building was almost fully constructed.

The Capitol was built at a naturally elevated location in the city center, on a narrow isthmus between two of the city's lakes, Mendota and Monona. Its dome mirrors that of the US Capitol in architectural style, made of white Vermont granite and flanked by four wings of equal size.

Edgar and Marie Smith's home sat just a block from Vilas Park, a large public space with an adjacent free zoo. The Henry Vilas Zoo was named for the young son of Colonel William F. and Anna Vilas who had died due to complications from diabetes. The family donated the land to the city and stipulated that the park and the zoo always remain accessible to everyone and admission free. Neighbors in the Vilas Neighborhood could hear the lions roar.

Arthur and Ethelyn paid her parents 20 dollars per month in rent and evenly split with them the cost of utilities and other expenses. Arthur was earning 125 dollars a month at the lab, supplemented by the 30 dollars per month the couple received from the buyers of their Washington, DC, home. They bought a car and joined the First Methodist Episcopal Church in downtown Madison. Ethelyn joined the Ladies Aid.

Arthur's financial ledger chronicled expenditures in categories such as groceries, meat, milk, household running expenses, household permanent, clothing for each member of the family, and "Better Life," which included spending on such things as going to the movies, dining out, and donations to the church and to charities.

The Koehlers took trips to Niagara Falls and California, the latter sparking a love of the western part of the country with side travels to Cripple Creek, Colorado; the Grand Canyon; Catalina Island; and Portland, Oregon. Arthur loved the outdoors, and the family picnicked and camped all along their journeys.

By 1916, plans were underway to build their own home a few blocks from Ethelyn's parents, and Arthur took a large role in the process. He had helped his father build a new farmhouse, putting up studs, nailing on sheathing and siding, shingling, laying floors, fastening wainscoting, and helping with the painting, so it was no surprise he felt comfortable supervising the building of his new family home.

The land cost $1,400, and contractors cost $1,850. Arthur paid for it by borrowing money from two banks and his parents. When it was completed in 1917, the two-story Arts and Crafts–style home featured a den just off the entryway and a small living room on the other side. A brick fireplace separated the living room from the dining room, where all the family meals were eaten. Wainscoting made of the best wood available lined the lower few feet of all the first-floor walls.

The dining room led out to a back porch that ran the entire width of the house. A small kitchen, with a built-in nook for breakfasts, was at the back of the first floor. A side door adjacent to the kitchen led outside and to steps heading down to a basement full of the results of fruit and vegetable canning and also Arthur's tools.

On the second floor were the bedrooms, four in all, and the house's sole bathroom. They would need the extra bedrooms, as Kathryn, whom they called Katie, was joined by Ruth in August 1918. In addition, Arthur's younger brothers Walter and Alfred often stayed with them while they were taking classes at the university.

The Koehlers continued to travel throughout the 1920s, making multiple visits out west, to Yellowstone, Salt Lake, the Black Hills and Badlands of South Dakota, and back a couple of times to Colorado. The family traveled around the upper Midwest, including Minnesota and northern Wisconsin, as well as out east to Gettysburg, New York City, and Washington. All the while, Arthur taught his girls about trees and Ethelyn shared her passion for bird watching.

Arthur and Ethelyn bought lots along Lake Mendota, west of the city, in 1925, and Arthur supervised the construction of two cottages, primarily for summertime use. One was "Big Cottage," for his family's use; the other, "Little Cottage," was intended for visitors and for renters. The land and construction cost just under $8,000.

Arthur corresponded with his brothers and father throughout this time with a circular letter that traveled from one Koehler man to the next, with everyone responsible for updating his own personal and professional life for everyone else. Arthur created his first efforts in spirals on two paper disks in an effort to make his brothers laugh. The goal was to be true to the concept, with each word following the next clockwise in a circle, expanding from the center out to the edge of the paper. He attached his pen to a second pen that wrote on the paper attached to the side of a large grindstone wheel that Ethelyn was drafted to turn. At the beginning of the fourth side, Ethelyn turned it too fast, leading to scribbling and requiring Arthur to explain to the rest of the Koehler men that he "forgot the outer edge of a disk moves faster than the center. You see I am not faking this. It is such natural slips that a good detective looks for in the genuineness of a piece of work."

They called their never-ending correspondence *The Flying Dutchman*. The name could have had a few different meanings. First, "Dutchman" was common slang at that time for a German. Second, one of the most famous baseball players of the era, the German-American Honus Wagner, was nicknamed "The Flying Dutchman" for the way he flew around the bases. Or, maybe they named it for the phantom ship and its crew doomed to never finding port, celebrated by Richard Wagner's opera, *Der Fliegende Hollander,* or *The Flying Dutchman*.

Whatever the genesis of its name, the missive allowed the Koehler men to share their successes and failures, worries and dreams. They wrote about their jobs, families, and every other topic

Louis, Ottilie, and their five sons who lived to adulthood. From left, in order of age: Hugo, Arthur, Ben, Walter, and Alfred. (Courtesy: George E. Koehler)

imaginable. Following one trip to California, Arthur wrote, "The reason why I did not stay is that nobody offered me a job. There are two places in the world, where I would like to live, namely, Berkeley, California and Madison, Wisconsin."

Ethelyn became more active with their church, and the family attended regularly. She enjoyed handicrafts, bird watching, and hosting various groups at the house. However, the Koehler girls, Katie and Ruth, would say Ethelyn's chief "project" arrived on May 5, 1930, in the form of a baby boy, George.

"Ruthie! Ruthie!" Katie yelled, running down the block after hearing about his birth. "George is here—and we love him." Katie was sixteen and Ruth eleven when George arrived. Arthur and Ethelyn were forty-five and almost forty-two, respectively.

Times were tough as the Great Depression swept the country. No raises were offered at the lab, and Arthur supplemented his income with book royalties, lectures, investments, and real estate. He was able to maintain the family's quality of living during an era few others would. The family spent eight dollars on a new baby carriage since the last one had been sold years earlier.

Their youngest child would give them numerous scares in his early days. On September 18, when George was just four months old, Ethelyn put him down for an afternoon nap on a thin rubber sheet spread on her bed, leaving a young couple, Bill and Helen Hildebrand, to babysit.

"George caught hold of one corner of the sheet and pulled it over his face," Arthur would write in *The Flying Dutchman* of October 22, 1930, explaining that the baby had swallowed part of the rubber blanket. "[Helen] said she heard a peculiar noise coming from the room, so she looked in and she found him unconscious and blue in the face. . . . [Her husband, Bill] is a medical student and he happened to be [there]. She called him and he used artificial breathing on him and he soon come to enough to breathe himself."

Katie recorded in George's baby book that "George was unconscious for about six hours—till 9:30 PM. At ten o'clock, Mother fed him a little weak formula milk and he went right to sleep and slept till 6 o'clock, when he was just as normal and happy as ever." The incident would be reported in the *Wisconsin State Journal* two days later under the headline "Student's Efforts Save Child's Life."

About a year later, George drove his "Kiddy Kar" down the cellar stairs, leading to profuse bleeding and a scar under his lower lip.

In far more peaceful moments, Arthur often took his son out for evening walks, politely touching the brim of his hat if a lady were to pass by. George would sit on his lap, drawing "monkey faces" on his face using a mechanical pencil with the lead withdrawn.

In 1932, Koehler's division continued to collect and care for wood samples, microtome sections, and photomicrographs. The Forest Products Lab had outgrown its space on the University of Wisconsin campus, and Congress authorized a new building. The facility was constructed for $735,298, west of campus, adjacent to the railroad tracks. Everywhere one looked in the new building, there was wood: wood floors, walls, desks, chairs, and stair railings. The entryway floor was inlaid with several wood species.

The southeast corner office at the top of the new building belonged to the head of the Division of Silvicultural Relations. Koehler could sit at his desk there with a clear view of Lake Mendota.

By 1932, Arthur belonged to the American Association for the Advancement of Science, Sigma Xi honorary scientific fraternity, the Society of American Foresters, and the International Association of Wood Anatomists and was an associate editor for the *Journal of Forestry*. He was also supervising efforts to measure the relation of growth conditions to wood quality in southern hardwoods and conifers. In addition to his management role, he worked in the lab himself, furthering work that had started in 1920 to recognize wood of abnormal shrinkage, so that it could be guarded against or properly diagnosed immediately if troubles arose.

He was subpoenaed in early February 1932 to travel to Lake Charles, Louisiana, for a case involving a failed piling at the city's harbor. At that time he was also working on a technical paper about raised grain and starting on another one dealing with causes of brashness (tendency to break) in wood.

Arthur was content at both work and at home. He and Ethelyn had purchased a new Studebaker to replace their old Dodge and an 8-millimeter movie camera to capture family moments on Adams Street and their travels around the country. The family was doing

Arthur moved to Madison in 1914 to work at the Forest Products Laboratory. He and Ethelyn, shown here with their two youngest children, George and Ruth, in 1930, also had an older daughter, Kathryn. (Courtesy: George E. Koehler)

well. Katie was studying sociology at the University of Wisconsin, living at home. Ruth was enrolled at the newly opened Madison West High School and enjoyed birding and playing piano, just like her mother. And Arthur was having a ball with George, making him laugh by tossing him into the air in the front yard.

At work, he kept on his desk a clipping from the *Forest Service Bulletin* of August 22, 1927, that he glanced at whenever he needed inspiration. "We like to talk of the importance of our vanishing timber supply and the need of conserving it," the passage read. "But more important than the number of board feet of lumber in a forest is the spiritual medicine it contains for what ails us, particularly us of the U.S.A. There is nothing like the sun-dappled aisle of a forest to foster in the human heart a new sense of humility, a fresh appreciation of privacy, a better perspective regarding the values of life. And if any people ever needed these things, we do."

He'd soon find out exactly how true that prophecy was.

3

Before there was Lucky Lindy or the Lone Eagle, there was Slim. Charles A. "Slim" Lindbergh was just another eighteen-year-old on the University of Wisconsin campus without direction—at least, that's what his professors thought. A tall, lanky kid from Little Falls, Minnesota, he had arrived in Madison in 1920 on his Excelsior motorcycle, late for registration and his first mathematics class.

He picked Wisconsin because it had the best engineering school close to his hometown. His father had been a US Congressman for a decade before returning to his Minnesota farm. His mother, Evangeline, decided to go to Madison with her son and had arrived in town before him. She found them a third-floor apartment blocks from campus on North Mills Street and got a part-time teaching job at Emerson Elementary School on the city's east side. She initially found Madison "a queer place" and never completely embraced its charms.

"I couldn't understand why his mother would leave her husband in Minnesota to be with her son in Madison," Slim's engineering school friend Delos A. Dudley would later write in his book, *My Lindbergh Papers.* "However, I asked no questions and no explanations were given."

Their apartment featured a two-foot by three-foot picture tacked to the back of the entrance door. The picture showed a high-speed train with black smoke pouring out of its stack and "US Mail" displayed on each of its three cars. In the foreground, next to the embankment, was a ditch in which, Dudley remembered, was "a hen running at top speed, pursued by a rooster running at even greater speed. I do not recall if the title of this gaudy picture was 'The Fast Mail' or 'The Fast Male.'"

Delos met Slim through a mutual friend, Dick Plummer, who knew that both young men liked to ride motorcycles. All three were freshmen in the Engineering College. Dick and Delos would ride on Sunday mornings, sharing a rebuilt Harley-Davidson, with one riding perched on the gas tank since there was no buddy seat. Slim brought along his Excelsior.

During the winter, a ski jump was set up at the top of a hill with a landing along frozen Lake Mendota. Slim wanted to take the jump in his motorcycle, but until he could figure out how, the steep, winding road down from the jump back to campus would have to do. It started as a straightaway before a sharp turn onto Park Street.

"Dick and I shuddered," Delos remembered. "We did our best to talk him out of it, but Slim was adamant. We rode down Park Street to the hill. Dick and I remained at the bottom, stationing ourselves and my bike out of harm's way. Slim rode up the hill, then out of site [sic], as he rounded the curve.

"Soon Slim and his bike came into view, picking up speed all the way down. He reached the bottom, attempted the turn, but the cycle and Slim hit the curb and both were slammed into the fence. Now neither Dick nor I wished to copy this feat of willpower and grim determination."

Both rider and cycle were fine. What happened next, though, confounded Delos.

> Slim said, "If I had applied power as I hit the turn, I could have made it."
>
> Dick and I watched in amazement as Slim mounted the cycle and turned up the hill. Dick and I resumed our position of safety. Slim and the cycle came down as fast as before. On reaching the bottom and beginning the turn, Slim put on power. They rounded the curve and straightened up on Park Street. Slim had ridden down the hill, around the sharp corner, and had not touched the brakes.

Lindbergh chose to show neither willpower nor grim determination in his studies, though. He was put on probation after his

Charles A. Lindbergh became the most famous person in the world when he successfully flew across the Atlantic Ocean. For a short time during his two years at the University of Wisconsin, he lived in an apartment connected to the home of Arthur Koehler's in-laws. (Courtesy: Library of Congress)

first semester for poor grades in chemistry and math and for failing English. While he was interested in solving his calculus problems, he had no desire to copy the solutions. "Why should I hand in this paper?" he said to Delos. "The instructor knows the answers."

More why's came from his frustration with his English class. "Why should one spend the hours of life on formulae, semi-colons, and our crazy English spelling?" he would later be quoted in the book *Lindbergh* by Scott Berg.

Lindbergh did excel in one area on campus, as a member of the school rifle and pistol teams. Whether upright or prone, outside or inside, firing .22-caliber rifles or Colt .45-caliber pistols, he regularly shot perfect scores. For fun, he liked to shoot quarters out of a teammate's hand from fifty feet away.

"[He] was a crack shot," Delos later remembered. "He established a record for hitting consecutive bull's eyes. As far as I know, that record was never equaled, not even approached. Lindbergh told me he never drank tea or coffee because caffeine was bad on the nerves, that he had to have steady nerves in order to shoot at his best. I was a good shot too, having been awarded a 'Qualified Marksman' medal in the R.O.T.C. However, I could not compete with Lindbergh."

The team finished the 1921 season ranked as the best in the country, and Lindbergh was its best marksman. But shooting a rifle and pistol would not get him through college, and he was flailing. He didn't know what came next.

As he and Delos spent a good amount of time in the latter's basement, building a propeller-driven ice boat made with cast-off airplane parts, conversation turned to possible careers.

"Why don't you learn to fly an airplane and go into the flying business?" Delos asked.

"After you learn to fly," Lindbergh said after thinking for a moment or two, "being a pilot would be like driving a car. It wouldn't be exciting."

Yet the allure of the air did intrigue him, certainly more so than his classwork. He didn't think "God made man to fiddle with pencil marks on paper. He gave him earth and air to feel. And now even wings with which to fly."

Delos found an aviation magazine and sent off for flying school brochures for his friend. He dropped them off at Lindbergh's apartment. Slim's mother overheard the conversation, and as Delos was leaving, she said to him, "If Charles goes to a flying school, I will hold you responsible."

At the start of his sophomore year, Lindbergh resolved to do better, but it wasn't meant to be. As he would later be quoted in *Lindbergh*, "I have not been a good student. My mind has been the partner of my body rather than its master. For so long, I can sit and concentrate on work, and then, willy-nilly, my body stands up and walks away—to the shores of Lake Mendota; to the gymnasium swimming pool; to my motorcycle and distant country roads."

His mother had left during the summer for Detroit and a full-time teaching job. Needing a place to live, Charles moved into an apartment farther away from campus, just across from Vilas Park. The home, at 1803 Vilas Avenue, was connected to 1202 Grant Street. It was owned by Edgar and Marie Smith and had at one point been occupied by their daughter, son-in-law, and granddaughter, Ethelyn, Arthur, and Katie Koehler, who now lived only a few blocks away.

On those "walks away," Lindbergh likely passed Arthur Koehler on the streets of Madison's near west side. Or perhaps they saw one another when the Koehlers visited their relatives' home for supper. If they did, it never registered with the scientist.

When Lindbergh left the university on February 2, 1922, he was two days from his twentieth birthday. He wouldn't return to Madison until five and a half years later, on August 22, 1927, flying his *Spirit of St. Louis* over forty thousand people who had packed into Camp Randall Stadium to honor him. He would help dedicate the school's Memorial Union later that day.

What happened in between those two dates would give Slim a couple of new nicknames and make him the most famous man in the world.

Soon after leaving Madison in 1922, Lindbergh went to flying school in Nebraska, quickly becoming a barnstormer, doing daredevil stunts at fairs in Kansas, Colorado, Nebraska, and Wyoming. He'd walk on the wings, parachute down from the plane, and then, since it was a fairly low-budget outfit, he'd be the prime mechanic tasked with keeping the plane in one piece.

Two years after that, he enlisted in the army, graduating from its flight-training school as the best pilot in his class. He was then hired by the Robertson Aircraft Corporation of St. Louis to fly the mail between St. Louis and Chicago.

But delivering the mail didn't evoke the sensation that Lindbergh sought, even though twice he had to evacuate his plane by parachute. After all, as he had told his friend Delos Dudley years earlier, "After you learn to fly, being a pilot would be like driving a car, it wouldn't be exciting."

For years, since before Lindbergh had entered the UW, aeronautics' Holy Grail had been there for the taking. A New York City hotel owner had offered a prize of $25,000 to any pilot who could make it nonstop from New York to Paris. Many aviators had been killed or injured trying to earn the money. Lindbergh was sure he could do it if he had the right airplane. He convinced nine St. Louis businessmen to finance most of the cost of a plane he helped design. He would chip in $2,000 of his own savings. He placed the order with Ryan Aeronautical Company in San Diego on February 28, 1927, and he remained there for the two months it took to build it.

The plane would be called the *Spirit of St. Louis.*

Lindbergh felt confident after flying the plane on May 10 and 11 from San Diego to New York City with an overnight stop in St. Louis. That flight took twenty hours and twenty-one minutes, a transcontinental record at the time.

Word quickly spread that this Missouri-based mail pilot just might earn the $25,000 that so many had tried for and failed to achieve since 1919. It was less than two decades since Orville and Wilbur Wright had first conquered the air in Kitty Hawk, North Carolina.

Lindbergh's mother visited him just before he sought to cross the Atlantic. "For the first time in my life," she told her son, "I realize that Columbus also had a mother."

Hundreds turned out at Roosevelt Field in New York on the morning of May 20. Originally called Curtiss Field, the airfield had been renamed in honor of Teddy Roosevelt's son, Quentin, who died in World War I. At 7:40 AM, with 451 gallons of gasoline and five sandwiches, Charles Lindbergh boarded his craft.

He was asked by a reporter if the food would be enough for the journey. "If I get to Paris," Lindbergh replied, "I won't need any more, and if I don't get to Paris, I won't need any more either." Twelve minutes later, at 7:52 AM New York time, he took off with the crowd cheering loudly. Lindbergh never heard it over the din of his plane—a din he'd become accustomed to over the next day and 3,600-plus miles.

The world waited anxiously. Even humorist Will Rogers found no reason for humor while Lindbergh's fate remained unclear. "No attempt at jokes today," he wrote in his nationally syndicated column. "[Lindbergh] is somewhere over the middle of the Atlantic Ocean, where no lone human being ever ventured before. He is being prayed for to every kind of Supreme Being that had a following. If he is lost it will be the most universally regretted loss we ever had."

The image of a sole pilot trying to achieve the previously unachievable captured America like nothing else had. "Alone?" asked an editorial in the *New York Sun*. "Is he alone at whose right side rides Courage, with Skill within the cockpit and Faith upon the left? Does solitude surround the brave when Adventure leads the way and Ambition reads the dials? Is there no company with him for whom the air is cleft by Daring and the darkness is made light by Emprise?"

Lindbergh fought fog, fatigue, and fear, and at 10:21 PM Paris time on May 21, 1927, thirty-three and a half hours after taking off, the *Spirit of St. Louis* landed at Le Bourget Field. Bedlam ensued.

"Speaking was impossible," he would recount in his book *We,* published in 1927. "No words could be heard in the uproar and nobody apparently cared to hear any. I started to climb out of the cockpit, but as soon as one foot appeared through the door I was dragged the rest of the way without assistance on my part. For nearly half an hour I was unable to touch the ground, during which time I was ardently carried around in what seemed to be a very small area, and in every position it is possible to be in. Everyone had the best intentions, but no one seemed to know just what they were."

He wrote that a French general told him, "It is not only two continents you have united, but the hearts of all men everywhere in admiration of the simple courage of a man who does great things." The son of America would quickly be adopted by the world. Theatre audiences in Berlin erupted at the news of his success. An Indian publication outside Bombay proclaimed, "Few things have so deeply stirred the hearts of India. . . . The triumph he has achieved is a matter of glory, not only for his own countrymen, but the entire human race."

Before traveling back to America a few weeks later by boat, he would meet the president of France in Paris; King Albert in Brussels; King George V, Queen Mary, and the Prince of Wales in London. Hundreds of thousands of residents across Europe strained to see him wherever they could get a glimpse, including those near the Eiffel Tower who looked skyward to watch for the *Spirit of St. Louis*.

His return to the United States evoked continued chaos. In Washington, President Calvin Coolidge promoted him to colonel in the Army Air Corps Reserves and introduced him to the country on live radio. Lindbergh spoke only 106 words, mainly about cooperation between America and Europe, and yet 30 million people were riveted to every word. He would leave DC with his image on a ten-cent postage stamp, the first time a living American had earned that honor.

New York came next, with multiple parades in different boroughs, each drawing hundreds of thousands of screaming citizens. Then it was back to St. Louis and the same story: hundreds of thousands of people attended a ticker-tape parade, casting phone books into the sky to celebrate the accomplishment. He had received 3.5 million letters, 100,000 telegrams, and 14,000 parcels since landing in Paris.

Over the next three months, Lindbergh would fly his plane to 92 cities in 49 states, give 147 speeches, and ride in 1,290 miles of parades in an effort to promote commercial aviation. He also received $5 million worth of offers, including movie roles, product endorsements, and public appearances. The offer that he immediately accepted, for a fee of $50,000, came from the Guggenheim Fund for the Promotion of Aeronautics and is what would take him back to Madison later that summer. His appearance in Wisconsin that August was attended by the governor, the mayor, and even some of the professors who had given him failing grades just a few years earlier.

Arthur Koehler's first acknowledged brush with Lindbergh would be in the New Orleans *Times Picayune* newspaper of March 26, 1928, when a picture of the scientist taken at the Southern Pine Association's thirteenth annual meeting just happened to be next to an article and picture of Lindbergh in Washington. That led to a mention in jest in the Forest Products Laboratory bulletin about a "well-known countenance and a familiar bald head" being spotted next to the famous aviator.

Lindbergh returned to Madison the following spring to accept an honorary degree from the school that had flunked him out. On the same stage, in front of thousands of graduates' families and onlookers who simply wanted to see Lindy, Arthur Koehler would receive his master's degree in forestry.

The Lone Eagle remained a worldwide phenomenon. As Fitzhugh Green, who helped put Lindbergh's accomplishments in perspective in the pilot's autobiography, wrote:

> Whether it was his modesty or his looks or his refusal to be tempted by money or by fame that won him such a following we cannot say. Perhaps the world was ripe for a youth with a winning smile to flash across its horizon and by the brilliance of his achievement momentarily to dim the ugliness of routine business, politics and crime. Many said that his sudden meteor-like appearance from obscurity was an act of Providence. Whatever the reason for it all, the fact remains that there was a definite phenomenon of Lindbergh quite the like of which the world had never seen.

The normally reserved Minnesota farm boy was uncomfortable with the attention. Newspaper stories of his engagement at the end of 1928 to Anne Morrow, the daughter of Ambassador

On the spring day in 1929 when Lindbergh accepted an honorary degree
from the school that had flunked him
out, Arthur Koehler was receiving his
master's degree in forestry on the same
Camp Randall Stadium stage. (Courtesy:
George E. Koehler)

Dwight Morrow, usually included words like *seclusion*. Charles and Anne's subsequent marriage and pregnancy made front-pages and radio newscasts worldwide.

Charles A. Lindbergh Jr. was born on June 22, 1930, on his mother's twenty-fourth birthday. Little Charlie, or the Eaglet to the papers (Young Charles to his family), became the world's most famous baby, a seven-and-a-half-pound instant celebrity.

"No royal child, for whose arrival a nation waited with anxious interest, ever attracted more public speculation before its birth or was watched more closely afterward," the United Press wire service reported. "Would it be a boy or a girl? Would he be a flier like his father? Numerologists, astrologers and others wrote articles on the subject. . . .

"The baby's first picture—his orange juice diet—any change of nurses, all were duly recorded in the press in greater detail than if the youngster had been heir to the throne."

There were novelties to commemorate the event, of course. Hawkers peddled post cards, songs, and miniature airplanes all adorned with Lindy's photo. Word that the baby's first book was to be *The Painted Pig,* written by his grandmother, Elizabeth Morrow, warranted a special dispatch from the wire services.

And so when Arthur Koehler picked up his *Wisconsin State Journal* on March 2, 1932, his attention wasn't drawn to the story about the record temperature of 56 degrees set in his hometown the day before, nor to the follow-up report about three men rescued after having falling through the ice on Lake Mendota. He didn't focus on the notice that Albert Einstein, "famous scientist and ardent pacifist," could be speaking later that spring on campus nor on the Ripley's Believe It or Not feature about two men from Rhode Island who played dominoes continuously for twenty years.

No, like other folks in the 98 percent of Madison homes that subscribed to the local paper, Arthur Koehler was captivated by the double-decker headline: "Lindbergh Ready to Pay $50,000 Ransom Demanded for Return of Kidnaped Baby." And he reacted like any father with a son—his was just forty-eight days older than Charles Jr.—would.

"I looked across the breakfast table at my smallest child, a baby son, and I suppose I shuddered," he'd later tell *The Saturday Evening Post*.

His next reaction was less predictable:

> Then, I read further in the newspaper about that homemade ladder left behind by the fellow who had done the crime and I grew excited. You see, that ladder, because it was made of wood, seemed just like a daring challenge.
>
> Within a few days after that I wrote a letter to the Lindbergh baby's father, saying I thought it might be possible to trace that ladder's members until the wood matched up with other wood so as to compromise the man involved. Of course, I'm no Sherlock Holmes, but I have specialized in the study of wood. Just as a doctor who devotes himself to stomachs or tonsils or human vertebrae narrows down his interests to a sharp focus on the single field of his pet passion, so I, a forester, have done with wood.

Koehler didn't hear back. Lindbergh was receiving thousands of similar offers to help, "each writer," as Koehler would later describe it, "adding to the task of those who tried to sift the grain of that correspondence from the chaff."

The problem for the New Jersey State Police from the beginning was the lack of investigative "grain." But this much was certain: on March 1, 1932, sometime between the hours of 8 and 10 PM, the twenty-month-old with the golden curls had been taken from his crib in his second-story nursery. Left behind was a smudge of yellow mud, then another and another, leading to a bedroom window whose shutters remained open. On the radiator grille that comprised the window sill was an envelope containing a ransom note demanding $50,000, of which $25,000 was to be in twenty-dollar bills, $15,000 in tens and $10,000 in fives.

Flipping on the light just as his wife arrived at the nursery, Lindbergh would turn to Anne, seven months pregnant with their second child, and utter the words that would crush parents around the world.

"Anne, they have stolen our baby."

Arthur's own son, George, was 48 days older than Charles A. Lindbergh Jr. Koehler said when he read about the kidnapping, he "looked across the breakfast table at [George] . . . and I suppose I shuddered." (Courtesy: George E. Koehler)

Lindbergh had purchased the five hundred acres perched high on the south face of New Jersey's Sourland Mountain specifically because it was both remote and close to New York City. He had flown over the area and picked the spot from the air, as it was marked by a large oak tree along the edge of the woods where he would eventually build their home. Neighbors would call that tree the Lindbergh Oak. The land was the highest point in New Jersey; indeed, it was the highest point between New York and Philadelphia.

The simple two-story whitewashed stone home north of the village of Hopewell would soon be overwhelmed by New Jersey State Police officers, reporters, and gawkers. A mud-spattered press corps traipsed all over the active crime scene and were allowed to use the garage as a headquarters, where Lindbergh's personal attorney, former WWI army officer Colonel Henry Breckinridge, served them coffee as they filed their stories for worldwide consumption. They speculated more than reported, though, due to the lack of concrete information.

It had to be an inside job, they wrote, after Anne's mother wondered how a kidnapper would know the family was still at Hopewell and not back in New York or at her home. Reporters mentioned that police were scouring the area over Sourland Mountain "into the dense tangle around Devil's Cave and Roaring Rocks, an isolated region which rumor says is inhabited by numerous moonshiners."

They passed along Anne Lindbergh's "heart-broken appeal" to the kidnappers about the diet she had been feeding her son since he began fighting the cold that had kept them in Hopewell that night. It included milk, cooked cereal, one egg yolk, and two tablespoons of stewed fruit. That story ended with the reporter writing, "Follow her request and you may in some small part redeem yourself in the eyes of a contemptuous world."

Hyperbole was not at that moment in the vernacular of Colonel H. Norman Schwarzkopf, who ran the New Jersey State Police. He went on live radio the night after the crime to state quite plainly that "It behooves every law-abiding citizen to co-operate with the police." Further, he encouraged people to report any sightings of unfamiliar infants in their neighborhoods and said, "Failure to solve this crime will jeopardize every home and strike terror in the hearts of all parents."

Congress immediately went to work, calling back to its calendar previous legislation two lawmakers from Missouri had introduced as local authorities were becoming increasingly frustrated by different state statutes governing kidnapping and ransom requests. The bill, which sought to prohibit the interstate transportation of kidnapped persons, had been bogged down by supporters of the Tenth Amendment, which states that powers not expressly granted to the federal government by the Constitution are in the purview of the states.

That opposition quickly faded, though, after what became commonly referred to as the Lindbergh kidnapping. The Federal Kidnaping Act would be passed the next month and signed into law by President Herbert Hoover, who immediately offered New Jersey authorities the support and assistance of the federal government's Bureau of Investigation, run by J. Edgar Hoover.

The original "Major Initial Report," filed by Corporal Joseph A. Wolf, one of the first officers to arrive at the Lindbergh estate the night of the kidnapping, illustrated the problem for detectives. Wolf wrote, "The Kidnappers consisted apparently of a party of at least two or more persons." Yet, after detailing the description of the crime and the premises, the column next to "COMPLETE LIST OF SUSPECTS" read "None at this time."

Further, the "COMPLETE LIST OF EVIDENCE" listed only three items. Police at the crime scene had found a ransom note and a carpenter's ¾-inch wood chisel that measured 9½ inches in length with a wood handle and a cast steel blade. The biggest piece of evidence left behind was a ladder, found sixty or so feet from the home, lying on the ground. It was a three-piece sectional ladder—that much anyone could have deduced. One of the bottom two sections was split where it joined the other, indicating that it had been broken during its use in the crime. Again, it didn't take an expert to figure that out.

Police immediately placed the ladder up against the nursery window on the east side of the home in what reporters called "part of their frantic efforts to solve the mystery." It appeared that only the bottom two sections had been needed to ascend to the nursery, but police displayed all three sections for the news photographers. Trooper Frank Kelly, New Jersey State Police's fingerprint expert, dusted the ladder and found no apparent fingerprints. Investigators found an imprint from the ladder left in the mud and an ambiguous footprint left by a moccasin or a sock, but nothing conclusive. Any other physical evidence could have been overrun by the lack of sensitivity to the crime scene by the reporters, the authorities, and others visiting the Lindberghs at Hopewell.

Over the next week the Lindberghs would receive two more ransom notes, one by mail and the other delivered to Lindbergh's attorney, Colonel Breckinridge. One upped the ransom demand to $70,000, and the other rejected any intermediary the family would appoint to negotiate for the safe return of their child.

Shortly thereafter, Dr. John F. Condon, a retired Bronx school principal, wrote a note to his local paper offering to act as a go-between for the Lindberghs and the kidnappers and to contribute $1,000 of his own money if it led to Charles Jr. coming home safely. Condon's request was granted by the kidnappers via a letter sent back to the newspaper. He adopted the code name "Jafsie," a play on his initials, in his interactions with the kidnappers and was told to keep the police out of the negotiations for the boy's safe return. Lindbergh approved of Condon's intervention, even if the authorities did not.

Meanwhile, police were probing the Lindberghs' servants with questions and forcing them to provide alibis. Henry "Red" Johnson, the boyfriend of the baby's nursemaid, Betty Gow, was immediately taken in for questioning, but all authorities discovered was that he was in the country illegally.

Koehler wasn't the only one who read the initial United Press report, which stated, "With cold daring, the actual kidnaper crept up a short sectional ladder into the second-floor nursery," saw the accompanying picture, and felt compelled to share his personal observations on the evidence with either Lindbergh or the authorities investigating the crime.

O. A. Ross, a consulting engineer with offices in Los Angeles and New York, sent a typewritten letter to Lindbergh on March 3 advising him that "this form of telescoping ladder is extensively

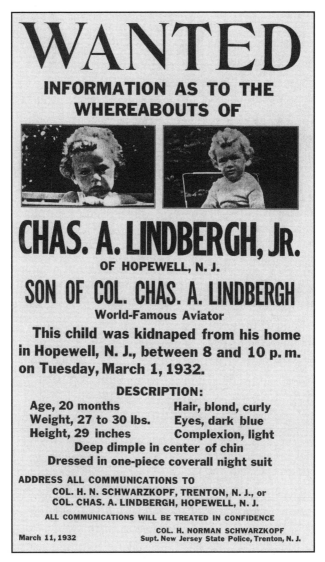

WANTED

INFORMATION AS TO THE WHEREABOUTS OF

CHAS. A. LINDBERGH, JR.
OF HOPEWELL, N. J.

SON OF COL. CHAS. A. LINDBERGH
World-Famous Aviator

This child was kidnaped from his home in Hopewell, N. J., between 8 and 10 p. m. on Tuesday, March 1, 1932.

DESCRIPTION:

Age, 20 months	Hair, blond, curly
Weight, 27 to 30 lbs.	Eyes, dark blue
Height, 29 inches	Complexion, light

Deep dimple in center of chin
Dressed in one-piece coverall night suit

ADDRESS ALL COMMUNICATIONS TO
COL. H. N. SCHWARZKOPF, TRENTON, N. J., or
COL. CHAS. A. LINDBERGH, HOPEWELL, N. J.

ALL COMMUNICATIONS WILL BE TREATED IN CONFIDENCE

March 11, 1932

COL. H. NORMAN SCHWARZKOPF
Supt. New Jersey State Police, Trenton, N. J.

This poster was distributed to law enforcement agencies nationwide for help solving the crime. Col. Norman Schwarzkopf, the head of the New Jersey State Police, said, "If the kidnapper came into this room and told me he had kidnapped the baby, I'd have no case against him." (Courtesy: New Jersey State Police Museum) used by WINDOW WASHERS. Have you recently had such a man working for you? Also have you recently had any common labor working on the grounds? I am an investigator and from facts disclosed believe that the 'job' is a local one and that your child is not far away, perhaps in Trenton."

He went on to "suggest that at least a part of the ladder be taken apart for inspection of the nails used. The manner in which the nails were driven should indicate wether [sic] a skilled carpenter or not made up the ladder. A skilled carpenter can tell you this." He concluded by offering to come to "Hope well" and help "without expense to you, if you so wish."

Ross followed up by sending "Col. N. Schwartzkoph" a note the following day suggesting that "as the ladder seems to be the only tangeable clew left by the perpetrators, this article should be analized from every angle possible."

And if the New Jersey authorities weren't busy enough, Ross suggested "the questioning of all milk delivery men in the territory of Hopewell" as it might disclose if a customer was taking an additional quart of milk daily.

L. Hyman from Atlantic City sent in the second of his handwritten notes on Saturday, March 5, suggesting that the ladder is similar to those "used in the Bronx ship yard. Ascertain if it is one of those and which men used that ladder at the ship yard. All the ladder handlers at the ship yard should be questioned. Note if any of those men are missing and their whereabouts Tuesday night. Only those men using that kind of ladder could put one of them together and set up at the house."

Thomas Bow sent in a note from Congers, New York, with a hand-drawn front view of the ladder and a side view. Pointing to the front view, he asked whether the ladder rungs had been removed "and [the] underside—at joints . . . examined for fingerprints?" Pointing to the side view, he said, "No two wood chisels will make the same markings on wood—The same type of peculiarities exist as on a bullet discharged from a gun."

Alfred Hearn wrote to authorities from Providence, Rhode Island. As someone who had worked in the lumber business, he said, "I am writing this not as a crank but, in the spirit of doing what little I might to restore Little Lindy." After describing what he surmised from the pictures, he explained, "The fact that the rungs are flush with the uprights shows the ladder was originally meant to be telescopic. Boats that pull up to a wharf or dock use this type of ladder due to the fluctuation of the tide."

There was, as the Bureau of Investigation would later state, a "mass of misinformation received from the well-meaning but uninformed, and a deluge of crank letters written by insane persons, nitwits, persons with a degraded sense of humor and others with fraudulent intent."

The Lindberghs believed the crank letters were "standing in the way of progress," and some politicians proposed adding crank letter writing to the kidnapping legislation Congress was forwarding to the president.

The authorities were doing what research they could on the ladder, taking it first to Assistant Director of Construction Squire Johnson with the New Jersey Division of Architecture and Construction. Johnson was the first person with any wood knowledge to look at the ladder. He declared the ladder's rungs in all three sections to be white pine and all of its runners or rails to be short-leaf yellow pine. He identified the dowels attaching the three sections of the ladder as maple.

Johnson's initial notes state that he "wouldn't say it was a good carpenter that made it. One man did the entire job." He also believed the person who made it "either got tired while making it or was in a hurry to finish the job," because the runners were marked for saw cuts that were never made and that "the ladder was made especially for the purpose." Further, despite somewhat large distances between the ladder's steps, "it is an easy ladder to climb for any person used to climbing."

Finally, he stated that the wood used in all but one of the ladder's runners came not from a building, but from crating used in shipping machinery or some similar object or material.

Yet, when he issued his final report to Schwarzkopf a couple of days later, Johnson dispensed with much of what he had earlier reported. His March 10 report told the colonel that "this ladder was constructed by two different persons," not one as he had earlier believed.

Besides a ransom note and chisel, this telescopic ladder provided the only physical evidence left behind at the scene of the crime. Numerous times, detectives simulated how someone could have entered through the toddler's second-floor nursery window. (Courtesy: Dr. Regis Miller/Forest Products Laboratory)

Further, he now said he believed the two smaller portions of the ladder "were constructed by a left handed person, inasmuch as the saw cuts on the rungs of these two sections, by virtue of the splintering or break which occurs at the bottom of every saw cut, indicate that they were sawn by a person who wielded the saw with his or her left hand."

More evidence leading to his conclusion was that the ladder "had been placed on the right hand side of the Nursery window which would be the normal side for a left hand person to work from."

He expanded about the type of person who could operate a ladder like this. "This would be an extremely difficult and if not impossible ladder for a short person or a tall person unversed in climbing to have negotiated. It is considerably more difficult to descend a ladder of this description than to ascend, particularly if both hands are not free.

Also intriguing was Johnson's revelation that a three-foot-long piece of maple "of the identical size and quality as that used in the dowels for assembling the ladder was discovered today in the corner of the Library in Colonel Lindbergh's [home]."

But the most concrete lead Johnson offered stemmed from his original belief that the runners were possibly "part of a crate used for protecting bath tubs in transit." He came to that conclusion because, he said, the wood used in the runners was a "cheap common variety of yellow pine and is not the size or grade commonly used in building construction. It is more commonly called box wood . . . used for the construction of crates." He told authorities that material of a similar grade and age had been found at the State Village for Epileptics at Skillman, New Jersey.

It was the investigation's most tangible lead related to the ladder. Johnson and Sergeant William T. Gardiner of the NJSP headed to Skillman to meet with the head of the facility. The two checked the wood pile and all the wood on the grounds. They found two pieces of the same material but not of the same length as the runners used on the ladder.

The next day, March 8, they procured the names of men who worked on jobs at Skillman and who lived in that vicinity. Gardiner and Johnson interviewed Fred Tomaske, Pete Messenio,

The nursery window where Charles A. Lindbergh Jr. was abducted held few clues for law enforcement officials. The first ransom note to the famous family was found on the window sill. (Courtesy: Dr. Regis Miller/Forest Products Laboratory)

Joseph Del Vilchio, Frank Amalfitano, and Joseph Ruggear. They searched each man's wood piles and found no crate lumber.

The next day they checked yet another man's home and came up empty in the search for crate lumber, so they went back to Skillman to see if they had missed something. They hadn't.

Two more days led to more home wood pile searches, one toolset inspection, and a pile of dead ends. Five days in all following up on Johnson's crate lumber theories had led to nothing.

So now detectives were left looking for a left-handed carpenter who wasn't too tall or too short and who knew how to climb and who had access to crates that might have transported materials like bathtubs.

Not much to go on. The investigation continued.

Sergeant E. Paul Sjostrom of the NJSP went over the ladder thoroughly to "secure the fingerprints in the position the wood would have been held while sawing." He tried all the positions that a ladder could have been held by a left-handed or right-handed person. He discovered five prints, two on the third rung of the first section, one on the fourth rung of the second section, and two more on the second rung of the third section. The fingerprints were then photographed by Trooper Frank Kelly.

Lieutenant Arthur Keaten interviewed Reginald Brown with the New England Organ Company in Boston. Brown reported that after his "examination of the ladder and my experience I have concluded that the manufacturer of the ladder not only possessed mechanical skills but also a knowledge of the standard type of ladder used as equipment for pipe organs."

So now the New Jersey police were on the lookout for a left-handed, pipe organ–fitting, seasoned ladder climber. They would make one more attempt to help the ladder bear witness.

On the recommendation of the New York City Police Department, they brought in Dr. Erastus Mead Hudson, an independent fingerprint expert, to see if he could find what police could not. Mead was a specialist in body chemistry and bacteriology, but while stationed in Liverpool during World War I he had witnessed Scotland Yard detectives taking fingerprints and decided to study the science of dactylography.

Hudson used a chemical called silver nitrate instead of the traditional police method at the time of using powder to lift fingerprints. The soluble silver nitrate reacts to the salt deposits found in sweat and that are present in most latent fingerprints. Ultraviolet light shows a fingerprint in a reddish brown or black color.

Using this cutting-edge technology, Hudson found five hundred or so latent prints on the unpainted wood ladder. While most were unusable, the findings showed just how many people had handled the ladder since that cold first night of March.

The investigation turned back to tracing the ransom money and interviewing potential witnesses and suspects.

On March 16, John Condon received a baby's sleeping suit in the mail, subsequently confirmed as Charles Jr.'s. On March 21, Condon received the eighth ransom note, in which the kidnapper insisted on total compliance and stated that the kidnapping had been planned for a year. A little more than a week later, on March 29, Betty Gow, the young boy's nurse, found his thumb guard, which he had been wearing at the time of the kidnapping, near the entrance to the estate.

Finally, on April 1, 1932, a month after the boy had been taken, the tenth ransom note instructed Condon about where to deliver the $50,000 ransom money the following night. The eleventh and twelfth ransom notes would lead to a cemetery meeting, with Lindbergh himself watching from afar, and the passing off of the money to a man with a heavy German accent that the authorities and the press would call "Cemetery John." After receiving the ransom money, Cemetery John gave Condon another note that provided instructions that the boy would be found on a boat named *Nellie* docked near Martha's Vineyard, Massachusetts. Two searches for the child, including one by Lindbergh himself, would prove unsuccessful. Meanwhile, Condon gave authorities details about Cemetery John so a police artist could create a sketch of the man.

Yet hope and clues dwindled. And on May 12, the tenor of the investigation would completely change. The body of Charles Augustus Lindbergh Jr. was found, partly buried and badly decomposed, about four and a half miles from the home where he had been abducted.

It was a gruesome discovery. His head was crushed, and there was a hole in his skull. Other body parts were missing. The coroner determined he had been killed by a blow to the head and had been dead for about two months.

Hudson, the fingerprint expert, offered an unsolicited theory, "without any doubt, that ladders similar in all particulars to the one used by the kidnapers, are used in South Carolina and Florida for the purpose of gathering fruit. If this is true, then there is in all probability another section of the ladder which has not been found, in which case its discovery would be of great value in establishing the identity of the kidnapper."

Schwarzkopf dispatched Trooper Frank Kelly to follow up in southern New Jersey with various people in the fruit business. Kelly first met Dr. Frank App, the general manager of Seabrook Farms, who said he had been in the fruit business his whole life and "would not state definitely that this type of ladder is used for picking in the fruit business."

To make certain, Kelly interviewed a number of Seabrook workers, including some who were "colored" and who grew up in the South. None had ever seen a three-section ladder constructed like that. Two sections used as a step stool, yes, but nothing like what was used in Hopewell for the kidnapping.

Two weeks later, with clues at a minimum, the New Jersey State Police offered a reward not to exceed $25,000 for information leading to the apprehension and conviction of the person or persons responsible for kidnapping and murdering the twenty-month-old.

Running out of leads locally, Schwarzkopf decided to take advantage of President Hoover's offer of federal government resources. Trooper Kelly was dispatched by his captain, J. J. Lamb, to take the ladder and the chisel found at the Lindbergh estate and a soil sample found under the window of the nursery to US Department of Justice headquarters at 18th and Pennsylvania Avenue in Washington, DC, two blocks from the White House.

John Keith was his contact at Justice. He would take Kelly to meet men from the Bureaus of Standards, Soil, Plant Industry, and Agriculture and the US Forest Service to see if they could discern anything "of value" from the clues Kelly brought to them. Trooper

Kelly stayed with the ladder until the end of the workday before it was "kept in a room locked up" and under guard until the following morning, when the investigation would continue.

Kelly would return first thing the next morning, and by ten AM he'd be back in New Jersey making a verbal report to Schwarzkopf before locking up the ladder in the cellar of the Lindbergh home.

During the ladder's trip to Washington, a Forest Service senior engineer, H. S. Betts, broke off a few small pieces of it and sent them to the Forest Products Laboratory in Madison to be conclusively identified. Upon receiving them, FPL Director Carlisle P. "Cap" Winslow, whose first job for the US Forest Service was investigative work to find better ways to preserve transmission line poles, would head to the office of the Director of Silvicultural Relations.

He closed the door and placed the samples on the desk of the country's top wood identification expert. "Arthur, drop what you're doing," he likely told him. "This needs to be identified as soon as possible. Don't tell anyone what you're doing."

At a lab accustomed to working with divisions of the military, secrecy was not uncommon. But this was what Koehler had written to Lindbergh about two months earlier, offering to help. As he later said, "I have spent many years studying the patterns of wood pores, the structure of its cells by species; how it grows, thickly in the years of rainfall, skimpily in years of drought. For me the world perhaps has too limited boundaries fixed by its kinds of trees and the wood they produce. I work all day on wood with microscopes, calipers, scales and even X-ray machines."

He sent word less than a week later to Betts that he had positively identified the seven samples of wood sent for his inspection. When he personally inspected the ladder at his office in Washington, Betts had labeled the rungs of the ladder 1 through 11 and the six rails (two in each of the three sections) 12 through 17. The numbers 18 and 19 were assigned to the dowels that connected the ladder sections.

Squire Johnson's report was flawed. While he had concluded that all the steps or rungs were white pine and all the rails or runners were shortleaf yellow pine, Koehler's microscope yielded different results.

At least one of the step samples, Number 11, the top step, was Douglas fir, as were two of the rails, Numbers 14 and 17.

Also, despite Johnson's proclamation that he had found maple in Lindbergh's library identical to the wood in the ladder's dowels, Koehler determined that sample Number 18 was birch, not maple, and said more specifically that it was likely paper birch.

He made that determination because, as Betts would record in his report to J. Edgar Hoover at the Bureau of Investigation, microscopic inspection showed it was "covered by a thin film which gives a fatty or oily reaction with a reagent known as Soudan IV. The material, however, has not penetrated the pores appreciably, indicating that it was put on sparingly, as linseed oil or wax that might have been rubbed on with a rag. This coating also indicates that it was part of a handle. Paper birch is used to some extent for the cheaper grades of long handles."

Further, Koehler thought he had struck gold with the discovery of a number of fibers, apparently textile fibers, "clinging to the loosened grain." Two were golden yellow; others were deep purple or white. They appeared to be wool and/or cotton.

Investigators would later discount Koehler's fiber evidence, because everywhere the ladder had gone to be studied it had been wrapped in woolen and cotton blankets that were golden yellow, deep purple, or white.

Hoover forwarded Betts's report, with Koehler's findings included, to Schwarzkopf. It did confirm to authorities that the species used in the steps and sides of the ladder were not grown in New Jersey. The Douglas fir and Ponderosa pine were western woods, while the southern yellow pine was from the southern part of the country, but all were frequently used throughout the eastern states.

Further, Betts pointed out that Rail 16 had "four rectangular nail holes made by old-fashioned cut nails." Betts also reported that at least two of the nails had been driven in at an angle.

Dr. K. F. Kellerman, the associate chief of the Bureau of Plant Industry, also sent Hoover a report on the ladder that would be forwarded to Schwarzkopf, saying that while he had seen ladders like this occasionally used on farms or in orchards, "we do not believe this type of construction is generally used in orchard work or that it is typical of any farming section.

"There is nothing either in the construction or the material used that would identify it either by locality or profession of the maker," Kellerman wrote, concluding, "We believe ladders of this character are used more frequently by mechanics and others doing light work around buildings than by farmers, although mechanics would almost certainly have better constructed ladders.

"We regret we can give no further or more definite information."

When he sent the federal bureau reports to Schwarzkopf, Hoover wrote, "the information contained in the reports by the several scientists is unfortunately very meager, but probably to be expected under the circumstances."

The investigation was, to use a metaphor Koehler and his colleagues might have, growing dormant. The leads were drying up.

But as Koehler knew, dormancy can be tricked. Without question, the growth and development in an organism's life cycle is closely linked to environmental conditions. But that environment can change.

He was plenty busy at work, packing up the office for the move to the new building later that fall and working on projects on reducing waste in logging and lumber manufacture, lowering costs to consumers, and improving the overall usability of wood. Testimony in two more court cases, one in Toledo and another in Cincinnati, was forthcoming.

Yet he felt there was more for him to give to the Lindberghs and the New Jersey State Police. They had taken the ladder many places, "always hoping it could be made to speak." Koehler believed he could create a "wooden witness."

Among the many quotes relating to forests and leadership he had been collecting was one from the nineteenth-century American clergyman Maltbie Davenport Babcock. "We think that conspicuous events, striking experiences, exalted moments have most to do with our character and capacity," Babcock once said. "We are wrong. Common days, monotonous hours, wearisome paths, plain old tools and everyday clothes tell the real story . . .

"The Work Shop of Character is everyday life. The uneventful and commonplace hour is when the battle is won or lost."

Koehler was willing to provide many uneventful hours to this ladder. That's what he did.

He just needed a chance.

4

Iva Marsh knew about struggle.

Growing up in Boston the daughter of a leader in the women's suffrage movement, she had learned the power of words, the power of knowledge, and the power of standing up for women's rights.

"Most women expect entertainment every time they leave their homes and that is something that I do not believe is right," she said. "I feel that, if a woman has reasonably good health and a reasonable amount of time, she should give of it to her community."

That is why when she moved to Wisconsin after the First World War, with her doctor husband and young baby in tow, she jumped right in to assume the telephone chairmanship of the Madison League of Women Voters. Roles on numerous other civic-minded committees followed, as did another child, leading to the near-constant presence of a telephone at one ear and, as she said, the smell of "the milk for the baby's bottle boiling over on the stove."

She was so busy one friend speculated whether she could handle any more responsibilities. To that, another friend suggested, "Sure, if we just give her a minute to put her baby in the ice box."

Marsh still wondered if that was a compliment.

What she knew for sure, as she looked out her on her Maple Bluff neighborhood that Wednesday morning in March, was that she needed time to process her thoughts. She looked out her front window at the maple trees along the street that gave the area its name and then walked to the back of the house and out to a tranquil and semi-frozen Lake Mendota. Usually this time of year there were some fishermen on the ice, but the weather had been so unseasonably warm the first couple days of March that the police and fire departments were warning people to stay off the lake.

Like so many others, she'd read the morning paper's news that Charles A. Lindbergh's baby boy had been audaciously kidnapped out of his nursery window, with his parents downstairs the whole time.

Marsh's husband was at work at the clinic and her kids were at Emerson School—coincidentally, the facility the kidnapped baby's grandmother had taught at less than a decade earlier.

All her life, she'd been taught self-determination. It led to confidence and self-esteem. She was now the president of the Madison League of Women Voters and in that position stressed empowerment and responsibility. "Unless the people of a country have a sense of responsibility about their government, there can be no true democratic government," she said. "All citizens must be imbued with a sense of individual responsibility for the future of the nation."

But now as she bowed her head and closed her eyes, she felt powerless. The mother of two herself, she had read how Anne Lindbergh was trying to go through her daily household tasks without breaking down. The newspaper said the distraught mother was remembering the "flier's motto—keep a cool head in emergencies," but the very next sentence described her "tearful eyes."

Marsh was interrupted by the sound of the phone. On the other end was a staffer with the local paper wanting to know what "the city's women leaders" thought of the crime. He was working on a story for the front page of the March 3 *Wisconsin State Journal*.

Mrs. Harry E. Marsh paused and in a firm, resolute voice said for publication, "There is no punishment adequate. They should give the most extreme punishment to kidnapers."

When the paper came out the next morning, her sentiments were echoed by women across Madison under a headline, "Madison Women Advocate Death for Kidnapers of Lindbergh Baby."

Mrs. James Jackson, who was the executive secretary of the local Girl Scouts council, said, "Punishment should absolutely be death without money being spent on trials."

Mrs. George Ritter, who ran the Madison Women's Club, said, "Kidnaping is inhuman. Persons guilty should be given the maximum punishment."

And Mrs. J. W. Madden, a member of the Madison School Board, said, "No punishment is too severe. Mothers are all in sympathy with Mrs. Lindbergh."

Their sentiment was shared by the editors of their paper, who wrote an editorial called "We Go Primitive." It read, "For several years there has been in the making an American revolution. It isn't 'red,' it comes from the right. It has smouldered in the breast of decent Americans everywhere. It is a revolt against the rule of crime. . . . The patience of the public is exhausted. The fury that makes mobs is near the surface of the law abiding citizens today."

Nationally, legendary humorist Will Rogers turned dark when discussing the fate of his friends' son. "Generally speaking, I'm not in favor of lynchings and mob law and that sort of thing, but I'd gladly be a one-man lynching party in this case."

As 1932 wore on, the authorities were getting angry as well. However, their anger was directed at the lack of credible leads and the abundance of incredible ones, like the one involving a former federal inmate named Fred Tomkins who insisted that a German acrobat, an Australian, and a powerful dwarf had pulled off the crime of the century. The story Tomkins told explained that the dwarf actually went up the ladder and into the nursery to get the baby. Of course, he didn't know their names, and they had all left the country.

The lack of news associated with the case was bad business for an industry eager to slake the thirst of a parched public. The media swarmed in June when Violet Sharpe, who had worked in Anne Lindbergh's mother's home, committed suicide by swallowing poison just before she was due to be interviewed by police for a second time. The first time she had curiously and clearly lied to authorities, but after her death she would be cleared of any involvement with the abduction. Yet the papers buzzed that she must have been involved.

Reporters jumped on the story of Gaston Means, a felon living in Washington after serving two years in prison for lying to Congress about his actions issuing liquor permits during Prohibition. He told Evalyn Walsh McLean, a local socialite and mining heiress, that he could procure the baby for a fee that kept growing until eventually it hit $100,000. McLean was the last private owner of the forty-five-carat Hope Diamond and had married the heir to a publishing empire, so money usually was not a concern. However, when Means kept promising Little Charlie and continued to fail to deliver, she called the police.

Hoover would later call Means, who at one time made a living as a private detective and a salesman before becoming a bootlegger, forger, swindler, and con artist, "the most amazing figure in contemporary criminal history." *Criminal* was the operative word in that description. Means would be convicted of larceny and sent to the Leavenworth federal prison for fifteen years.

The nonstop parade of cranks stymied Schwarzkopf and the others investigating the case. They just couldn't get a break.

As Dr. Carl J. Wardon, a professor of psychology at Columbia University, told the Bureau of Investigation in 1932, "A great number of these letter writers are persons mentally unbalanced. They are border line case paranoiacs. By that I don't mean they are insane but they are filled with delusions of grandeur owing to the Lindbergh case. They believe that Lindbergh may send them an answer which they can show to their friends. It makes them look important. Some of the writers of these crank letters are mono-maniacs, emotionally unbalanced. Some are evidently seeking publicity. If such letters could be stopped the real clue might be obtained."

Arthur Koehler wasn't a crank. He was a man of science who embodied the researcher's motto: "Go as far as you can see and then see how far you can go."

At the start of 1933, he wasn't pining away to work on the kidnap ladder because he was too busy already. In addition to studying the usual number of samples sent to the lab for identification, he was working to identify several hundred timber samples for the city of Cincinnati. Government workers there believed they were buying longleaf pine, which grows primarily in the southeast part of the country. It's a strong species, often used for lumber and pulp. The problem for Cincinnati was that only a few slivers under Koehler's microscope were longleaf pine.

He had also been asked by a ladder company in Toledo to defend their product against two painters who were injured when a ladder rung supporting one end of their scaffold failed. The workers accused the company of using "defective material or 'brash' wood, as the term goes, in the rung that broke." First he needed to test the other rungs. He found them to "show high resistance, slow yielding to pressure and a uniform splintering failure." Translated, it was good wood. Then he looked at the part of the ladder that had broken and found that it carried "a normal load although being bent far out of line." His conclusion was not one the painters wanted to hear. The ladder broke in all likelihood because of "severe damage in the earlier service life of the ladder, as may often happen." The ladder company would win its case.

Back in New Jersey, Schwarzkopf was fighting a different kind of battle than he'd been used to in World War I. In war, there are winners and losers, land and prisoners to be captured. Police work seemed more plodding, with far fewer casualties but far fewer victories as well.

He had been injured in a gas attack in the Second Battle of the Marne in 1918. He knew both pain and agony after seeing friends and ninety-five thousand French soldiers die during that three-week fight.

He was appointed to be the first colonel and superintendent of the newly created New Jersey State Police force in 1921 after he returned from the war. He was twenty-five years old, and his experience was rooted in the formalities, rules, and regulations of the military. That was what he knew, so that's what he brought to this new police force. Duty, honor, and fidelity would be its code.

Now, 5 percent of his enlistment was assigned full time to the Lindbergh case. Numerous others would play roles throughout the investigation. Still it wasn't enough. He needed help, and despite reservations about others grandstanding for credit, he turned to the Bureau of Investigation and J. Edgar Hoover.

Three months after the kidnapping, when the ladder first made its way to Washington, R. Y. Stuart, the head of the Forest Service, had suggested to Hoover that instead of having Koehler identify only the seven samples sent to him, "Possibly you wish all the parts identified." If that were the case, he said, "the Forest Service will be glad to send a representative from the Forest Products Laboratory at Madison, Wis., to wherever the ladder is stored to complete the identification of all parts and to make such further suggestions as may occur to him. This representative would bring with him the necessary apparatus for his work."

The day after the crime, Hoover had offered the federal government's facilities and resources to Schwarzkopf. He had passed Stuart's request on to Schwarzkopf, but the New Jersey superintendent did not initially accept the offer. Then, more than nine months after the toddler had been taken, on January 17, 1933, the head of the New Jersey State Police finally asked Hoover for help.

"Can you obtain for us the approximate cost of this service," he asked. "Said ladder is now being held at Troop C Headquarters, West Trenton, N.J.

"Thanking you for your continued cooperation and assuring you of our desire to be of service in each and every possible, I beg to remain,

"Sincerely yours, H. Norman Schwarzkopf."

Hoover would respond four days later that he had received the request and was "seeking advice as to the approximate cost of the service."

On January 25, Stuart wrote Hoover that it would cost approximately $150 to conduct the complete identification of samples. Hoover immediately forwarded the cost on to Schwarzkopf. Two weeks later, Schwarzkopf reiterated the request for a "more detailed examination" and confirmed that the total expense would be "approximately $150.00" before "respectfully" requesting that a representative come to New Jersey to inspect the ladder.

Stuart forwarded the request to the Forest Products Lab in Madison and Carlisle Winslow, assuring Schwarzkopf that Winslow would "detail the proper man to make the examination."

Winslow once again climbed to the southeast corner office and closed the door. Koehler's new workspace had windows all around. Looking east, he glanced at the State Capitol and the University of Wisconsin campus, before speaking to that "proper man."

His official note to Schwarzkopf read:

I shall be glad to detail Mr. Arthur Koehler of our staff to make further examinations of the wood in the ladder referred to. Mr.

Koehler is a specialist in the growth, structure and identification of wood and is well versed in wood properties and uses. I trust that he can be of assistance to you in this matter.

It is understood that his expenses will be paid by your organization. Since he will be traveling officially it will be necessary to keep his living expenses down to $5.00 a day. He would appreciate it if you would recommend a good, reasonably priced hotel to stop at.

It would be most convenient for Mr. Koehler to arrive at Trenton on the evening of February 27, but if the following day is an inconvenient time for you to see him, other arrangements can be made.

I suggest that any communications regarding this matter be addressed to me and marked "Confidential" on the outside, or if by wire that all reference to Lindberg be omitted, as we do not want to have the matter receive publicity here.

On February 26, 1933, Arthur Koehler was aboard a train for Trenton and looking forward to his first up-close look at the ladder. He didn't know he wouldn't be home again until the second week of April.

"As I sped eastward, I tried to visualize the paths that might lie ahead of me, the objectives that might develop and the guide marks that might direct me in a successful search," he would later remember. "The ladder had apparently offered no decisive clues to police experts. Would my wood detection methods prove adequate to this critical test, or would the ladder be as devoid of fruitful suggestion to me as to any layman? Well, the prospect was vague; it might somehow become clearer through my microscope. I determined to examine that ladder up and down, inside and out, without mental reservations."

Late on the night of February 27, Koehler arrived at the Trenton Rail Station, on Clinton Avenue along the Delaware River and the Raritan Canal. It was one of those great, nineteenth-century brick urban railroad stations with closed gabled bays in the front and back and large eaves to protect passengers from rain or snow. He went first thing the next morning to the State Police Training

School in the Wilburtha section of West Trenton, a series of red brick buildings, Craftsman-style, constructed not a decade earlier. They all had low-pitched roofs and extensive porches. The facilities, which were used for training, housing, and managing the force, comprised an oval-shaped courtyard with a giant US flag and the mess hall greeting visitors at the traffic turnaround.

Koehler duly noted the deciduous and coniferous trees symmetrically placed throughout the compound. The land used to be a farm, so its soil was good for growing.

Schwarzkopf's headquarters was not part of the compound, but he tended to hold staff meetings in his private dining room at the mess hall since it provided more space for his team. His office was across from the State Capitol and was staffed 24/7, as the colonel believed the public should always be able to speak with a trooper if need be.

Next to the mess hall was Building 7, along the southwest part of the courtyard. It featured seventeen windows on each side, a horse corral out back, and a full basement below that contained a holding cell. Built in 1925, it was the second structure at the complex to be completed and served as a barracks for the troopers before becoming the zone headquarters of Troop C.

Now it held arguably the most scrutinized piece of criminal evidence in the twentieth century.

Koehler walked up to the door with "old faithful," his favorite microscope, in one hand and the other extended to meet Colonel Schwarzkopf. Koehler was immediately impressed with the state police facility's "atmosphere of earnestness and hard work." After Schwarzkopf offered him the full cooperation of his force, he introduced him to Captain J. J. Lamb, who was in charge of the day-to-day doings of the Lindbergh investigation.

The two men walked Koehler over to the ladder. It was February 28, one day before the one-year anniversary of Charles Jr.'s kidnapping. The moment wasn't lost on Koehler.

"If it had been the steps to a gallows," he said, "it could not have repelled or fascinated me more."

For the next four days, he would inspect, examine, and analyze every piece of that instrument of evil.

Arthur Koehler would finally get an opportunity to study the kidnapping ladder in 1933, nearly a year after the crime. He would join the investigation after New Jersey authorities asked Bureau of Justice chief J. Edgar Hoover for help from the federal government. (Courtesy: Dr. Regis Miller/Forest Products Laboratory)

His first reaction was disdain. "What it seemed to speak out loud was a charge against its maker, indicting him as a slovenly carpenter," he would later remember.

"Those carpenters who build things for experiments and tests out at our laboratory, you can't hurry them. If you say, 'Just knock these boards together because I'm in a hurry,' you hurt their feelings. They simply have to do a good job, their best because their trade has old, old traditions.

"But this ladder was shamefully done."

It was a telescoping ladder, a hybrid between a stepladder hinged in the middle and a full extension ladder, meaning it was either extendable or compressible in nature, as its sections overlapped. The three sections before him were strangely narrow, in Koehler's view. Their width decreased from 14 inches at the bottom to 11 inches at the top, so that they "could be nested together for transport purposes."

Each section was 6 feet, 8½ inches long, so together they reached a total height of 18 feet with overlapping parts. Immediately he could see why Squire Johnson had believed its wood had come from crating stock. The material, Koehler observed, was "flimsy," its construction, "at best, slipshod."

The ladder hadn't been jointed together carefully. All the maker had done was overlap the uprights some eight inches and pinned them with ¾-inch dowels running through bored holes of that diameter. The support for the joints was "inadequate," which was proved when, sometime during the crime, the lower ends of the middle-section uprights, starting at the holes, had split.

"There had been some kind of accident," Lamb said to Koehler when he showed him the ladder for the first time. Further, he told Koehler it did not appear that the third, or top, section would have been needed for access to the nursery. The combined length of the two bottom sections was sufficient to get to that second-floor window.

Koehler shifted his attention from the rails to the rungs, more aptly described as cleats. They were atypically square-edged, not round, and those on the top two sections were recessed or hammered into the uprights. Further, he noticed that the notches mortised by the chisel in the side rails were uneven.

"It clearly was a job no man had pride in," he later remembered. "For a job that was to pull down $50,000, it showed poor foresight. The only piece of good workmanship on the ladder is that most of the nails were driven with the head of the nails flush with the surface of the wood, without making dents with the hammer around the nail head, as most 'wood-butchers' are apt to do."

Interestingly, the rungs were spaced 21 inches apart, "abnormally" far by Koehler's estimation. Traditionally, ladder rungs are anywhere from 10 to 14 inches apart. Whoever had built this had wanted fewer steps to navigate.

That was the clinical, once-over picture. Next, Koehler would perform the "autopsy."

The ladder had to be taken apart. Every rung, every rail was numbered and measured again, calipered for width and thickness, identified by species, and scrutinized for every mark, man-made or machine-made in nature. Koehler explained to the law enforcement officers,

> There are in the United States about 160 species of wood that are sufficiently abundant to be designated as commercial. Some of these are easy to identify exactly; others are almost impossible to distinguish from their nearest relatives, but any one can be quickly assigned to a narrow group by those who know the signs. For instance, there are about 40 American pines, but they fall into three groups of species at most having the wood virtually alike, and these are usually close neighbors geographically.
>
> Barring finer structural details, the criteria of wood identification are the annual growth-ring structure, the pore or resin-duct structure and the cell structure, besides helpful incidental features such as knots and other defects.

Tree rings, or "annual growth layers," Koehler explained, can be seen with a simple handheld magnifying glass. Each ring tends to mark the passage of one year in the life of the tree. The science of tree-ring research, or dendrochronology, was not yet known to a mass audience, and certainly not to the New Jersey State Police. A. E. Douglass was working in the field at the University of Arizona, but he was still four years from opening the country's first laboratory on the topic.

Douglass, Koehler, and other experts knew of only one year in history, 1816, when rings were missing in oak and elm trees in the northeastern United States. In the "Year without a Summer," as it was called, temperatures worldwide had decreased by almost 1.5 degrees. It snowed the first week of June in upstate New York and Maine, and lakes and rivers as far south as Pennsylvania remained frozen until August, choking off tree growth throughout the region.

That was the anomaly. The norm could offer terrific clues to wood identification.

Cutting crosswise into a tree trunk shows the observer the growth layers as rings, while cutting lengthwise of the trunk and through the center shows them as parallel bands. For identification purposes, Koehler preferred to cut along the side of the trunk to get "the so-called tangential section, which affords the most highly figured view of the layers as they emerge at the surface in flowing curved contours."

By looking at the rings on the ends of lumber, Koehler could roughly estimate the size of the trees the wood came from. "Sharply curved rings throughout [the wood] indicate small trees, usually the 'second growth' from lands previously logged over. Rings whose curvature is slight indicate large trees from virgin stands."

The size of the trees could also be indicated by the diameter of the heartwood, or the darker-colored core, found in all pine logs and most other tree species.

But over the next four days, Koehler found the formal identification of the wood species in the ladder "to be no mere academic exercise." It was a "pick-up job," meaning it appeared the person who built it simply picked up what lumber the kidnapper had at his disposal.

"The different kinds of woods used in this ladder indicate that the maker had a limited amount of material to choose from," he reported to the New Jersey State Police.

Koehler identified each piece of the ladder with a number. The bottom cleat or rung was Number 1; the top cleat or rung was

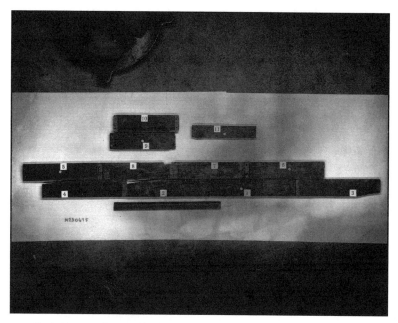

The ladder was disassembled for a closer examination. Each of the rungs (1-11) and the rails (12-17) were numbered for the investigation. (Courtesy: Dr. Regis Miller/Forest Products Laboratory)

Number 11. The ladder rails ran from Number 12 on the bottom left to Number 17 on the top right.

He set about his inspection. Starting from the bottom of the ladder moving upwards, the uprights or rails on the first section, Numbers 12 and 13, measured ¾ by 3⅝ inches, as finished at the mill. The standard piece of lumber in the industry measured 1 inch by 4 inches (1x4) before it was processed at the mill to a traditional ¾ by 3¾ inches. Numbers 12 and 13 also had sharply curved growth layers and a very small amount of heartwood, indicating they came from a smaller tree. Koehler labeled them examples of "North Carolina pine," a term that came about because lumbermen from that state were the first to cut and market wood from smaller trees. The wood was not exclusive to North Carolina and could be found in other southern states.

Further, Koehler noted in his official report, the grain of the bottom uprights "matched end to end, showing that they had been cut from a single strip more than 13 feet long, likely the standard 14-foot length for lumber coming from the mill."

The rails in the middle section, 14 and 15, were the same length as those in the first section, but were Douglas fir, grown largely in the Rocky Mountain west. It had become common in eastern markets, though.

Koehler knew this was not decorative wood. This was practical wood.

"Both the pine and the Douglas fir uprights were so-called 1-by-4-inch stock, mill-dressed, of the type of material commonly used for crating, and in the big cities, for underflooring," he said.

During its late-May 1932 inspection of the ladder, the Bureau of Soil in Washington had found that Number 14 had a large spot of red iron oxide roof paint on it. To Koehler, that meant it had possibly been used as scaffolding or for some other construction purpose.

The rails on the top section proved "a study." Number 17, on the top right, he identified as Douglas fir like the rails in the section beneath it.

Number 16 on the top left, though, was different from the other five rails "in very striking respects." Like Rails 12 and 13 it was North Carolina pine, but Rail 16 was a more knotty type of lumber than the others. And there were other major differences to indicate it had not come from the same tree that produced the others.

First of all, it had not been machine planed like the others, but was hand-planed on both edges. That suggested to Koehler that it had been worked down from a wider piece of wood. It was also slightly narrower than the other rails.

"Why he planed both edges of rail 16 is a mystery unless it was rough edged to begin with," he said in his report to Captain Lamb and Colonel Schwarzkopf. "The edges were not always at right angles to the face, and scratches made by the plane wobbled back and forth along the edge. . . . the scratches left by a hand plane on both edges of this rail were exactly the same as those on one side of each of the [cleats], proving conclusively that they were made by the same plane, and presumably at approximately the same time, probably when the ladder was made."

He came to that conclusion because "a plane would hardly show the same pattern due to dullness for a number of years."

Rail 16 also contained four nail holes made previously by square-cut or 8-penny nails made of iron. They had been in use since the early nineteenth century but had been phased out at the end of the 1800s as it became much cheaper to make round wire nails from soft steel. By 1913, 90 percent of nails made were wire nails. Square-cut nails were still used in some home constructions, however.

The spacing of the nail holes indicated the board and the nails had come from a "building of some kind."

Now, two of the Douglas fir rails had a few irregularly spaced round wire nail holes in them as well, leading him to surmise these pieces of wood, too, had been used before, but their randomness of placement gave no suggestion as to what they had been used for. Rail 15 had one wire-nail hole near the top, one near the middle, and one near the bottom, all driven from the left side of the rail. Rail 17 showed one wire nail hole near its lower end and two in its middle.

A couple of the nail holes showed evidence of rust on the inside, but it was impossible to know if that was from using rusty nails, or because the wood had gotten wet, or because the silver nitrate used to find fingerprints on the ladder had gotten into the holes. Koehler didn't have time at that moment to dissect the wood around the holes for further inspection, and he wasn't sure if he did that he'd find something more. The fact that most of the nail holes did not have discoloration in them indicated the wood hadn't been exposed to nature after it was logged.

The nails in Rail 16, though, were more "significant." None showed signs of discoloration or rust around the heads and around the nail holes, telling Koehler definitively that the original "board had been nailed in a place sheltered from the weather." Specifically, he believed it had come from a "protected location inside a building."

He speculated it came from "the interior of a crude building, possibly an attic, shop, warehouse or barn."

"Although cut nails do not rust as easily as wire nails," he concluded, "if the wood had been nailed down outdoors in the early days when cut nails were commonly used, and had been exposed to the weather since then, there should have been considerable rust and discoloration around the nails."

Further, he believed "the boards were pried off whatever they were fastened to and the nails were driven out from the back side. There were faint indentations near the nail holes on the back sides as if a pry had been used, although the impressions are faint, indicating that the nails were easily pulled."

Moving on to the cleats, or rungs, Numbers 1 through 10, they were made of a soft wood, Ponderosa pine, or California white pine, as it used to be called. Number 11, the topmost rung, was Douglas fir.

Numbers 1 through 8, when placed together end to end into two strips of four each, "could be matched together sufficiently well so that there is no doubt that they were made from one board cut in two lengthwise," according to Koehler. That said, they didn't match sidewise perfectly, measuring about 5½ inches in width when the standard width of dressed lumber is 6½ inches. Even though there was an inch of wood missing between them, Koehler was convinced they had come from the same tree as their outer edges, when matched together sidewise, were perfectly square.

The inner edges of Numbers 1 through 8 were planed with the same hand plane that had worked on Rail 16. The ridges or scratches the planer left were distinctive.

Numbers 9 and 10 did not match up with Numbers 1 through 8, either endwise or sidewise, but they did match together quite nicely. They, too, had the same planer marks as Numbers 1 through 8 and Rail 16.

The ends of Numbers 1 through 10 had all been cut with a saw that did not leave coarse saw marks or break out the wood on the far side. "A fine saw," Koehler deduced and said the sawing seemed to have been done at a 45-degree angle, indicating it was at table or workbench height when it was sawed.

Number 11 was the odd one of the rungs, coming from Douglas fir but not appearing to match the ends of any of the three Douglas fir rails (Rails 14, 15, and 17). There was nothing particularly distinctive about it.

None of the rungs showed any appreciable signs of wear. They weren't worn down from painters or home builders or apple pickers climbing on them. According to Koehler, the evidence indicated that the ladder "had received no previous usage."

In essence, he was reinforcing what authorities already suspected: the ladder had been built specifically for this crime.

The dowels, or pins, used to connect the ladder sections, Numbers 18 and 19, were birch, likely white birch found in the Northeast. They were 1 foot, 3¾ inches long and 1 foot, 2 inches long, respectively. The growth rings didn't show perfect matching, so there was no evidence they came from the same piece of wood.

Both showed faint spiral marks from a lathe and were covered with something like linseed oil, but dirt had gotten into the pores to make that identification difficult. Koehler believed "their fair but not perfect smoothness and thin coating indicate that they were made for a semi-refined purpose, where they would be handled but would not be used for an ornament."

He thought maybe they had come from the handle of a toy rake or a small broom.

Koehler also inspected the chisel found near the ladder. The chisel used to make the mortises for the ladder cleats had been sharp, sharper than the hand plane for sure, and Koehler reported that it had cut the wood smoothly along the grain with no scratches. He said it was not possible to determine the width of the chisel used in building the ladder. He initially did not try to compare the chisel found at the scene with the chisel used in the construction of the ladder, but its impact left an impression nonetheless. Authorities also wondered if the chisel could have been used as the blunt instrument causing the hole in the skull of Charles Lindbergh Jr.

"For all my cold and calculating science," Koehler later said. "I could not touch it without a sense of horror."

On March 4, 1933, he turned in his thirteen-page report and some diagrams to support his assertions. Schwarzkopf and Lamb immediately devised a plan of action and implemented it two days later.

"An obvious thing to do was to make a canvass of territory adjacent to the Lindbergh home to see what house, yard or scrap pile might have furnished the kind or kinds of lumber found in the ladder," Koehler said. "Since the kidnapper appeared to have been sufficiently familiar with the place to know where the nursery was located, the possibility that some of the workmen or others living in the vicinity might have taken lumber for the ladder from the premises and committed the crime was not to be overlooked."

The New Jersey State Police detectives who went with him were Nuncio "Nick" DeGaetano and Lewis Bornmann. Both had been promoted from trooper to detective four months after the kidnapping. DeGaetano had been one of the first officers to arrive at the crime scene that night and had discovered the footprint under the nursery window. More importantly to Koehler, Bornmann was the detective who had found the ladder several yards away from the house.

Koehler was a scientist, used to taking detailed notes. And as a government scientist, he was painstaking in chronicling in his daily reports his every move when he wasn't in his Madison laboratory. As he drove up the long road to the home, Koehler realized this was not a time to sightsee or to be awestruck. He would inspect all of the woodwork in the home, from the basement to the attic.

There was no Ponderosa pine and only some North Carolina pine of a wider stock found in concrete forming, attic floor, and roof boards. It didn't match anything in the ladder. The three men didn't find any Douglas fir, either. They took slivers off the back of some enameled interior trim in the home's library, because Squire Johnson had earlier said it matched what he believed to be the maple wood in the dowels.

Johnson was wrong on both counts. The dowels were birch. And Koehler's microscope helped determine that the wood from inside the library was yellow poplar.

On that first day in the field, they found a birch dowel at an old deserted stone house in the Lindbergh neighborhood and would take it to headquarters. More exciting for Koehler, they went to the home of neighbor Charles Schippel, who wasn't there to let them in. Instead of waiting, Bornmann boosted Koehler by the foot and they got in through a window.

"I was just like a burglar," he said later.

Schippel had remodeled his home within the last year or two, which was obvious because he had unpainted lumber exposed to the weather and it showed no signs of wear. Koehler and the detectives took shavings from a piece of wood with red paint on it to analyze back at Troop C Headquarters because Rail 14 had red paint on it.

"Surprisingly primitive places were visited," he said later about their investigation. "A condition of living existed in some of the hill country that one would associate with the less accessible valleys of the Appalachians rather than with a country only 50 miles from New York City and 40 miles from Philadelphia."

The next day, they went back to the Lindbergh house to look at the old "Gate house" and "Chicken house" at the entrance of the property and the garage, where they found an old hand plane said to belong to the superintendent during construction of the Hopewell home. Koehler tried it on some soft pine nearby, and the markings didn't match those on the ladder.

They also inspected the pile of waste wood left over from the construction of the home. Again, they found no clues.

They went to nearby Princeton, New Jersey, to speak with George Matthews, a contractor on the Lindbergh home, to see if any Ponderosa pine had been used in its construction. Matthews said it had not.

They traveled to the nearby Miller and Sons lumber yard to ask about the use of North Carolina pine, Ponderosa pine, and Douglas fir in that area. They went to Trenton to ask the Updike-Kennedy Company folks the same questions and found out the North Carolina pine was "used for crating by the potteries."

Koehler, Bornmann, and DeGaetano spent the next two days visiting nearly a dozen lumber yards in New Jersey near New York and in Staten Island. Few outlets were using Douglas fir. More had Ponderosa pine, but nothing matching the marks on the ladder. Repeatedly they heard that North Carolina pine was not used in Jersey but was found in subfloors and concrete forming in New York City and Brooklyn.

So that's where they went next.

On March 10, Bornmann and Koehler drove to New York City. Their first stop at 74 Greene Street, at Olney & Warren's, who manufactured planing mill machinery, brought nothing but derision.

"We were given rather casual attention," Koehler reported, "with off hand remarks that there would be no chance of tracing the peculiar marks on the edge of the N.C. pine used in the bottom rails of the ladder."

Then, they went to the Production Machinery Sales Company, 52 Vanderbilt Avenue, which sold woodworking machinery. There they were told the marks on Rails 12 and 13 were "due to a bolt on the cutter projecting beyond the knives, or to some sharp projection on the guides, but that those things might occur on any planer and could not be traced to any particular make or type of machine."

On to the Berst-Forster-Dixfield company, 1602 Craybar Building, which distributed dowels. While the people they spoke to were very courteous, they offered little productive information.

The pattern continued. They heard that Douglas fir was not normally used in New York and the vicinity, but maybe in crating or bulkheading in freight cars.

Despite the dead ends, Schwarzkopf was pleased with his new wood expert and the leads he was pursuing. He sent Carlisle Winslow a telegram: "Request permission for Mr. Koehler to continue investigation for week longer stop thanks for cooperation."

Winslow responded that that was "satisfactory" before issuing a gentle reminder. "Assume you will continue to cover his expenses," his return Western Union telegram stated.

First thing the next morning, Saturday, Koehler and Bornmann met with H. C. Padon of the Yates-American Machine Company at 405 Lexington Avenue in New York City. Yates-American was one of the largest manufacturers of planers in the country. Padon believed the peculiar markings "might possibly be due to a chip being firmly lodged between one of the knives and the block of the cutterhead, or to a projection on the guide." Worse for the detective and the scientist, he thought that "it might occur on any type or make of planer."

From there, they headed down to the docks, visiting first a wood products company that supplied boat builders and then three more outfitters. They had no luck finding ¾-inch birch dowels on the water.

So then Koehler went to a number of hardware shops and stores that had household articles on display in lower Manhattan. He was trying to prove his theory that the ladder pins were made from some type of handle. He spent the afternoon at large retail stores, ostensibly to find ¾-inch dowels, and was successful. At Wanamakers, they were used in painted toy broom handles and in apparently shellacked long dustpan handles. Macy's also had the painted toy broom handles, plus mop and dustpan handles with a transparent coating on them. Woolworths, opposite Macy's, had toilet brushes with painted and uncoated ¾-inch handles.

The team took Sunday off before heading to Philadelphia on Monday. During a stop at the Sears, Roebuck plant there they found rugs rolled on bamboo sticks, oil cloth on a hollow cardboard core, and toy broom handles made of conifer, not birch. They searched the toy, kitchen, sporting goods, and hardware departments but found nothing.

The Pennsylvania Lumbermen's Association allowed them to attend a meeting of its members where they inquired about North Carolina pine and Rail 13. The association's members looked at the evidence and said that "it might be used for many purposes, including trim." They thought it came from farther south than

North Carolina, perhaps Georgia. They were surprised it had been dressed to 3⅝ inches and not the more common 3¾-inch width.

At another toy maker, Heintz Manufacturing on Front and Olney Streets, they discovered that the company's toy garden sets used to use ¾-inch birch dowels had been turned over to another company.

Back they headed to New Jersey and more meetings with lumber companies, one of which suggested that the source or outlet for the North Carolina pine might "be traced through wholesalers, as they keep a record of sales for several years back."

On the morning of March 15, Koehler went through the left door at the mess hall into Schwarzkopf's private dining room, where he met with Captain Lamb, Lieutenant Keaten, a federal Department of Justice agent, and other New Jersey State Police officers. Koehler briefed them on what he knew and, more importantly, what he thought they could learn.

"Good police work and science are similar," he once said. "Both are investigative in nature and usually entail much legwork and drudgery."

This case appeared to be no exception. Schwarzkopf, with no other viable leads to pursue, asked Koehler to continue and sent Winslow in Madison a long note explaining why he needed to keep the country's top wood scientist on the case—indefinitely. He told Winslow that Koehler was "making progress," and that meant "more angles to be looked into and investigated. He continued,

> In handling a matter of this kind it is our policy to exhaust the possibilities of the matter in hand. The progress made so far thoroughly justifies a continuation of our investigation and forcefully brings to attention the necessity of exhausting every possibility of obtaining information.
>
> Under these circumstances, it is respectfully requested that Mr. Koehler be granted an extension of time to work with us, in fact an extension long enough to satisfy the absolute completion of the investigation and the exhaustion of the possibilities of obtaining information. Daily discoveries and contacts lead to further possibilities and it is impossible at the moment to estimate just how long it will take to complete this phase of our investigation.

After promising Winslow that he would continue to pay Koehler, this military man who had little to be happy about in his floundering investigation became effusive in his praise for the scientist. "Our contacts with Mr. Koehler have been such, up to this time, that we have learned to feel the utmost confidence in his ability and integrity," he wrote. "I feel that the earnestness and interest, as well as the effort and ability, which he has so generously displayed, is deserving of the highest commendation."

He copied R.Y. Stuart, the head of the Forest Service, who was first to respond, saying he was "very glad indeed to know that the cooperation that Mr. Winslow and Mr. Koehler of the Forest Products Laboratory have been able to extend to you has been satisfactory. . . . It is my sincere hope," he continued, "that Mr. Koehler will be able to find some clue, however small, that will be of some use to you."

Winslow also expressed his contentment that the partnership seemed to be going well and told Schwarzkopf that he had wired his charge to continue "his work with you for whatever period of time he feels desirable. I am quite satisfied to rely on your and his judgment as to how long he should stay," his letter read. "I, of course, hope that his work with you will lead to something of definite and tangible value in the important problem which confronts you."

Meanwhile, Koehler and Bornmann were back at the Institution for Epileptics at Skillman for a second time, and again they found no wood similar to that used in the ladder. Over the next week, they racked up the mileage, going to Massachusetts, New Hampshire, and back to New York City. They visited lumber yards, broom handle companies, and furniture warehouses. They brought samples, Rail 13, Rail 14, and Dowel 18, to show their interview subjects. They learned that Douglas fir samples could be roof boards or door jambs and that birch dowels could be flag sticks or chair stretchers.

Finally, back at Troop C, Koehler would look again at Rails 12 and 13, the North Carolina pine boards cut from the same piece of wood. He had initially noticed depressions on the wave crests on one edge of Rail 13 and thought it was a compression from the building of the ladder. But with his "old faithful" microscope there to help him out, he discovered that the depressions were actually cut away.

That meant the wood had been treated or trimmed *before* it became part of the ladder. He knew Rail 16 and the rungs had been hand-planed with the same instrument, but that likely remained in the possession of whoever made the ladder and thus would need to wait until an arrest was made for comparison purposes.

However, the machine planer marks on Rails 12 and 13 might be able to be traced. Koehler knew he needed to go back to New York City. With Bornmann alongside him, he went back to the Yates-American Machine Company in the Chrysler Building. A representative from the S. A. Woods Company joined them. Between them, the two companies manufactured about 90 percent of all the machine planers used in planing mills nationwide.

They agreed the depressions were likely due to a projection on one of the knives in the side cutter head of the machine that had planed the wood. That meant the distance between the depressions would indicate one revolution around the side of the wood. There were six individual knife cuts on the edges per revolution and eight individual knife cuts per revolution on the top and bottom faces of the rails.

Bornmann could follow along so far, but the conversation soon eluded him.

"Assuming a speed of 3600 r.p.m. for the side heads," Koehler said to the group, "the rate of feed through the machine was calculated as 258 feet per minute and the revolutions of the top and bottom heads as 3304 r.p.m."

The resulting conclusion, however, Bornmann could understand. One of the edges of the two rails was off. It wasn't planed smoothly. The planer had left telltale marks on it that, if the tool had been working correctly, would not have been there. It was a clue, albeit a difficult one to trace.

"The fact that the top and bottom heads apparently revolved at a different speed than the side heads indicated that the machine was not electrically driven," Koehler wrote in his report. The Yates and S. A. Woods representatives agreed, saying it sounded "reasonable," but they didn't think there were many machines like that in operation in the North Carolina pine district and that "such machines probably were equipped with automatic feeding devices since it is impracticable for a man to feed the machine by hand."

Koehler would leave the seeming contradiction of whether the planer was automatic or manually fed for later. He had the outline of fingerprints on the rails in question and needed to get back to Troop C Headquarters so he could more precisely measure those markings.

After what he called a "careful check up," he calculated the distance between revolution marks on the distinctive edge of Rails 12 and 13 was 0.86 inch. There were six knife marks per revolution, and the width of those knife marks was 0.143 inch. On the faces, or the top and bottom, the distance between the revolution marks was 0.937 inch. They showed eight knife marks per revolution and were 0.117 inch wide.

He submitted the supplement to his report to Captain Lamb along with illustrations backing up the numbers, diagrams highlighting certain features of the ladder, and drawings of the planing marks. He explained that a machine with different speeds for its top and side heads is belt driven, not electrically driven, and that it would have had an automatic feeder.

Koehler's next step was to send a letter to Yates-American and S. A. Woods headquarters, asking if and where they had sold planers in the eastern United States that might "do the work indicated by the planer marks on the North Carolina Pine rails Nos. 12-13." Koehler also decided to send a request to J. A. Fay & Egan Co. in Cincinnati; the company usually dealt with smaller woodworking machines, making it unlikely it would provide useful information, but Koehler wanted to be thorough. So he prepared another letter, this one for the West Coast Lumbermen's Association in Seattle to see if it knew which mills might have had planers that could have left the marks in question.

"An attempt is being made to trace the origin of the lumber in the ladder used for kidnapping the Lindbergh baby, and your cooperation is solicited," the letter began. Koehler went on to describe the distinct revolution marks and knife cuts on the North Carolina pine's edges and faces and asked the companies if they put out a machine that did such work.

"Finally one edge of the 'North Carolina' pine used in the ladder shows rough work, as if the knives had not been jointed or the spindle was loose in the bearings, and a projection on one of the knives cut out a short, shallow groove each time it came around, which may make it possible to locate the particular mill that dressed the stock."

Koehler and Bornmann started visiting homes again in the area, looking at wood samples and bringing planers and other woodworking tools back to headquarters for further inspection. They looked through chicken coops, basements, pottery stores, barns, attics, backyards, and wood piles. The end result was a lot of stories for Koehler to tell his wife in the strictest of confidences, but no evidence. Yet their efforts weren't completely unproductive.

"The net result of this preliminary search was to exonerate adjacent residents from any suspicious connection with the ladder and this was something gained," he would later write.

At the end of March, Koehler took a day trip to Washington to meet with his colleagues, H. S. Betts and Arthur T. Upson, who ran the National Lumberman's Manufacturers Association. From there, he went back to Philadelphia, to the freight yards of the Pennsylvania and Reading Railroads to look for 1x4 North Carolina pine strips.

As the calendar turned to April, Koehler had been gone from home a full month, and like M. M. Baringer, whom he met at Hill's Refrigerator Factory in Trenton, he remained "at a loss to explain the shallow interrupted groves on . . . rails #12 and #13." Bornmann told his superiors that the ladder investigation "can be advanced no further at the present time," until replies came to the form letters Koehler was preparing to send out to planer manufacturers.

The detective's summary of their status wasn't all that encouraging. Starting with the dowels or pins connecting the ladder sections, they knew they were white birch, but it was "of a common variety and could have been purchased or picked up at any one of a thousand different sources, therefore must be eliminated as a possible lead to the solution of this crime." When it came to the Ponderosa pine rungs, "the only possibilities" were the hand plane marks, but they needed to find a suspect before they could make any comparisons.

As to the Douglas fir Rails 14, 15, and 17, Bornmann said the general opinion of lumbermen interviewed and of Koehler was that the rails provided "no possibilities," due to a lack of distinguishing marks.

"The only possibilities," he wrote, "lie in the North Carolina pine rails #12 and #13." But even they didn't offer much hope, according to the detective. "It is the consensus of opinion of most of the lumbermen and woodworking machinery manufacturers interviewed that there is a bare possibility that these yellow pine rails can eventually be traced to the mill from which they originated."

Further, "the only one who would be in a position to have noticed indentation marks made upon one of the edges of these rails, and which indentation marks are the only characteristics whereby this lumber might be traced would be the operator of the planer at the time this stock had been run through. He would have to view this lumber and the indentations thereon, inasmuch as, he is the only one who was in a position to notice any peculiarities or defects in the planer and would remember correcting same."

Bottom line: he thought the services of Arthur Koehler could "be dispensed with for the time being."

The scientist, however, was more optimistic, still believing the wood could talk.

Koehler headed back to Madison and his lab. Winslow would arrange a strictly private workspace and all the necessary optical equipment needed. Parts of the ladder could be sent there under strict guard. Privacy was vital. Even Cora Bilsey, his secretary, would be sworn to secrecy.

"I concluded that it had not divulged all its clues, and I resolved to study it," he later said. "Really study it, this time."

5

General John Pershing had been in France less than two months when he knew what needed to happen. The French and British wanted not just US military help in their battle against the Germans in World War I, they also wanted our lumberjacks. Trained lumbermen were desperately needed to build plank roads at the front, bomb proofs to protect from shelling, barbed-wire stakes, and ties to repair or build railroads.

So America's top field officer cabled the War Department asking for a force of "lumberjack soldiers," capable enough to cut upwards of 25 million board feet per month. A year later, the requirements of the American Expeditionary Force would be more than 73 million board feet per month.

In May 1917, the 20th Engineers began accepting 250-man companies across the Atlantic Ocean. Over the next twelve months, forty-seven more companies of forest and road engineers would go to southwestern France. A forty-ninth would go to England to help cut lumber for the British government.

The Landes forest, or *La foret des Landes* in French, is the largest maritime-pine forest in Europe, bordering the ocean on the west and with rivers running every other direction. It is rare in that it is a manmade pine plantation, created in the eighteenth century to prevent erosion. In its early days, residents needed stilts to get across the wet terrain, but by the time the American servicemen got to the 3,900-square-mile forest, it had been rehabilitated.

Interestingly, the pines surround a natural forest created by the glaciers, with oak, alder, birch, willow, and holly trees. Commercial interests wanting wood, paper, and pine resin had dominated the area in the decade before the war, so the infrastructure was in place to support the army's needs.

To staff the forestry units, the call went out to men with lumber companies and associations, to men who grew up on farms just like "Black Jack" Pershing in Missouri, and to men who simply liked getting their hands dirty. They came from every state in the Union, hardy and resourceful, to help. As Lieutenant Colonel W. B. Greeley told *American Forester* magazine after the war ended in June 1919, "They came straight from her forests and sawmills, trained in her woodcraft, with all of the physical vigor, the adaptability to life in the open and the rough and ready mechanical skill of the American woodsman. They knew their work and were ready to put all that they had into it."

Edward Manning Davis and John Brown Cuno were two such men. They willingly cut fuel wood, hauled logs, and built sawmills and docking facilities for landing soldiers, their shoulders aching from long, back-straining hours of chopping and hauling lumber.

They may not have been on the front lines, facing fire, but still Greeley said of providing the infrastructure to win the war, "It is doubtful if American resourcefulness was ever put to harder test than during the first months of forestry work in France."

Cuno was in one of the first lumberjack companies after receiving his undergraduate degree in forestry from Penn State University and a master's degree in the same topic from the New York State College of Forestry in 1915.

He was working for a lumber company in Columbus, Ohio, supervising the felling and scaling of timber, when the signs of war emerged. He wasn't a farm boy, having grown up in Brooklyn as the son of an editor before earning a first lieutenant commission as the supply officer for one of the forestry battalions.

Davis was born on a farm in Iowa and raised in small-town Connecticut. He had started at Carnegie Institute of Technology in Pittsburgh before moving back to Iowa for family reasons after his freshman year and finishing his undergraduate degree in forestry at Iowa State College in Ames in 1917. While on campus, he worked in the school's forest nursery.

He was working for the US Forest Service in Priest River,

Idaho, when the war broke out. Then he was a private in the 17th Company of the 20th Engineers, serving as an acquisition specialist, a tree scaler, and an instructor in forestry at a French university.

When Cuno, Davis, and their fellow lumberjack soldiers returned from France in the spring and summer of 1919, their legacy was impressive. They had built and operated eighty-one sawmills, cutting two million feet of lumber, ties, poles, and piling every day. In their first year alone, the forestry troops would cut 300 million board feet of lumber and ties, 38,000 piles, nearly 2.9 million poles of all sizes, and 317,000 cords of fuel wood.

"It is impossible, in a few words, to tell of the labor, the Yankee ingenuity, and the resolution to back up our fighting doughboys which were called for to win these results," Greeley wrote. "Nor is it possible to describe the pressure upon all of us . . . when every lumberjack in the regiment felt the tenseness of the final grapple and put everything he had into it."

Both Cuno and Davis wanted to continue their careers in forestry. Both knew the preeminent place to do so was the US Forest Service, particularly the Forest Products Laboratory.

Davis arrived at FPL in October 1922 after working as a wood inspector for the Erie Railroad Company in Georgia and as a yard foreman with a lumber company in Kansas City. He was hired as a wood technologist and while working there finished up his graduate work in forestry at Iowa State in 1925.

In 1932, he was put in charge of the lab's efforts to study how different hardwoods act when put through woodworking machines like a lathe or a planer. This came on top of the work he'd already done on machining defects on native softwoods in the south, north, and east. He had also completed studies on density, rings, and growth in southern pine and had testified for the government as an expert witness in a case before the Federal Trade Commission.

Cuno's path to Madison took him first to Washington, DC, where he served as the Forest Service's liaison with the army and navy. After working there as an associate wood technologist, he was transferred to the Forest Products Laboratory in 1926 to work on research in logging, milling, and wood utilization.

In 1932, he co-wrote a technical bulletin for the Department of Agriculture about sawmill and logging activity in the pine forests of North Carolina.

Both men's performance reviews at the laboratory gave them very high marks in dependability, thoroughness, initiative, and having a "scientific or professional attitude; fairness, freedom from bias."

They were trusted employees, much like their colleague Arthur Koehler.

Koehler knew when he returned to Madison and his familiar surroundings in early April 1933 that the investigation of the kidnapping ladder needed to center "more and more closely on the machine planing that the lumber had received at the mill." The marks on Rails 12 and 13 had been "recorded in the faint transverse waves and ripples that the fast revolving cutters leave on the wood surface."

The question was whether it was possible to find a sawmill with equipment that had the defining characteristics found on those bottom uprights of the ladder. It wasn't necessarily a needle in a haystack, but it wasn't Koehler's expertise, either.

But it was Davis's expertise. He was FPL's expert on planing.

Lab director Carlisle Winslow believed that Davis and Cuno, military men who had served their country with distinction, could serve once again—and keep their communications about it to a minimum.

And secrecy was paramount. Koehler, who in his letters to his brothers discussed everything from the boils he'd been fighting to his political views, never mentioned his efforts on this case. "My work in the East is in a state of 'unfinished business,'" he wrote them on April 21, 1933. "Some day maybe I will tell you all about it."

He did tell Davis everything about his investigation. Koehler double-checked his measurements, his observations, and eventually his conclusions with his colleague.

Davis knew that in a typical mill planer machine, a rough board would be gripped between two steel cylinders before the feed rolls, which push and revolve the board forward at a constant speed. Past the rolls are sets of knives, positioned above and below the board. These are called cutter heads. The knives are fixed at equal spacing

Two months of dead ends on the East Coast led Koehler back to Madison and a private workspace to continue studying the ladder. "I concluded," he said, "that it had not divulged all its clues." (Courtesy: Dr. Regis Miller/Forest Products Laboratory)

around cylindrical drums that Koehler would describe as looking like a "paddle wheel."

The cutter heads would be positioned at the distance wanted for the thickness of the lumber, with the knives extending crosswise to the width of the board. They would then revolve at a high velocity and "dress," or cut, the board's upper and lower faces. Past the face cutters are the upright cutters. The number of blades in the upright cutters varies, and while they also revolve quickly, they're not necessarily spinning at the same speed as the face cutters. They dress the edges of the board as it is fed through the planer.

The process wraps up when two outgoing feed rolls, which are timed exactly with the first pair, make sure the board gets out of the planer. If none of the settings are manually changed, board after board should have the same markings from the planer, cut after cut.

Koehler had deduced in New Jersey that Rails 12 and 13 had come from one board cut in two, giving a "twofold record of the planer cycle, which was of great value in checking observations." Davis confirmed there was no conspicuous evidence of "nicks or dull spots" in the planer knives and that the faint intermittent grooves on one edge of each upright were sharp cuts, not so-called "chip marks," which can happen if a chip sticks to a knife edge.

He recalibrated Koehler's measurements and backed up that there was one revolution every 0.86 of an inch on one edge of Rails 12 and 13. Further, they found there were six "short, shallow, equally-spaced waves" impressed on the surface in that distance. That meant there were six knives dressing the edges of the lumber.

Turning to the faces, they calculated that a periodic but slight irregularity happened in the planing every 0.93 inch on the top and bottom of the wood. The two scientists noted there were eight knife cuts every 0.93 inch per revolution, indicating there were eight knives dressing the faces of the lumber.

Koehler called these results "a kind of time-clock record." Davis knew that upper and lower face cutters of planers in eastern pine mills were usually driven at roughly 3,000 revolutions per minute, or 50 per second. The wood traveled an inch every one-fiftieth of a second.

Doing the math using the calculations he and Davis had come up with, Koehler determined that meant Rails 12 and 13 were fed through a planer at around 230 feet per minute. That was fast by eastern mill standards, more than twice as fast, in fact, as the typical pace. The cutters dressing the edges went even faster than those cutting the faces, since they made a complete revolution while the feed was going a shorter distance.

What this all meant was that the machine that cut the ladder's bottom uprights had six knives cutting its edges and eight knives cutting its faces, that the edge cutters went faster than the face cutters, and that the machine that did it was really fast.

They still didn't know though exactly how it all had happened. But wood wasn't supposed to look like this, and likely the person who had dressed it had eventually spotted the abnormalities himself. Koehler and Davis were banking on that possibility.

By now, Koehler had heard back from the three major companies who manufactured planers that fit the general descriptions laid out. He met personally with representatives from Yates-American in the company's Beloit, Wisconsin, headquarters after he returned from New Jersey. There he received a list of 420 firms the company had sold similar machines to, from New Jersey to Alabama. The planers in question were the A-4 and A-5 versions, as well as the company's models number 94 and 95. S. A. Woods Machine Company in Boston sent a list of thirty-six firms that had purchased its #404B planer model. Fay & Egan out of Cincinnati responded that it had not sold any of those machines.

From April 10 to 13, 1933, Koehler wrote a form letter to all of the firms on Schwarzkopf's New Jersey State Police Department stationery and with the colonel's signature.

"An effort is being made to trace some North Carolina pine used in connection with a crime," the letter began. "We are trying to trace it to the mill that dressed it and from the mill to the consumer. Fortunately there are several identification marks on the lumber which may make it possible to do so, and your cooperation is solicited."

After laying out the details of the planer in question (eight knives in top and bottom cutter heads, six in the side heads, and so on), the letter asked the companies if they had dressed 1x4-inch North Carolina pine on it "within the last 3 or 4 years." Koehler added that the wood in question was not finished, but "a common or box grade."

If they had such a machine, he said he would write with more particulars to determine if "it was dressed at your mill."

Then, as if to assuage any fears, he wrote, "You may be assured that giving this information will not involve you in any way, but that in so doing you may be rendering the public valuable service. May we request that you keep this matter confidential, since publicity might frustrate our plans."

The initial response was not good.

The Scarboro-Safrit Lumber Company in Mount Gilead, North Carolina, wrote back to say, "We beg to advise that we do not have a planer or matcher carrying 8 knives in the top and bottom cutter heads. We have never dressed any of our lumber on this kind of a planer."

The Fairfax Manufacturing Company in Orangeburg, South Carolina, had a planer with six knives each on its top and bottom cylinders, as did the A. C. Tuxbury Lumber Company, which wrote, "This eliminates us as a possible source of supply for the lumber mentioned in your letter." The Douglas Machine Company in Luverne, Alabama, had twelve knives on top and bottom of its planer.

The Shippen Hardwood Lumber Company was "unable to give you any light or data to the machine work etc. that you are seeking." The Whittle and Slade Lumber Company in Eufaula, Alabama, wrote that its planer "does not answer" to the description given.

The Dickson-Henderson Lumber Company in Ocilla, Georgia, couldn't help because it was out of business. The Traylor Engineering and Manufacturing Company in Allentown, Pennsylvania, couldn't help because it didn't use 1x4-inch pine in its plant.

As April progressed, the investigation did not, even as Koehler spent all of his "spare time" tracking down leads. A number of letters were returned marked "Unclaimed," "Unknown," and "No such post office in State named." Those who did respond weren't any more helpful.

Victor W. Stewart with the Colonial Pine Company in Petersburg, Virginia, did "not believe that we will be able to be of any real assistance to you in this matter."

The Woodward Lumber Company in Augusta, Georgia, insisted it was "regretting our inability to help you in this matter." The Jeffreys-McElrath Manufacturing Company was "very sorry." The E. S. Adkins & Company representative in Maryland told of the "slight difference in pine that grows in this section and that grown further south."

Others recognized what case they were being asked to help with, even if they couldn't. The J. E. Paterson Lumber Company in Mobile, Alabama, wanted to "assure you that it will be treated confidentially." The Wisconsin Alabama Lumber Company wrote, "We are sorry we are unable to assist you in tracing this lumber as we would like nothing better than to help apprehend the perpetrators of this terrible crime."

Maybe summing up what others were thinking, if not saying, was the representative who responded from the Kentucky Lumber Company in Columbia, Mississippi. "We wish that we could be of some service to you," he wrote, "but this is impossible."

At the same time he was pursuing the North Carolina pine connection, Koehler was actively trying to trace the planing of the Douglas fir rails, Numbers 14, 15, and 17. Bornmann had believed them to provide "no possibilities" because they didn't have distinguishing characteristics, but Koehler and Davis, upon taking a closer look in the lab, found one in particular. Every eighth planer mark was more pronounced, indicating there were eight knives in the upper and lower cutting heads, one of which was "not lined up perfectly with the others."

Plus, one of the fir rails had a patch of red paint on one edge and one face that was about half the size of a hand. It had been identified by the federal Bureau of Chemistry and Soils as red iron oxide roof paint, but Koehler had learned it was also used in cargo shipments to mark off different lots.

Koehler knew Douglas fir came from the Rocky Mountains and forests west to California, so he reached out to the head of the West Coast Lumbermen's Association, run by Lieutenant Colonel

W. B. Greeley, who had also served in the 20th Engineers during World War I. Koehler hoped to get a list of mills that shipped Douglas fir out to the Atlantic Coast.

Greeley's associate, C. J. Hogue, who was in charge of trade extension and technical service for the association, responded to Koehler that there was "very little possibility" that lumber would have been shipped from the interior of the country to the East by rail, because the freight charge would have been too high for such a low-grade wood. Therefore, they concluded it likely had been shipped by boat.

In an April 19 note to Captain Lamb, Koehler deduced, then, that it "practically eliminates the possibility of its having come from Pittsburgh, Buffalo, Chicago or any number of inland towns which would make it impossible to trace it."

Working on both the pine and the fir, Koehler believed that "it should be possible to narrow down the origin of the lumber a great deal more than with only one kind of lumber to work on."

He was also working on the birch dowels, believing them now to be yellow birch, since it weighs significantly more than white birch. He sent back Number 18 to Lamb by registered mail after the paint expert at FPL also checked it out and concluded that the surface coating on the dowels came from handling, not manufacturing.

That said, Koehler and Davis had reason to hope. Fourteen firms out of the 456 queried replied that they had planers that fit the general specifications, including the Woodville Lumber Company in Crawford, Georgia, which indicated it had an A-5 Yates-American model and was willing "in any way to help you check up on this question."

The Waccamaw Lumber Corporation in Bolton, North Carolina, responded that it had two high-speed planers that were the models in question, but it doubted how much it could help, as its planing mill foreman had recently died.

Others like Keystone Lumber in Pittsburgh; Halsey Lumber Mills in Charleston, South Carolina; Roper Brothers Lumber in Petersburg, Virginia; Millen Lumber in Millen, Georgia; and American Car and Foundry in New York continued the conversation, as they, too, had at least one of the planer models in question.

A follow-up letter, also written by Koehler but sent out by Schwarzkopf, went to all of the companies who had answered in the affirmative. If Schwarzkopf's name and location had not tipped them off about what crime he was writing about, the next letter was even more blunt.

"The following request is made of you in the strictest confidence, being in connection with the Lindbergh kidnapping and concerns lumber which we are trying to trace and which is a part of the ladder used in this kidnaping and your cooperation is solicited," it stated before explaining in an enclosed two-page, detailed description Koehler had prepared on Rails 12 and 13 and an exaggerated sketch of the planer marks on the edges of the North Carolina pine. The letter continued,

> The three most logical theories so far developed as to the cause of the shallow interrupted grooves are: 1) A groove cutting knife was inserted in one of the side cutter heads merely for balance but was not set back far enough to completely clear the wood, therefore, it cut a shallow groove each time it came around; 2) a groove cutting knife was ground down to a straight edge, except for a small projection which remained on the edge and cut the shallow groove each time it came around; 3) the edge of one knife was badly damaged except for a portion 0.2" wide which was the only part of that knife which did any cutting.

But then, as if owning up to the long odds investigators faced, the letter read, "We suggest, however, that you consult with your planing mill foreman and develop your own theory as to the probable cause of the shallow interrupted grooves. . . . It is the general opinion that whatever caused the shallow interrupted grooves was something unusual and would be remembered by the planing mill foreman."

It was not as if there weren't doubts about Koehler's and Davis's conclusions to date. The engineers at Yates-American looked over one of the rails and concluded that both sides of the board were planed with six-knife heads, not an eight-knife head and a six-knife head as the FPL scientists had reported. This led Koehler to second-guess himself in a note to Captain Lamb, saying that "perhaps we have put too much emphasis on the 'peculiar markings' on the edge of the rails 12 and 13."

He'd further second-guess himself when H. A. Perkins, the president of the Production Machinery Sales Corporation in New York City, was brought to Trenton for his own analysis of the ladder, paying particularly close attention to Rails 12 and 13. In his forty-five years of experience, including twenty-five as the founder of the American Woodworking Machine Company, he had become known "as an authority on woodworking machinery." Perkins, who refused to be compensated for his efforts aside from his train fare to and from New York, believed that the edges of the rails in question had been planed with a six-knife head on one side and a four-knife head on the other.

Responding to Perkins's analysis to Lamb, Koehler said, "Anyone who wishes to make a different interpretation than I made of the planer marks should be encouraged to do so, especially if he thinks that with a different interpretation his machine set-up would fit the case. We can later straighten out any differences of opinion."

Koehler continued to soldier on despite the doubts. Letters to lumber mills were all fine and well, but he knew he needed wood to analyze. He encouraged Schwarzkopf to send out yet another letter to the now thirteen companies with the planer models in question, asking for two pieces of wood, preferably from two separate strips, of 1x4-inch North Carolina pine, two to three feet long, dressed on the machine in question.

Koehler wanted the lumber to be as clean as possible, but at the same time he wanted samples from at least two years earlier, nothing recently dressed, as the crime had been committed in March 1932. He was presuming that the ratio of the speed of the side heads to the horizontal speeds, and likely to the feed as well, hadn't been changed in that time.

In the June 23, 1933, correspondence, the head of the New Jersey State Police encouraged the companies to send the samples directly to "Mr. Arthur G. Koehler, US Forest Products Laboratory, Madison, Wisconsin," for a "critical check-up of the stock used in the ladder in question."

Koehler received dozens of wood samples every month at the

Forest Products Laboratory, and by including the fake middle initial that had appeared on his high school graduation program, samples related to the Lindbergh case could go straight to the top of the pile. At the same time, a package addressed to "Arthur G. Koehler" would not draw any extra attention from his colleagues.

Schwarzkopf concluded, "No letter of transmittal need accompany any samples sent to Mr. Koehler, as the assumed middle initial in his name will indicate the purpose of the material." Twelve of the companies agreed to send in samples.

This is where John Cuno's knowledge of sawmills and logging activity in North Carolina came in. There was a chance that many of the mills in that region had second-hand planers and thus would not be on the original list from Yates-American or S. A. Woods.

So Koehler and Cuno consulted the *Lumberman's Directory*, which held a list of all the sawmills in the country, and found those listed that were planing North Carolina pine or shortleaf pine from New Jersey to eastern Alabama. After they crossed off those firms they had already written to, the list included 1,140 companies.

Koehler asked Lamb if he could correspond with them directly instead of using Schwarzkopf's letterhead and signature. The captain, though not quite clear about what his wood expert was doing, still agreed.

Koehler used much of the same phraseology as in the other form letters except with no mention of Lindbergh, saying only that FPL was "assisting the police department of an eastern state in tracing the origin of some lumber used in connection with a major crime." His letter ended with the familiar request that the recipient "keep this matter confidential as far as possible, since publicity might frustrate our plans."

In response, eleven more mills reported having planers that fit those characteristics and saw fit to render a "valuable public service" by shipping their wood to Madison, Wisconsin.

The E. H. Barnes Company in Norfolk, Virginia, sent its two pieces of 1x4-inch wood by parcel post. So, too, did the J. H. Steedman Lumber Company in Clayton, Alabama, along with a note from the owner saying that his company was "only too glad to be of any help to you of any nature in this matter. If the above does not cover the subject and is not full enough kindly advise and we will be glad to go into the matter of shipments more fully or as full as we can."

In all, from April to September, Koehler sent out 1,596 requests to lumber mills and companies on the eastern seaboard. In return, he had received twenty-three samples that met the general requirements laid out.

The width of the individual knife cuts from the Roper Brothers samples from Petersburg, Virginia, and from the Millen Lumber Company in Millen, Georgia, were close to those on measurements of Rails 12 and 13. The distance between revolution marks on the Steedman Lumber samples from Clayton, Georgia, was only .01 off from those on the rails. Lipscomb Lumber in Henderson, North Carolina, had only six knives on its cutter head, not eight as hoped for.

Koehler and Davis put each under the microscope. They measured each to the hundredth of an inch. They looked at the sides, the edges, and the faces.

And then they looked at a set of samples sent in from South Carolina. First Koehler, then Davis. Then Koehler again.

The two scientists looked at each other and knew. They had found their match.

6

Joseph Jennings Dorn removed his black fedora and wiped his brow as he climbed the steps leading up to his porch with its paired Ionic columns. He looked back at Gold Street and waved as a passing car tooted its horn and a man's voice yelled, "Evening, J. J."

He didn't know who the driver was, but no matter. A lot more people knew J. J. Dorn these days than he was familiar with, due to any number of his activities, not to mention his surname.

The name Dorn in McCormick, South Carolina, in 1933 was arguably the city's most famous. William Dorn, J. J.'s great uncle, had discovered the second richest vein of gold in South Carolina's history in February 1852 at the site that would be called Dornsville before eventually becoming McCormick, on the Palmetto State's western border with Georgia.

William Dorn had been a farmer who became obsessed with gold prospecting a decade earlier, testing and examining a host of nearby sites. The area included flat, sandy terrain surrounded by extensive pine forests. Dorn would convince a neighbor to allow him to prospect on his land, and in a mere eight years the mine produced more than $900,000 of gold.

Gold in that part of the country was along a geologic belt, discovered from North Carolina into north Georgia. Along his neighbor's land, William Dorn excavated a two-hundred-foot-long trench, and with the help of slave labor, he prospered.

Williams's brother, James, was a successful farmer himself, and his son, J. M. Dorn, was described as "one of the leading men of affairs of Dornsville," owning a saw and grist mill and a cotton gin. However, the next generation of Dorn men would eclipse the business acumen, if not the wealth, of their great uncle.

J. J. Dorn took off his gray suit coat as he passed under his home's open port-cochère with extended roof brackets. The two-story brick home, one of the few brick structures in McCormick, was constructed in the Colonial Revival style just a couple blocks off of Main Street. It was designed by J. C. Hemphill, who had served as a drafter for Thomas Edison.

The brick helped it stay cool during the typical South Carolina summers, of which this August of 1933 was no different. Dorn pulled a handkerchief out of his pocket and dabbed his hairline, which for a man of fifty-eight was hanging in there, even as his gut was starting to hang out. He was overweight by about forty pounds, all of it seemingly showing in his stomach, leaving his tie unable to reach his belt buckle.

He began leafing through his mail. It was a nightly chore, as he received correspondence at so many places and for so many different positions.

With his brother, Martin Gary Dorn, J. J. owned more than a dozen sawmills in South Carolina, sixteen cotton gins, and the M. G. and J. J. Dorn Lumber Company. J. J.'s other activities included serving as president and treasurer of the McCormick Manufacturing Company, president of the Dorn Banking Company, a founder and vice president of the People's Bank of McCormick, and director of the South Carolina Power Company. Plus, he ran a farm with a "fine herd of Hereford cattle."

The diversity allowed the Dorns to survive first the boll weevil outbreak that devastated the area's cotton crops in the early 1920s and then the Depression, which saw McCormick lose more than 15 percent of its population as jobs dried up faster than the South Carolina soil in summer.

After running the county highway commission and the city's public works commission and serving as a trustee on the local school board and as a town councilman, J. J. had been convinced in 1930 to run for state senate. Elected as a Democrat—everyone was a Democrat in South Carolina in those days—he focused mainly on economic issues during his tenure, serving on the banking and insurance committee as well as the commerce and manufacturer's committee.

To be civic and social, he was a member of a number of groups including the Masons, the Knights Templar, the Temple of Shriners, the Elks Club, and the Lions Club.

J. J. Dorn was a busy man.

He said hello to his wife, Honora, and inquired about his daughter, Mabel, a teacher in the rural school district where he had received his only education. Then he turned his attention once again to his mail. The pile seemed to get larger every day.

What caught his attention was another package from the government, this one from a laboratory in Wisconsin. The earlier letter had come from up north, from the Schwarzkopf fellow who was running the Lindbergh kidnapping investigation. Well, the letter hadn't said that in as many words, but even though Dorn lived in small-town South Carolina, the local *Journal and Review* out of neighboring Aiken had covered Lindbergh's plight from cover to cover, and Dorn knew that a letter from the New Jersey State Police asking about wood had to do with that ladder they had found at the scene of the crime.

The new letter hadn't come from the authorities, though, it came from someone named Arthur G. Koehler, who ran a division at the Forest Products Laboratory called "Silvicultural Relations." Dorn didn't know what that meant, but he did know something about wood. He was hands-on at the lumber mill, which was located on the line of the Charleston and Western Carolina Railroad. He and his brother not only provided the locals with the wood they needed, they also shipped product all over the Atlantic seaboard.

In his letter, Colonel Schwarzkopf had asked him to send some samples of yellow or North Carolina pine to Koehler as part of the investigation. They were interested in the speed of his planer and how it dressed 1x4-inch rails in the process. Dorn had instructed his foreman to comply with the request.

Now, Koehler wrote,

Recently, I received from you, evidently at the request of Col. Schwarzkopf, two pieces of 1-inch yellow pine lumber cut from the same stick measuring 3-$\frac{20}{32}$ inches wide and three pieces cut from another stick measuring 3 $\frac{7}{32}$-inches wide. All of these pieces were cut to a length of about 9½ inches.

The pieces which are 3 ²⁰/₃₂-inches wide have practically the identical spacing of planer marks on the faces and edges as were found on the yellow pine ladder rails under investigation, but quite different from those on the pieces 3 ⁷/₃₂ inches wide. Evidently the two original sticks were dressed on two different machines, or possibly the same machine but the speed of feed was faster for the narrower stock.

Before we go any farther, I wish you would send me a few more pieces of the stock which is 3 ²⁰/₃₂ inches wide, for a further check on the planer marks. If you can find some that were dressed a year or so ago on the same machine, so much the better.

Koehler had enclosed two self-addressed government franks, so Dorn could send the samples without postage. He also asked the South Carolina lumberman whether his planer was of the "high speed type in which the stock goes through at the rate of about 250 feet per minute. It is belt driven instead of having an individual motor for each cutter head. Am I correct?"

Dorn wanted to help, but this was getting time-consuming, and he had a number of businesses to run. He set the letter aside, telling himself to come back to it.

In Madison, Arthur Koehler had been positively giddy after seeing the first samples from the Dorn Lumber Company—the first to match the marks on Rails 12 and 13. On the same day he sent the letter to Dorn asking for more wood, he had sent one to Schwarzkopf updating him on his progress. "At last," he wrote, "I received a piece of lumber with planer marks apparently identical with those on the N.C. pine rails. They were received from M. G. and J. J. Dorn, McCormick, S.C."

He went on to comment about how few samples he had received overall. Then he expressed some doubt about the Dorn sample he had just complimented. "I might add that one of the edges of the stock from Dorn shows defects in the planing similar to, but not so pronounced as those on one edge of rails 12 and 13, although they have the same spacing," he concluded. "I hope additional material will show these defects more definitely."

He included a table comparing measurements from the sides and edges of Rails 12 and 13 and the two samples sent in from the Dorn mill. It was the "A" sample that best compared.

While the width of the individual knife cuts from the sides of Rails 12 and 13 was 0.117 inch, sample "A" from Dorn was 0.115 inch. The distance between the revolution marks on the kidnapping ladder rails was 0.93 inch; on the Dorn sample it was 0.92 inch. The number of knife cuts per revolution was eight in both.

On the edges, the similarities continued. The width of the individual knife cuts from 12 and 13 was 0.143 inch, and from Dorn sample "A" it was 0.144 inch. The distances between revolution marks were 0.86 inch and 0.87 inch, respectively. The number of knife cuts per revolution was six in both.

While Dorn was living his life and working his multiple businesses plus serving his constituents at the South Carolina State Capitol, Koehler was anxiously awaiting more samples.

He was also fighting a dizziness that seemed to come and go. Focusing on work helped. So did the Liggett's milk sugar that his brother, Alfred, the doctor, recommended. It was better than the laxative and visit to the oculist that his personal physician had suggested.

When Dorn didn't respond to his letter within a week, Koehler wrote again to remind him. He wrote him again nine days later as a second follow-up.

"Since the letters were not returned you evidently received them, but possibly on account of other work have misplaced them," Koehler wrote, enclosing a copy of his original letter. He ended with a handwritten encouragement to the typed letter that read, "P.S. Please keep this matter confidential as far as possible. AK."

The scientist was persistent. Dorn liked that in a man and thus proceeded to have his foreman ship Koehler four samples of 1x4-inch stock that same day.

Koehler and Edward Davis immediately put them under the microscope. Koehler briefed the New Jersey State Police the next morning. "Where these show the planer marks clearly they show practically exactly the same spacing as those on rails 12 and 13, both for revolution marks and individual knife cuts," he wrote to Schwarzkopf before expressing some doubt.

"They do not show the peculiar planer markings as on one edge just like they are on rails 12 and 13, but they do show faint uniform intermittent marks of the same spacing as on the rails, which may or may not be due to being made by the same machine—I can not tell.

"Since the field was canvassed about as thoroughly as could be done by mail, and since these are the only samples that I received which have the same spacing of planer marks as on the rails, the lead may be worth following up further."

Even more curious, though, the other two samples sent in the second batch from Dorn showed a wider spacing of the planer marks, indicating they were dressed on a "more rapid feed" than the wood whose marks matched Rails 12 and 13. Unfortunately for Koehler, those also did not show the distinctive "grooves" or "indentations" found on the kidnap rail.

So he suggested a trip to McCormick and a thorough "check-up of [the Dorn] stock, and particularly as to whether the defect in the planing of one edge of rails 12 and 13 could have been formed at their mill, thereby definitely pinning down the mill at which the lumber originated."

If he could do that with any reasonable degree of certainty, the detectives could track where it was sold, thereby bringing the wood and the case closer to a potential suspect. Then again, he openly stated that his proposal, "if carried out, may prove to be a 'wild goose chase,' but it is the only lead that I have left, unless use can be made of the hand plane marks later if the problem gets closer to solution through other channels."

Finally, it was out in the open. A "wild goose chase."

That's what the New Jersey authorities felt they'd been on since the beginning of the investigation. They expected more science—even if they didn't understand it—and less speculation from their wood expert.

Schwarzkopf didn't acknowledge the doubt in his reply, simply stating, "It is our wish that you proceed to [McCormick] so that nothing will be omitted on this check up."

So Koehler plodded on, sending yet another letter to Senator Dorn, asking for more information, this time about where the mill sold its lumber and more.

"Can you let me know what your market is for 1x4 North Carolina pine, or was a year and a half ago?" he wrote. "That is, do you sell it all through commission men or do you sell it direct to box factories or such? To what part of the country did it go a year and a half to two years ago? Do you have records of your sales during the last two or three years?" He concluded his letter by writing, "I may be in your section of the country later and call on you, do not go to too much trouble now."

Too late for that. Dorn was now fully engaged with the thought he might be helping, albeit in a small fashion, in solving the murder of the Little Eaglet.

He replied within a day to Koehler's questions. They were selling the lumber through wholesalers and in markets from New Jersey to Rochester, New York. He had all the sales records and invoice files and said that it would likely take a day to get the files together.

"Will be glad to do this for you when it becomes necessary," Dorn concluded. "If you are in this section will be glad for you to call by."

In a follow-up letter to New Jersey, Koehler once again prepared the state police for the possibility he could come up empty in South Carolina—that ten months of study, nearly twenty form letters, and numerous hopes could be dashed.

"I feel encouraged in the way this matter is narrowing down," he wrote. "Of course, I realize that even if we locate the mill that dressed the lumber there still is plenty of chance for getting stuck."

Koehler wrote to Schwarzkopf again just a week later, once again hopeful. For a man of science, he was also being guided by emotions. "I feel that as long as I have been delegated to assist in this work I am going to do as thorough a job as possible," he wrote. "And, as I said before, the fact that the possible origin of the North Carolina pine is narrowing down so tremendously, gives me great encouragement."

He asked that Lamb send one of the bottom rails (Rail 12 or 13) to McCormick or cut the rail in two and send half to the Dorn mill with a letter of introduction in case his Forest Service badge didn't cut it. Schwarzkopf responded in the affirmative on both points.

The first week of November 1933, Koehler was once again on a train heading to the unknown, excitement building with each

Planer markings on Rails 12 and 13 led to a trip to McCormick, South Carolina, and the M. G. and J. J. Dorn Lumber Company. Koehler told Schwarzkopf that it could "prove to be a 'wild goose chase,' but it is the only lead that I have left." (Courtesy: Dr. Regis Miller/Forest Products Laboratory)

passing mile. He wondered if the mill foreman would remember that his machine made that defect. For that matter, he wondered if it was the same mill foreman who'd been there a year and a half earlier.

He speculated about how the spacing of the planer marks on the uprights could match the Dorn samples and yet contain none of those "grooves" or indentations.

McCormick wasn't an easy place to get to. Koehler could figure out how to make it to Atlanta easily enough and even to Calhoun Falls, about twenty-five miles away, but the train didn't go straight to McCormick. So he got off at the town along the Georgia–South Carolina border at midnight and took a bus the next morning, November 7, to McCormick.

There were at least seven structures located on the Dorn grounds. Some were simply roofs on poles, erected to cover dozens of piles of wood. Just a few trees dotted the outlying part of the complex. Thick black smoke came from a stack in one building. Koehler knew that had to be where the dressing happened, and so that's where he went to meet Senator Dorn.

He shook hands with the portly senator in his omnipresent black fedora. Mill foreman J. P. Rush was on one knee looking at one of the wheels on the pulley he supervised when Koehler came in. Rush wore overalls, long sleeves, and a brown hat. His jacket hung on a hook attached to one of the many wood beams throughout the building.

Sawdust hung in the air and covered the unfinished floor. Over their shoulders, Koehler saw one #404B fast feed planer and matcher from the S. A. Woods Machine Company, outfitted with eight-knife round top and bottom cylinders plus six-knife round self-centering side heads.

The Dorns had bought the machine, a type "F" heavy double profiler complete with countershaft devices and spindles, and one Rogers type G-32 fully automatic knife grinder with emery wheel leather belts and an emery wheel dresser for a total of $5,447 on March 20, 1929. They had the receipts to prove it. Koehler would want to see those.

"The package you were expecting came yesterday," Dorn told his visitor.

Koehler opened it in front of them to display a piece of wood that he explained was part of an instrument used in the crime of the century. Dorn and Rush looked at it carefully as Koehler explained in specific detail why he had arrived, hat in hand and hope in heart. He showed them the eight-knife and six-knife planer marks on the ladder rail and the spacing between them that matched the samples from their mill.

They nodded their heads before he explained the key factor missing between the samples and the ladder upright. There were those shallow intermittent grooves, or indentations, on the kidnap ladder rail and nothing similar on either set of Dorn samples.

"It awakened no special recollections," Koehler would later write, "apart from the general recognition that it might have come from there."

The men decided to sift through old lumber around the yard to see if they could find any similarities. To the naked eye, they found scraps that matched both the slower and faster variations in the rate they were dressed, but no detectable grooves on any stock.

It was unlike any mill Koehler had studied, and he didn't understand it, but Dorn did.

"I'll tell you," he said. "The largest feed drive pulley that came with our planer gave us too fast a feed, and the next smaller one gave us too slow a feed for much of stock. So, we bought a pulley of intermediate size from a hardware merchant over here in Augusta, Georgia. That pulley was not standard equipment, but we have used it quite often, and if the ladder uprights were dressed with it, that would explain the matter."

They'd bought the third pulley in August 1929, six months after buying the standard planer and matcher from S. A. Woods.

The men decided to test things out right there. Rush asked the others to stand back and proceeded to dress three separate pieces of 1x4-inch North Carolina pine. One was treated on the largest pulley, another on the smallest, and the third on the intermediate, nonstandard equipment.

They held up each next to the kidnap ladder sample. The first showed marks that were spaced farther apart than those on the ladder rail. The largest pulley went too fast to have dressed the

J. J. Dorn owned the mill with his brother. A pulley they bought from a local hardware shop dressed the lumber that made up Rails 12 and 13. Their detailed sales records also significantly helped Koehler's research. (Courtesy: Dr. Regis Miller/Forest Products Laboratory)

lumber. The second showed marks too close to one another. The third could not have made Koehler happier.

"Sure enough, the planer feed, when driven by the pulley obtained in Augusta, gave exactly the same spacing of planer marks on the edges and sides as were on the ladder!" he later wrote. Because the "pulley was not obtained from the manufacturer of the planer . . . therefore, it is unlikely that another machine would have the same sized pulley, even if the machine were otherwise the same."

Thus, he concluded, "That left practically no doubt that the mill that dressed the uprights of the bottom section of the ladder had been located."

As for the grooves, or indentations, Koehler deduced that those went away when the knives were sharpened. "Here today and gone tomorrow" is how he described them.

Rush told the men he usually dressed ten to twelve carloads of lumber before resharpening the top and bottom knives, and anywhere from twenty-five to thirty cars before resharpening the side heads. That was provided he didn't hit a nail or break a blade in the process.

They moved to the office and turned their attention from wood to a wood product: paper. Now that he had a time frame, Koehler needed sales records. He knew the rails had been dressed by that intermediate pulley, which the Dorns had purchased in September 1929. He decided to cast a broad net and asked Dorn to provide records for any North Carolina pine dressed and sold between August 1929 and March 1, 1932, the date of the kidnapping.

Koehler felt a jolt of energy. The investigation had life. The "wild goose chase" would continue. Even if it remained a challenge, to say the least, the North Carolina pine tree that had produced the wood in Rails 12 and 13 had come from McCormick.

The men pored over the company's sales account sheets covering that thirty-month time frame. Under the heading "Manufacturers of building material, rough and dressed lumber, North Caroline Pine roofers a specialty," they found numerous handwritten entries of lumber being shipped all over the eastern seaboard. Dorn sold to wholesale dealers, the lumber loaded on cars run by the Charleston and Western Carolina Railroad Company. There were records of wood sold and sent to Connecticut; Maryland; New York City; Norfolk, Virginia; Philadelphia; Trenton, New Jersey; Staten Island; Massachusetts; and other places on the East Coast.

Dorn's records indicated date sent, destination, dealer to whom shipped, car initials, car numbers, board feet in question, and the width of the lumber shipped.

Koehler smiled. Dorn was a man with an attention to detail, like himself. He gathered up the records, thanked his hosts profusely, and took the bus back to Calhoun Falls to board a train to Trenton. It was time to brief Schwarzkopf, Lamb, and the others.

On the way, he crafted another letter to be signed by the colonel to send to the places the forty-six carloads of 1x4-inch North Carolina pine had been shipped. He chose to focus on those lumber buyers north of the Potomac River right off the bat, figuring wood of this quality was so common, it likely had not been transported a long distance before being used in the crime. He arrived in Trenton at 2:45 PM on November 9.

"We are trying to locate the place where some 1x4" North Carolina pine lumber was obtained and used in connection with a crime," his note read. "It is definitely established that the lumber was dressed by the M. G. & J. J. Dorn Company, McCormick, South Carolina. Their records show the following destinations for dressed 1x4" stock purchased by you. Please let us know as soon as possible the names of the respective firms to whom the lumber was shipped so that we can contact with the firms directly in tracing the lumber.

"We are interested only in shipments over the period given, and only in 1x4" stock dressed to ¾ inch thickness and 3-¾ inches width."

The original measurements of Rails 12 and 13 were closer to 3⅝ inches wide than 3¾ inches. In fact, one end was just 1⁄32 of an inch shy of 3⅝ inches wide.

Initially, he had wondered whether they had been dressed to the thinner width, or if they had been dressed to the wider width and had simply shrunk over time. From his experience at the lab, he knew that some types of wood shrink excessively along the grain, while in other, more normal wood, the "longitudinal shrinkage is negligible."

He deduced that the wood had shrunk after manufacture, and since one was still a trifle wider than 3⅝, both must have been 3¾ inches wide at the time of dressing. That would help, as there were eighteen carloads of lumber shipped north that had been dressed at 3⅝ inches wide. They could now be eliminated from the search.

Schwarzkopf, who had charged his expert with the directive "that nothing will be omitted," assigned Detective Lewis Bornmann to continue his work with Koehler. The two men were once again tasked with traveling around the area to find lumber from South Carolina with the missing grooves.

"The temporary character of the blade defect causing the chip marks made that slight grooved pattern seem a really priceless indicator to guide us to perhaps a single shipment and locality," Koehler later told a reporter. "But inasmuch as the shipments began more than two years before the kidnapping and this hunt was beginning a year and a half after that event, the trail was cold enough. Still, it was a trail."

The day after arriving back in New Jersey, he and Bornmann were on that trail. Eighteen of the shipments in question had gone to that state (fourteen to Manville and four to Trenton), to two factories.

The rest of the shipments would not be in such close proximity to Troop C Headquarters. On November 16, the two men left New Jersey, and for the next week and a half put a significant number of miles on the squad car. They started in New York City, where eleven of the shipments had been sent, six to Brooklyn and five to Manhattan. First, they visited the National Lumber and Millwork Company, which had received a shipment of 1x4-inch lumber from the Dorn mill in November 1931. National said it didn't have any left and that starting in spring 1930 its sales had been cash only—with the Depression raging, every dime was vital to the business's survival. Further, the wood could have gone to any of National's five-hundred-plus customers who bought in small lots.

Later that day, Koehler and Bornmann headed up to Poughkeepsie, New York, to visit a firm that had received a Dorn shipment in October 1931. A sample taken from a 1x6-inch board found at the J. S. Keathing yard showed the familiar planer marks, but records showed the company didn't get 1x4-inch wood from South Carolina until after the kidnapping in March 1932.

From there they went to Germantown, New York, to the Leland L. Crawford Lumber Company, which had received a McCormick shipment on November 6, 1931. They did not have any of their stock remaining.

The Fishkill Landing Lumber Company in Beacon, New York, had two pieces left from the carload they had unloaded in September 1930. It showed the characteristic planer marks of Dorn's machine, but not the defect on the edge.

Next up was the Cornell-Haverland Company in Pleasantville, New York, where Koehler and Bornmann were told the company "had none of the stock on hand since common lumber is like sugar in a grocery store in that it sells if nothing else does."

They stayed the night in New York City and visited four companies the next day only to be told none of the Dorn stock was still on hand. There was little evidence at any of the four as to where it had gone.

A company in Stamford, Connecticut, had received more than eight thousand board feet of the North Carolina pine from the Dorn mill in August 1931. Nothing to see there. Koehler and Bornmann moved on to New Haven and the Lampson Lumber Company, which did have around a quarter of the carload it had received on September 17, 1931. The planer marks were evident, but the defect on the edge was not.

Still, this wood did show a narrow intermittent indentation produced by a defect in one of the knives. It was narrower and closer to the edge than on the kidnap ladder rails, but it was worth checking out. The plant manager sent them to a nearby house where some of the shipment had been sold. With a light on an extension cord, they could see the faces and edges of the lumber used for shingle lath. The marks were identical with the marks on the lumber still in the yard. As Koehler would write in his field reports, that showed "that a defect in one of the planer knives may persist through perhaps a whole carload and undoubtedly through many thousand board feet before it is remedied by resharpening."

After hitting another dead end at another New Haven yard,

Koehler and Bornmann went on to a Boston firm that had received 18,597 board feet from the Dorn facility in June 1931. The company had been liquidated and had practically no lumber on hand. Three other stops in Boston also led to nothing.

From there they drove to Springfield, Massachusetts, and for the first time encountered some resistance when a local company didn't want to answer their questions. Finally they got through to the manager who, after they explained what they were doing, put the full resources of the company at their disposal, even though he was "certain none of the lumber was now in [his] yard."

They spent the next day, November 24, tracing where the Springfield company had sold the lumber. They stopped at a Miss La Brie's apartment and were told the stock was under wall board and no longer visible. They found some stock at the unfinished home built by J. A. Garneau, nailed to the base of the studding and in the garage. Leo De Blois, a contractor in the Springfield suburb of Longmeadow, had used 1,900 feet of the 1x4-inch North Carolina pine for shingle lath. A. R. Cuzzane lived nearby and had used the 1x4-inch lumber under his shingles. It was visible to a light on an extension cord.

After measuring some of these samples, Koehler ruled out the Springfield yard as the source. He saw the general irregular planing marks, but no edge defect, so the two men were on their way back to Connecticut before the day was over. One lumber yard had no samples left, and another had gone out of business two years earlier.

They went back to New York City, where they stopped at a yard in Brooklyn. A fire a week after the kidnapping had destroyed much of the lumber and all the sales records. A nearby lumber company had some of the scorched remnants of lumber, but after two hours of wandering around the yard, Koehler and Bornmann found none matching that from the Dorn mill.

Their search had yielded lumber dressed on the fastest pulley in South Carolina, but none with the planer defect on the edge. They had traced the lumber from the yard to homes, hen coops, dog kennels, attics, and basements, but came up empty. The following week they planned to head to lumber yards in Baltimore and Philadelphia, both of which had received a shipment of the 1x4 North Carolina pine.

After taking Sunday, November 26, off, they were back in New York City, this time at the Queens County Lumber Company, which had received a shipment from McCormick on December 3, 1931. All the company had left was around fifty pieces that it had used to build small bins for storage of lumber and molding in the yard.

Koehler didn't tell the dealer what he was after, only that he was trying to trace some lumber used in connection with a crime. The dealer said to him, "You got a hopeless task. They tried to trace the lumber in the ladder used for kidnapping the Lindbergh baby and did not succeed."

One look led Koehler to believe he would prove that dealer and every other doubter wrong.

"I got it! I got it!" he wrote to his wife, Ethelyn, immediately after getting back to the Hotel Lincoln in Manhattan around noon. He went on,

> I found the lumber yard that handled the particular shipment of lumber from which part of the ladder was made. It is located in Brooklyn. That lumber, you remember, showed a defect in the planing of one edge and this yard still had some lumber on hand with that same defect in it. Since that defect is due to a dull knife it would be removed in the next sharpening which was every ½ to 2 days and therefore, it is impossible that it would also show up in the next shipment of 1x4 stock which was made 25 days later . . .
>
> Considering the seeming impossible success that we had so far it ought to be possible to finish the job.

He concluded by asking Ethelyn to "Keep it quiet, for if reporters there or anywhere got a hold of it, there would be a stampede."

Two days later, the night before Thanksgiving, he wrote to his wife again, from the Hotel Hildebrecht in Trenton. This time, he was less self-congratulatory.

"Well, I was all wet in what I wrote Monday, but I am dry again," he started.

Although I was sure that the defect in the planing of one edge of the lumber we found in Brooklyn was the same as on the ladder, that lumber was dressed at a faster speed as I could see by the width of the planer marks. Of course they had only a little left in the yard and knowing that it is a simple matter to change the speed, I thought that some of that shipment might have been dressed at a slower feed. So I asked the lumber dealer if he knew where some of the lumber went to. He said the first half of the carload all went into some 2-family flats in the Bronx and the rest went to miscellaneous places.

He explained how he and Bornmann tracked down the contractor who built the homes. Even though most of the wood would have been used in subfloors, they had gone to visit the site anyhow to see if there were any scraps used around basements. The contractor "seemed to know the occupants and walked right into the basements except one which was locked." They found no 1x4 pine. Koehler told the contractor they were very eager to see some of the lumber, so he took out a skeleton key and said, "I try this" and proceeded to go into the locked basement, where they found 1x4 pine that matched what they'd found at the yard.

"That wasn't so good," he wrote to his wife, "for now I wasn't so sure that the ladder came from the Brooklyn yard, and my enthusiasm curve took an abrupt drop. I had also noticed that the planing defect on the lumber was not as close to the corner of the edge as on the ladder. Evidently, they had removed the cutter head and put it back on between the time the ladder rail was dressed and the Brooklyn shipment was dressed—at least as much as we saw of it."

"*Und dann ging mir ein Licht auf!*" he wrote in German. Ethelyn, who had taken eight German courses in college, knew what he was saying, roughly: "And then, a light went on."

However frustrated he was by coming so close at the Queens County Lumber Company, Koehler was so close. He had traveled two thousand miles and figured he was "hot at last" in his quest.

"Perhaps the previous shipment would also show the defect," he speculated before quickly digressing, "Oh, if I hadn't been to McCormick and learned all about their practices how could I have managed?

"Now the previous shipment of 1x4 was made 10 days earlier to the Bronx—I have a complete list of their shipments. Ordinarily, they should have re-sharpened their knives several times . . . for they were dressing a carload a day."

Koehler and Bornmann decided to focus on the previous shipment, dated November 24, 1931, on the itemized sales sheets they had from the Dorn mill. The latter one happened twenty days later to Youngsville, Pennsylvania, and dressed wood ⅛ inch narrower than the stock they were looking for. They figured they could rule that out and head to the Bronx.

As he continued in his letter written the night before Thanksgiving to Ethelyn, they went again to the Bronx to visit the National Lumber and Millwork Company, which had received that previous shipment.

> We had been there once before, before we went to New England, for it seemed like a likely spot and their lumber from McCormick came in about 2½ months before the kidnapping. He had told us then that he had none of the lumber left—that was nearly two years ago since he got it and he said so again today. But we had learned by this time that lumber dealers don't always know their own business so we asked him if we could go in the yard and look around.

After getting permission, they immediately found a pile of new 1x4 lumber that had come from the Dorn mill just four or five months earlier. That wasn't what they were looking for, but at the bottom of the pile were some old pieces.

As he told Ethelyn, he didn't see any other way to check it out but to have them take down the whole pile of wood.

> I wanted to see it awfully bad. I couldn't get around the back to see if any protruded so I crawled over and sure enough long ends of the old stack was sticking out. I asked Bornmann to get me a hand saw and I cut some off and also picked up some broken pieces off the ground which had been there for some time as I could see.

Tracking down lumber shipments from South Carolina, Koehler visited the National Lumber and Millwork Company in the Bronx, where the foreman pulled a piece of lumber for him from a storage shed. "One look was enough!" he wrote his wife. He'd found the place where the wood for Rails 12 and 13 had been sold. (Courtesy: Dr. Regis Miller/Forest Products Laboratory)

I took them out to the light and while I could not be sure that they did or did not come from McCormick on account of being badly discolored, I decided to take them along for further scrutiny but one thing was sure, they did not show its defect on one edge that I was looking for. By this time stock in Detective Co Ltd was pretty low.

It was lunchtime in the yard. As the foreman and one of his helpers sat down to eat, Koehler strode up to him for a conversation.

"Are you sure that the lumber in the bottom of this pile was from the shipment from McCormick in December 1931?" Koehler asked him.

"No, I'm not sure," replied the foreman. But then he said, "I built a coal bin from scraps in that pine shipment."

He put down his lunch, and the men proceeded to the coal bin. They cut off a protruding piece only to find out it was Douglas fir, not North Carolina pine after all.

Koehler's shoulders sagged.

"I got one other idea," the foreman said. "In the summer of 1932 I built some bins in the shed for moldings and miscellaneous lumber and I am quite sure that was from the car." He had his colleague take a saw, crawl through to the back of one of the bins where there was overhanging lumber, and cut a sample for Koehler and Bornmann.

"Make sure you get a good piece—about 18 inches long with square edges," Koehler shouted to the man wedged inside the storage shed.

"He soon had it off and crawled back with it," Koehler wrote to Ethelyn. "One look was enough! Here was the defect and the lumber was dressed at the same speed as the ladder rail. We thanked the men for their trouble, they did not know what it was about, and went back to the hotel. There we compared it with a piece of the ladder rail which we carried with us and the planer marks and defect were identical. If it hadn't been for a slight difference in grain you would think the two were cut from the same piece."

As he further examined the Bronx lumber, he discovered a defect in the planing of the face that was apparent on both the

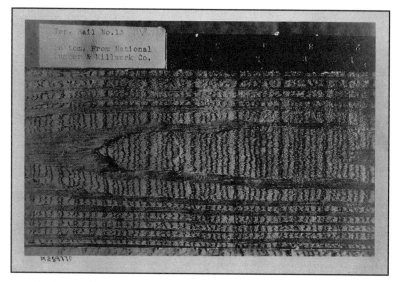

Koehler would later prepare this slide to show the similarities in the rails and the lumber sample from the Bronx yard. The investigation would hit a dead end when he discovered the company only did cash sales during the Depression. (Courtesy: Dr. Regis Miller/Forest Products Laboratory)

ladder rail and the sample. He hadn't noticed it right away because it was stained by the silver nitrate that had been used to take fingerprints off the ladder. But the sample had a second defect that did not show at all on the ladder uprights.

That second defect reinforced Koehler's belief that this Bronx yard had to have sold the lumber in question because it was not found in the sample shipped ten days later to the Queens County Lumber Company. The ladder lumber had to have come from the earlier part of the shipment, while the National Lumber and Millwork sample came from the latter part of the carload.

"This conclusion is made because defects in knives do not disappear as more lumber is dressed, and if the face knives had been sharpened the other defect in one of the face knives would also have been ground out," he wrote in his official report of the visit.

He took it back one step further just to make sure and found the shipment before National Lumber and Millwork had gone to Pennsylvania and had also been dressed ⅛ inch narrower than the ladder rails.

"No doubt now remained," he later told a reporter, "that the retail source of the lower uprights of the ladder had been found and its location was in the Bronx, New York City."

Bornmann's colleagues at the New Jersey State Police immediately went to work investigating the National Lumber and Millwork Company. They now knew the wood had been bought after December 1, 1931, but that's about it.

"I have not yet decided what the next move will be," Koehler told Ethelyn.

That's because the most logical move had been ruled out during his earlier visit. When he and Bornmann had asked to see sales slips, they were informed National Lumber and Millwork had stopped selling on credit in the spring of 1930. Arthur Koehler had found the yard that sold the lumber that made up Rails 12 and 13 only to come up short in finding a suspect. He was shaken.

"It was a hard blow," he told Ethelyn.

It was harder still for the Lindberghs and for the investigators working the case. One of their most promising leads had hit a brick wall.

7

Acting Lieutenant James J. Finn, known as Jimmy to his friends, stared at the three-foot-long New York City map on his office wall day in and day out, looking at the pattern for another clue, something he might have missed, anything that could help him solve the crime that had harmed a man he knew personally.

Green, red, and black pins dotted the boroughs, primarily in Manhattan, the Bronx, and Brooklyn, with a few more placed in Queens. The pins marked locations where $4,200 of the $50,000 Lindbergh ransom money had turned up. Green represented the twenties, red the tens, and black the fives.

The fifty-two-year-old Finn had been with the New York Police Department since 1905. As "one of the smallest men in the department," he didn't really look the part of a cop, but he reportedly made up for that by being "handy with his fists." The newspapers of the day described him as "a slight, nervous and sharp-visaged man."

He would later be described by historian Barry Levy as "not unhandsome, but perhaps unremarkable describes him better. Straight, dark, close-cropped hair parted in the middle accentuated a well-proportioned though square, honest face atop a sturdy but lithe frame. Maybe he is best described as inconspicuous—hardly a disadvantage in his line of work. His pale blue eyes constantly flitted about absorbing details, betraying the sharp intelligence behind them."

It was that intelligence that had defined his tenure with the NYPD. Within only ten years on the force, he was a detective sergeant in charge of some officers in the gangster unit, getting written up in the newspapers for "suppressing violence, dispersing gangs and capturing persons in possession of revolvers."

The New York Times reported that he battled Prohibition violators like the "Hudson Dusters," the "Dopey Benny [Fein] Gang," "Terry Riley's cohorts, the legions of Johnnie Spanish and Humpty Jackson, [and] the car barn outfits in the early '20s" before losing a battle of his own. The politics of the department, insiders speculated, led to a demotion and a walking beat, first in the Bronx and then on Staten Island.

A new police commissioner led to a promotion back to the rank of detective sergeant and eventually to an assignment that was the envy of millions of Americans and others worldwide. By 1927, Finn was on Charles Lindbergh's security detail, serving as one of the aviator's bodyguards when he returned to New York for a ticker tape parade after his successful flight over the Atlantic Ocean.

After the event, Lindbergh sent the police commissioner a note commending Finn and the others on the detail for their "remarkable" work in light of the "tremendous problem" they adeptly handled. He shook each of their hands and thanked them personally before leaving for St. Louis.

During the assignment, Finn became close with Harry Bruno, Lindbergh's press secretary. They stayed friendly through the years, and rumor had it that Finn had been socializing at Bruno's home the night Lindbergh's little boy was kidnapped.

Bruno recommended to Lindbergh that the NYPD put Finn on the kidnapping case, and the aviator asked the commissioner if he could "borrow the detective." His request was granted, and Finn became the NYPD's point person on the crime. More tellingly, he had access whenever he wanted to the victim's family. The Lindberghs trusted him even if the New Jersey State Police believed the NYPD wanted all the publicity surrounding the investigation.

For example, in a letter to his wife in December 1933, Arthur Koehler recalled a meeting with Colonel Schwarzkopf, Captain Lamb, and the other officers in New Jersey where half of the meeting was "devoted to discussing the importance of keeping the investigation quiet. We are no longer to mention the true purpose of the investigation even to reputable businessmen for they all have axes to grind with the papers or politicians." He explained,

Not only would publicity hinder our work a great deal, but they don't want the New York Police in on it because they would take all the glory and the local papers would stand by them. They say there is nothing the New York Police would not to do to have a story to spill about this case. . . .

They said if either the police or the papers knew what I was doing I would have a "tail," that is, one following behind to see what I was doing and a photographer handy to take my picture if I picked up a piece of lumber to examine it.

Finn and his unit at the NYPD didn't have time to worry about the ladder. They were tracking the ransom money.

An Internal Revenue Service accountant named Elmer Irey had the idea to make a majority of the $50,000 ransom twenty-dollar and ten-dollar gold certificates, along with some Federal Reserve notes. Great Britain had dropped the gold standard in 1931 in an effort to prop up its currency and its banks to deal with the Great Depression, and FDR had taken notice. The economic theory was to inflate the value of money in an effort to prevent an economic downturn. By requiring banks and citizens to turn in gold in exchange for standard currency, Roosevelt believed the Federal Reserve could inflate the country's money supply.

Irey knew Roosevelt didn't like the gold standard, and indeed, the president would severely restrict gold's use in the United States in the spring of 1933. Congress enacted a joint resolution a month later nullifying the right of creditors to demand payment in gold if dollars were not available.

The new economic policy doubled as a crime-fighting one. In the context of the Lindbergh investigation, this dramatically limited the yellow-seal notes still in circulation nationwide and drew attention to whoever possessed the currency.

The rest of the ransom money was in five-dollar United States notes with red seals and red serial numbers. FBI records show the ransom included 2,000 five-dollar bills, 1,500 tens, and 1,250 twenties. All were printed in 1928.

The authorities had taken down the serial numbers of the 4,750 bills in the ransom bundle and sent a list, fifty-seven pages long, to banks around the country. Despite efforts to keep that information private, it was leaked by a bank employee and published in numerous newspapers just a month after the crime, in April 1932.

Finn's job became more difficult the longer the case went on without an arrest. Two years after the crime had been committed, he continued to visit bank officials and tellers around New York, reminding them of the type of currency to look for. He had searched a list of those who had rented safety deposit boxes in the early months after the kidnapping, holding the signatures of those individuals to compare against any future suspects.

Finn was working on the money angle in concert with the federal government's Bureau of Investigation, in particular Special Agent Thomas Sisk, a serious young man with a black mop of hair on top, cut short on the sides per regulation. Clean cut and clean shaven, all the government agents dressed formally, in suit and tie.

The first money, a twenty-dollar bill, serial number B04173050, was identified by a teller at the East River Savings Bank on April 4, just two days after the $50,000 ransom was turned over. Finn received a list of the bank's depositors and he and others interviewed them, but turned up nothing worthwhile.

The next clue, a five-dollar bill, serial number B26909389, was deposited at the Bank of the Manhattan Co. on April 14, 1932, by the owner of Schraffts Stores, a lunchroom and candy and ice cream maker. The deposit contained money from all of the store's five branches in Lower Manhattan, at 31 Broadway, 48 Broadway, 181 Broadway, 281 Broadway, and 61 Maiden Lane.

It was more than a month before another bill turned up, on May 19. A five-dollar bill, serial number A85819751, was deposited at the Chase National Bank on 7th Avenue and 41st Street, as part of a deposit from Bickford's Restaurant at 225 West 42nd Street. Bickford's was regularly described as a "lunchroom," even if its extended hours provided customers modestly priced and quickly served meals at all hours of the day.

Finn talked to Peter Reilly, the night cashier at Bickford's, who didn't recall receiving any five-dollar bills until around 3:00 AM on the date in question. Between then and the end of his shift at 6:00 AM, he estimated he had seen about five bills of the five-dollar denomination.

"The bill in question was possibly presented by an unknown man apparently of Irish, Italian or possibly American extraction," the Bureau of Investigation report on the matter stated, "about 30 years of age; five-foot-eight inches tall, weighing about 150 pounds; with dark brown hair and eyes, tall flabby face; dark complexion; mild manner; had appearance of taxi driver or chauffeur, dressed in shabby clothes, old grey cap and grey suit."

The man Reilly described came to his attention because he had paid for a fifteen-cent meal with the five-dollar bill. The witness looked through the NYPD's and Bureau of Investigation's photo books but didn't find anyone who resembled the customer.

Another five-dollar bill, serial number B52611313, came to a different branch of the Chase National Bank on June 6. It was traced back to Brilliant Restaurant, located at the entrance to the Manhattan Bridge on Canal Street. It was a large restaurant catering to a transient clientele, authorities learned.

The cashier on duty that day didn't notice any of the six customers who had paid with a five-dollar bill during her morning shift, from 7:00 to 11:00 AM. However, after getting a description from detectives of "Cemetery John," the man who had picked up the ransom, she told them about a man who matched that sketch who visited the restaurant every other day.

So on June 7, Finn and his NYPD detectives and Sisk and his Bureau of Investigation agents went back to the Brilliant and waited. They watched William Heilewertz enter the restaurant and promptly took him back to NYPD headquarters for questioning.

The Brooklyn resident had seven cents in his pocket when he was picked up. The Polish immigrant had no criminal record, and after being sufficiently scared and investigated, police let him go, concluding he was not "Cemetery John."

This continued for the rest of 1932 like a slow leaking faucet. A five-dollar bill from the ransom money was tracked back to a gas station, another one to a woman "of good reputation and character" who received the money as part of her salary, and another to the Palace Café in Midtown Manhattan, which was "patronized for the most part by theatrical people," the Bureau of Investigation would later report.

A ten-dollar ransom bill showed up in the deposit from a cigar store in Queens. A five-dollar ransom bill came from a Manhattan sports shop. The electric company Brooklyn Edison turned in a ten-dollar bill in October as part of its collections. One of the Sheridan Cafeteria's 1,100 customers on November 19, 1932, passed a five-dollar bill associated with the case.

Each time, Finn interviewed the person who received the bill. Each time, he told them he was investigating a counterfeiting ring. He never mentioned Lindbergh or the kidnapping. And after each time, he placed another pin on his office map of New York City.

Sisk was also using this method to look for patterns, except he had large borough-specific maps of Manhattan, the Bronx, and Brooklyn at his office on Lexington Avenue in Manhattan.

For more than a year, Finn tracked ransom money, and after a break from late December 1932 to March 1933, during which none turned up, things began to get busy. In April 1933, bills turned up regularly, with five bills discovered between the twelfth and the twenty-second of the month. On April 27, Finn thought he'd caught a break with a five-dollar bill, serial number B-56667794. The detectives traced it to a man named Paul Yakutis, who ran a rooming house at 234 East 18ᵗʰ Street in New York.

According to phone records, Yakutis had made numerous long distance calls to a person named J. Fries in Youngsville, New York. Finn and his men discovered that a man named J. Fries had worked on the Lindbergh home as a steamfitter and had roomed with a Hopewell farmer whose son had served as a caretaker of the Lindbergh estate for a week while the butler was gone.

The NYPD put an undercover man inside Yakutis's rooming house and tracked Fries to Connecticut through his labor union, where he was tailed for a week before being brought to NYPD headquarters for questioning. It turned out to be another dead end, though, as Fries and Yakutis were cleared of wrongdoing.

As that investigation was underway, an even bigger break appeared to investigators. First, sometime between April 21 and April 29, fifty ten-dollar gold certificates were turned into the Federal Reserve by the Manufacturers Hanover Bank in New York. On April 29, twenty-four ten-dollar gold certificates of the

Lindbergh ransom money were turned over to the Federal Reserve by the Chemical National Bank and Trust Company.

Then on May 2, the Federal Reserve Bank of New York found 296 ten-dollar gold certificates and one twenty-dollar gold certificate, all from the ransom money. They had apparently been part of a single deposit a day earlier to teller James P. Estey. The deposit ticket in question bore the name "J. J. Faulkner, 537 West 149th Street."

The officers who raced to that address quickly discovered no one by that name living there. Police would interview a Jane Faulkner who had lived at that address some years back, but they could prove no connection.

Frustratingly to Finn, Estey said he had been very busy on the day of the deposit, as it had been payday for federal workers and he was in charge of counting the deposits from the armored cars. He said he didn't remember what "J. J. Faulkner" looked like or even whether it had been a man or woman.

Finn's efforts to discover who J. J. Faulkner was would be in vain. In hindsight, he likely knew he should have planned for a big expenditure of the gold certificates on May 2, as May 1 was the deadline President Roosevelt had set for citizens to turn in their gold certificates without penalty or punishment.

Meanwhile, the drip-drip emergence of the ransom bills continued. Clothing salesman Sidney Jacobson deposited a five-dollar bill at his local bank in early June. Jacobson remembered getting the bill from a woman for a fifty-nine-cent pair of gloves. He said she looked at him "in a very suspicious manner," but he couldn't remember anything else about her.

A ten-dollar gold certificate that came in from the First National Bank in Cooperstown, New York, was eventually traced back to a Mrs. John O'Neill, the wife of an East Springfield, New York, farmer, who used it to buy dry goods from another local farmer. Her husband said he had received the certificate from his local bank earlier that year, but no further leads came about, as the bank had closed in March.

And then the trail went dry for another five months until November, when bills once again turned up in banks, deposited from places like Penn Station and the Sheridan Square Theatre. At the latter, one of the cashiers remembered receiving the five-dollar bill in question because the man who spent it "virtually threw it, folded, through the ticket office window, causing her to look up at him in some anger." She hadn't talked with him but remembered him as being thirty to thirty-five years old, slender, about five-foot-eight and 155 or so pounds, with a thin face, light brown hair, high cheek bones, and "apparently American."

Other dead ends popped up between December and January. And then the leads went cold.

As the months passed and the calendar turned to 1934, hope faded. After February 13, no bills were discovered through the spring and early summer. The gap drove Finn crazy, with little to do other than study the three-foot map of Manhattan and the Bronx that started at his waist and traveled above his head. He looked at the bunches of pins and once again tried to make sense of it all. There was a thick clump of pins in Yorkville, a working-class neighborhood on the Upper East Side of Manhattan. Yorkville had significant populations of Czechs, Poles, Slovaks, Irish, and Hungarian residents, but it was known for its German flavor. Its main artery, East 86th Street, was sometimes referred to as the "German Broadway," with popular restaurants and ballrooms for waltzing and polka. The alleged kidnapper, Cemetery John, was described as having a German accent. Other clusters of pins were found across the Harlem River, in the east Bronx, and along the Lexington Avenue subway line in Upper Manhattan.

Finally the dry spell ended on August 20, when the Bank of Sicily and Trust Company turned in a ten-dollar gold certificate. Since Finn was on vacation with his wife and two daughters, federal investigators and a representative from the New Jersey State Police tracked the money back to the bank and discovered that seven of the last eight gold certificates found had been sequential.

Agent Sisk determined in his report that the sequential certificates indicated "almost beyond question that the person passing the ransom money was passing the gold certificates one at a time and still had in his possession a large part of the gold certificates paid as ransom."

Sisk and other federal agents visited all the banks in New York

City and the surrounding area, hundreds in all, to ask them to check for gold certificates matching the ransom numbers. Nine certificates turned up from local branches; another four were turned in to the Federal Reserve. A few were traced to corner grocery stores.

When Finn returned to work the first week of September, it was decided each organization, the NYPD, the Bureau of Investigation, and the New Jersey State Police, would place six men, eighteen men in all, undercover in the Yorkville neighborhood, where it appeared the ransom bills were now being passed. No two men from any organization were teamed up together. Despite fears they would bring more attention, the bureau stationed an additional ten undercover agents to watch street corner vegetable and fruit stands.

The net appeared to be tightening as more and more clues emerged. A ten-dollar gold certificate was traced back to the Charles Aiello & Sons fruit store on 2nd Avenue near East 83rd Street, and Aiello had a decent recollection of the man who gave him the money on September 5.

A twenty-dollar gold certificate was tracked back to the Exquisite Shoe Corporation, where it had been used for merchandise sold on September 7. Employees could provide no description, and the four customers who spent twenty dollars or more and whose names were known all checked out.

On the morning of September 18, Finn, New Jersey State Police Corporal William Horn, and the Bureau of Investigation's Special Agent William F. Seery visited the Wieland Bakery and Lunch Room at 1993 Webster Avenue. It had turned in a ten-dollar gold certificate as part of a deposit to the Irving Trust Company.

Finn interviewed Wieland, his family, and their employees about the customer who might have spent that ten-dollar gold certificate. He would head back to the office frustrated once again.

NYPD headquarters, at 240 Centre Street, was a Baroque-style palace completed in the early twentieth century by architects influenced by the 1893 Chicago World's Fair. It featured a beautiful, ornate dome on top and a fenced park along its north end.

For Finn, though, the building had been a source of frustration for the last thirty months. He was surrounded by clues and simultaneously by the realization that they hadn't amounted to anything concrete. A little boy was dead, and his parents, the world's most famous couple, remained frustrated at the lack of apparent progress in the case.

Finn, Horn, and Seery were back out after lunch when they got word to call the Bureau of Investigation headquarters. They were told that a ten-dollar gold certificate, serial number A-73976634-A, had been turned in to the Corn Exchange Bank Trust Company at the corner of Park Avenue and 125th Street.

When they arrived at the bank, the assistant manager, F. C. Dingeldien, gave them the bill in question. Finn looked at the front and saw nothing out of the ordinary, but when he turned it over he saw, written in pencil in the margin, "4 U 13-41." It was a license plate number that the bank workers hadn't noticed written on the bill.

The investigators got the list of deposit tickets from gas stations, figuring those businesses would have been most likely to take down a driver's license plate number, on September 17 and came up with Lind & Glantz at 2481 First Avenue, Dluka Garage, Inc., at 1725 Park Avenue, and Warner-Quinlan Oil Company, on the east side of Lexington Avenue between East 127th and 128th streets. The latter, a filling station, was closest geographically to the bank, so that's where Finn, Horn, and Seery went first.

There they met station manager Walter Lyle, with a dark mustache almost as big as the belt buckle on his uniform. He wore a black cap and black bowtie with his shirt sleeves rolled up over his elbows. Lyle told them he remembered the bill in question and the man who passed it. He had bought five gallons of special gasoline for a total of ninety-eight cents. When he presented the ten-dollar gold certificate, Lyle had questioned its value, to which the customer had said, "I have a hundred more just like it."

Not wanting to have to make good to the company, Lyle had written down the license plate number just in case the bank refused to accept the bill.

Lyle's paranoia would be Finn's good fortune. One call to the State Motor Vehicle License Division led to as solid a suspect as the case had had since March 1, 1932.

But if tracking the ransom money throughout late 1933 and early 1934 had produced leads, tracing the wood had not.

After finding the Bronx lumber yard where he believed the North Carolina pine in Rails 12 and 13 was sold and then discovering that the company took only cash, thereby dashing any hope of following that trail to a suspect, Arthur Koehler had turned his attention to tracing the Douglas fir rails. However, finding matching Douglas fir seemed as likely as finding a particular tree in a national forest. There were no defining planer marks on those rails. Koehler felt as if he was spitting into the wind.

As he wrote to his wife, "I can never be so sure of the fir as I was of the pine because it has no marks and no showing of a defect in the planer. Only the width of the knife cut is all I can go by."

That wasn't much of a lead at all.

As for the birch dowels used to connect the three sections of the ladder, Koehler believed they could have been part of a gymnastics apparatus. It wasn't very dirty, but the film on it suggested it had been handled a great deal. Maybe it had been held by sweaty hands.

On December 9, 1933, Arthur wrote to Ethelyn, reminding her that it was almost five weeks since he had left Madison.

"I suppose George has nearly forgotten me," he lamented. "Anyhow I am going to stick with this job just as long as they let me (except to come home for Xmas of course). They haven't said much till lately, but now they are letting out the magnitude of this job and what it means. It's an honor to be in on it but much more to have given them real aid and that is something that no one can beat me out of unless the N.Y. Police solve the mystery along different lines before the N.J. Police can make use of my findings."

As the New Jersey police force investigated the workers at the National Lumber and Millwork Company, Koehler was getting restless. He suggested to Lamb that they should check all the building permits taken out in the Bronx in the winter of 1931–1932, as he felt "quite strongly that the lumber was stolen on a construction job and not bought or stolen at a lumber yard."

Lamb rejected his attempt to play detective because to ask New York City officials for that list would lead to them asking why. Lamb and Schwarzkopf didn't want them to know why. The circle of people who knew what Koehler was working on was small: Schwarzkopf, Lamb, Lieutenant Keaten, Bornmann, DeGaetano, and maybe another detective or two, but that was it. No one from the NYPD or the Bureau of Investigation knew what Koehler was doing.

Koehler didn't listen. He followed his hunch to the New York City Public library, where besides the list of building permits he found "a lot of foreign looking and smelling people" as well as an "emaciated bed bug" crawling on his copy of *The New York Times*.

He, too, would get a map of the Bronx, hammer it to a piece of plywood in his Hotel Lincoln room, buy some colored pins, and plot the locations where the buildings were constructed. Unaware they were using similar methods, he and Finn were drawing the same conclusion about where the suspect lived. Koehler figured he studied that map often enough that he "could qualify for a taxi driver in New York if I should be without a job."

After finding out what Koehler was up to, Keaten once again reminded him of "the importance of keeping our work quiet."

Still the scientist pushed on, traveling on the train to Mosholu Parkway and the block of Decatur Street where John F. Condon lived. The former principal's involvement in the case seemed curious to all three of the law enforcement agencies trying to solve the crime. Koehler was equally suspicious.

"I was surprised at the old buildings on the street and the thought occurred to me that rail 16, which has cut nail holes in it, might possibly have come from one of those houses, or more likely a barn in which it was used to seal the inside against cold," he detailed in his official report.

"I talked to no one while in that section of the city," he added to reassure his New Jersey bosses that he was not drawing attention to himself. That wasn't good enough, and Lamb told him not to go into the Bronx again until other investigations there were complete. He wasn't able to go back to the yard where he had discovered the pine sample that matched Rails 12 and 13.

Instead, he was stuck going over more than 7,500 slips recording the Dorns' sale of Douglas fir to lumber yards. It was slow and tedious work, leading to hunches but not much more.

His letters home grew more sentimental as Christmas approached and he missed and worried about his family. "I've been wanting to mention for some time," he wrote Ethelyn on December 14,

> but always hesitate that it might be well for you folks to look out that you don't get kidnapped before I come home. It may sound far fetched and egotistical to infer that someone might try to kidnap you to get me off the job, and so it is—at least far fetched. Nevertheless, the kidnappers have nearly $50,000 to spend to avoid getting caught. However the idea is very remote, especially in view of the common belief among officials here that the kidnappers were a very amateurish bunch and not at all professionals. Just a little extra precaution might be well, especially with George. There, I got that off my mind.

To lighten the mood, he shared with her his dining experiences, with Bornmann, in particular, who liked to go to "high faloutin" restaurants since he was on "actual expenses," and Koehler was on a flat federal government reimbursement. Troop C Headquarters would further frustrate him by stating that if he wanted to go home for Christmas, he'd have to pay for the ticket himself.

"In a way, I don't blame them for that is what I would have to do if I were on a strictly Lab job if they wanted me here again after Xmas but since they are getting my time for nothing, they might overlook that," he wrote Ethelyn on December 19, the day before he was set to board a train for Madison. "What's more we don't know what to do next. That lumber yard in the Bronx seems to be OK."

Lamb would concur with that position, sending Koehler a wire in care of the Forest Products Laboratory on January 12 suggesting that he stay in Wisconsin until the situation warranted another trip out east. Over the next few months, Koehler would send letters to Lamb, trying to find a way to help but never quite matching the success and eventual dead end he had encountered with the North Carolina pine rails.

He kept up his investigation of Rails 14, 15, and 17, the Douglas fir uprights, and found lumber mills on the West Coast that had planer marks that were similar to those on the kidnapping instrument. Rail 14 had marks similar to those made at the Blanchard Lumber Company in Seattle, Washington, but its marks were "faint" and not as reliable as those on Rails 15 and 17.

Rail 15 had planer marks like those made by the Bloedel Donovan Lumber Mills in Bellingham, Washington. Rail 17 had planer marks like those made by Clark and Wilson Lumber Company in Linnton, Oregon.

Maybe more importantly for the investigation's purposes, all of those companies had sold 1x4-inch Douglas fir to three lumber yards in the Bronx: Butler Brothers; the Church E. Gates Company; and Cross, Austin and Ireland. Koehler had visited all three yards during his last couple of weeks out east and had acquired wood samples and sales slips in the process.

While at Cross, Austin and Ireland on December 14, he and Bornmann were going over sales slips in manager Arthur A. Tinker's office when two men, a large one and a small one, came in to buy a three-ply ¼-inch 24x48 fir panel for forty cents. They offered the sales clerk a ten-dollar bill to pay for it. It had been company policy during the Depression to avoid taking such large bills due to the numerous counterfeits in circulation, so the clerk asked if they had anything smaller.

The men said no, at which point the yard superintendent, William J. Reilly, passed the bill to the company treasurer in the next room to look over the bill before going to the safe to make change. The customers watched her, and before she made it to the safe the smaller man asked for the bill back. He pulled a five-dollar bill out of his pocket, for which the treasurer gave him five singles. He then pulled forty cents out of his pocket.

"Our queer customers," as Tinker would later describe them, next said that they were going to get something to eat at the lunch wagon across the way, and they'd be back for the panel afterwards. Reilly found the whole act "strange" and wondered why they didn't give him the change in the first place. What made it stranger is that the men disappeared, leaving their forty-cent panel behind, and their forty cents as well.

Reilly was suspicious enough that he looked out the window and wrote down the license number of the car the two men had driven to the lumber yard. Reilly said later that the number ended up matching the one written down on the ten-dollar gold certificate turned in by the gas station manager nine months later "although," as Koehler later questioned, "how that can be is not clear since the two occurrences were in different years," and drivers changed license plates each year.

Either way, Koehler had had no way of knowing his proximity to a potential suspect at that moment.

Now that he was back in Madison, Koehler asked Lamb to send him Rungs 1, 2, 7, 8, 9, and 10, all made of Ponderosa pine, so he could study their planer marks. Under the light available to him in New Jersey, he hadn't been able to identify their distinctive markings, but at the lab in Madison he had "various kinds of controllable natural and artificial lighting by means of which I can bring out the planer marks much better."

He used a very oblique beam of light on the samples in a dark room to detect even the minutest of ridges. The biggest challenge with tracing the Ponderosa pine rungs was that there were more than a thousand mills in the West shipping the lumber to the East Coast. That was a large canvas, but one Koehler thought he could narrow down if he could determine the number of knives dressing the wood's top and bottom. He already calculated there had been six cutting the side heads.

Koehler got permission from Lamb to cut a sliver off of Rung 2 so he could analyze it under the microscope. He found parallel slanting cuts at an angle of 21 degrees to the surface of the wood, made by exceedingly sharp knives and exactly one millimeter apart. He told Lamb that this was a "striking fact" that "would indicate strongly that the instrument was of foreign make, since we do not use the metric system much in this country."

Further analysis led him to conclude that six knives had dressed the Ponderosa pine in the top, bottom, and side heads and that the lumber had traveled through the planer at the rate of 0.56 inch per revolution of the top and bottom cylinders. That meant if the speed of a planer's cylinder was 2,700 rpm, then the speed of the lumber feed was 126 feet per minute.

Koehler sent another form letter to all the lumber dealers in the Bronx to see if they sold the Ponderosa pine in 1930–31 and, if so, where they had bought it from. He was looking in this case for 1x6-inch dressed stock.

By spring, not many retailers had answered Koehler's letter. In fact, on March 20, 1934, only eighteen of the sixty-six retail lumber dealers he had queried had responded. He was having better luck with the wholesale dealers but still didn't have answers from nearly a third of those questioned.

With Captain Lamb's permission, he followed up with the companies, writing, "Perhaps you considered the matter of no vital significance, and for that reason we wish to state that the inquiry is in connection with a criminal investigation about which we cannot go into detail at present, except to say that we do not expect your firm or any wholesaler to be involved."

He continued his checking, cross-checking, and rechecking of his samples and his measurements, but they still added up to just numbers and no suspects. As spring turned to summer, he sent the occasional update to Lamb about a mill that might have dressed the Ponderosa pine rungs or about three vertical marks on the right face of Rail 15 that apparently had been visible before the silver nitrate was applied for fingerprints.

He asked Schwarzkopf whether he should travel out west to visit the mills that might have provided the Ponderosa pine and the Douglas fir, but that trip was not authorized. By September, Koehler could only look at his map of the Bronx nailed to a piece of plywood and speculate.

Finn had done enough speculating over the last thirty months to know that he was tired of speculation. After getting New York 1934 license number 4 U 13-41 from gas station manager Walter Lyle, he called the state's motor vehicle division and was advised that plate belonged to Bruno Richard Hauptmann, 1279 East 222nd Street, in the Bronx, for a 1931 Dodge sedan.

Hauptmann's license described him as thirty-five years old, born on November 29, 1899, five-foot-ten, white, 180 pounds, with blue eyes and blond hair. Finn called Special Agent Sisk, who was at the New York office of the Bureau of Investigation with Lieutenant Keaten of the New Jersey State Police. The group met up and proceeded to East 222nd Street to begin surveillance of the home.

While Finn, Sisk, Keaten, NJSP Corporal William Horn, and Special Agent William F. Seery watched the house and the garage on one side, where he apparently parked his sedan, other agents immediately started digging into Hauptmann's life. They discovered he had a wife, Anna, and a roughly one-year-old son. The family had lived there since 1931. Hauptmann appeared to be unemployed. Copies of his driver's license and automobile registration were forwarded to the Bureau of Investigation laboratory to check against the ransom notes.

The Hauptmann home was the upstairs part of a two-story house in a predominantly German neighborhood. The Hauptmanns rented the flat, at the corner of East 222nd Street and Needham Avenue, which was a fairly unpopulated section.

The investigators decided to follow Hauptmann if he left the home for any reason. The original five on scene stayed on their shift from 4:00 PM until 9:00 PM that night, at which time two NYPD detectives and two NJSP troopers arrived in a Ford sedan. The second shift got out of the car and walked up and down Needham Avenue, directly in front of the Hauptmann home on several occasions, even peering into the garage at least once. In addition, they drove up and down East 222nd Street multiple times. At one point, a woman in the neighborhood came to the door with a dog and "sicced" the dog on the officers, causing quite the commotion. They were not the most subtle of detectives.

At 1:00 AM on the morning of September 19, Finn and Keaten discontinued the surveillance until 7:00 AM, as the officers at the scene had been stopped and questioned by precinct officers patrolling the neighborhood after a number of storekeepers and residents in the neighborhood complained, worried that a robbery was being planned. The surveillance team agreed to come back in the morning with a limited presence to avoid unwanted attention.

The federal agents, though, did not want to let the suspect out of their sights. Sisk instructed Seery to proceed to the nearest subway station as though he were heading home for the night but to return immediately to continue the surveillance. Sisk drove

Detectives from the New York City Police Department, agents from the Bureau of Justice, and troopers from the New Jersey State Police would stake out the house of Bruno Richard Hauptmann, at 1279 East 222nd Street in the Bronx after he bought gas with one of the ransom bills. A gas station attendant wrote down his license plate number. (Courtesy: Dr. Regis Miller/Forest Products Laboratory)

Keaten to his hotel and headed back to the surveillance location at 3:00 AM.

The next morning, all the respective agencies violated their agreement to keep a low profile by bringing numerous men to the surveillance. Before it could be straightened out, they spotted a man fitting Hauptmann's description leave the house at 8:55 AM, head into the garage, and drive out in a Dodge sedan with New York plates 4 U 13-41.

The agents, troopers, and detectives scurried into their respective vehicles to pursue. While the plan had been to follow him to see if he passed any more ransom money, Finn noticed him driving fast and constantly looking in his rear-view mirror as if to elude pursuit. One of Finn's officers pulled him over on Park Avenue between East 178th Street and East Tremont Avenue. Hauptmann was pulled out of his car and searched. Keaten pulled the wallet out of Hauptmann's back left pocket and found a twenty-dollar gold certificate, serial number A-35517877-A.

"What is this about, what are they doing, what is it?" Hauptmann asked the police officers.

"It's counterfeit money," Sisk responded as Seery searched his booklet listing the serial numbers of the ransom bills. "Did you purchase gasoline at a gas station at the corner of Lexington Avenue and 127th Street a few days ago?"

"Yes."

"Did you tell the attendant that you had a hundred more just like this twenty?"

"Yes, I said that," Hauptmann said.

Seery took a while to search the list of ransom bills, but finally on page 77, he found a match.

The police handcuffed Hauptmann and took him back to his house for an initial search of the property.

The world and Arthur Koehler would soon learn what they found.

8

While police were arresting Bruno Richard Hauptmann, Special Agent Charles Appel was ensconced in the Bureau of Investigation's crime laboratory. He had been there nearly every day since the summer of 1932, analyzing the handwriting from the thirteen ransom notes and comparing it to that of hundreds of suspects.

Like the others working the case, he'd had no luck finding the kidnapper.

But the balding, bookish, round-faced Appel knew from the beginning that science would help solve this case. Now he couldn't wait to get a handwriting sample from the German carpenter.

Appel was born in the nation's capital in 1895 and was a second lieutenant bombardier during World War I. Since joining the bureau in 1924 after going to law school at George Washington University, Appel had pushed for scientific detection in solving crimes, and his boss, J. Edgar Hoover, had encouraged him to pursue further studies.

He had taken classes in serology, toxicology, handwriting and typewriting analysis, and moulage (the making of casts, or impressions) at the Scientific Crime Detection Laboratory at Northwestern University Law School. The facility had been established after the St. Valentine's Day massacre in Chicago, when Al Capone's gang murdered seven members of his rival Bugs Moran's gang on February 14, 1929.

The crime so shocked one of the jurors in the case, a wealthy financier named Bert Massey, that he had bankrolled the creation of the lab at a cost of $125,000. Calvin H. Goddard, a New York forensic consultant, was hired to establish the facility. It was a challenge; forensic science was in its infancy, and Goddard later stated that many law enforcement officers were "quite satisfied with the 'good old fashioned methods'" and would "turn up their noses at anything that savors of science.

"This being the first time that a really comprehensive attempt to combat crime in all its phases by scientific laboratory methods had been undertaken in the United States, we had no precedent to go upon—at least on this side of the water," Goddard wrote in a 1930 *American Journal of Police Science* article.

In what is believed to be the first time science or medicine was used to solve a crime, a Chinese author wrote a book in 1248 describing how to distinguish drowning from strangulation. The first microscope would be developed roughly 350 years later, and a couple of centuries later, in the early nineteenth century, the first toxicology book was published.

Europeans were far more advanced in using forensic science to help solve crimes than Americans. Scotland Yard investigators used bullet comparisons to catch a murderer in 1835, and just a year later an English chemist became the first scientist to testify before a jury about toxicology results that concluded arsenic was present at a crime scene. The first police crime laboratory was established in 1910 by Edmond Locard in Lyon, France.

As the twentieth century began, the popularity of Sherlock Holmes, Arthur Conan Doyle's fictional detective who solved crimes using logic and science, was skyrocketing on both sides of the Atlantic.

Hoover wanted his agents to be up to speed on the latest, most modern ways to outsmart the criminals. In 1930, he had sent numerous agents to a conference Goddard hosted, at which the Chicago coroner said simply, "The only way in which crime problems in our American cities can be successfully attacked is by the use of modern scientific methods of investigation."

Rex Collier, a reporter for the *Washington Daily News*, was sold by Hoover on the new crime-fighting techniques and subsequently wrote on May 15, 1930, that the director was "progressive" and that his detectives were "ultra-modern" and were "being trained to out-Sherlock Sherlock Holmes."

Appel had been building contacts with forensic scientists and exploring what it would take to open up a forensics facility at the bureau, but he hastened his efforts after the kidnapping of the Lindbergh baby. In two memos to Hoover in July of 1932, Appel encouraged the creation of a "criminological research laboratory" that would become "the central clearing house for all information which may be needed in the criminological work and that all police departments in the future will look to the Bureau for information of this kind as a routine thing."

Hoover agreed and over the fall of 1932 set up Appel at the Old Southern Railway building in Room 802, a former break room for agents from the Identification Division. So, with stale cigarette smoke still apparent to those with a keen sense of smell, Appel went to work with his ultraviolet light machine, a kit to make molds of tool marks, a wiretapping kit, photographic supplies, chemicals, and a microscope on loan from Bausch & Lomb until the requisition to purchase one was approved.

He got a carpet from another unit, ordered custom cabinets to hold some of the new equipment, and began immediately to look at the Lindbergh ransom notes. It wasn't the only case Appel was working on. The first year of the Criminological Laboratory, he and his staff performed 963 examinations.

The following year, Appel was joined by an expert in chemical analysis, Samuel F. Pickering, and the lab was renamed the Technical Laboratory. At Hoover's urging, Appel was writing a manual called *Scientific Aids in Crime Detection*. While Hoover realized the scope of work Appel was undertaking, the director nevertheless wrote to an aide, "I fear we will all be dead of old age before Rip Van Winkle gets this done."

Appel completed the guide in the spring of 1934, moved the lab to the Department of Justice Building, and by fall had been joined by two more special agents. Appel would continue to focus on handwriting analysis and ballistics research. His new staff would pursue fingerprint technology, blood grouping, and infrared research.

Wood science, and even more generally botany, or the study of plants, were not on the list. Those were two fields of study reserved for the marble buildings of America's universities, not its police stations. The nexus of the two wasn't widely understood. Indeed, even Sherlock Holmes wasn't considered an expert in botany. When extolling his virtues and chronicling his knowledge in *A Study in Scarlet,* Sherlock Holmes's confidante, Dr. Watson, also listed his friend's limits, describing his friend's knowledge of botany as "Variable. Well up in belladonna, opiums, and poisons generally. Knows nothing of practical gardening." No, not even the world's most famous fictional detective solved crimes using wood identification or wood technology.

Koehler wasn't much of a reader, let alone of Sir Arthur Conan Doyle. When he had free time, as rare as that was, he preferred to spend it in his own basement, at his own workbench, and with his own tools. In addition to a full complement of carpenters' hand tools, he used a "buzz saw" (table saw), jointer (for planing one surface smooth), drill press, and band saw, all mounted with their motors on two stands. This was his headquarters for home improvements and repairs, and for the creation of the occasional family gift. By the fall of 1934, though, he spent less time at his passion and more time as an avid consumer of news—whatever he could find related to Hauptmann.

While he had received regular and prompt replies from Schwarzkopf and Lamb in the past, the duo had gone silent, not responding immediately to his note of Friday, September 21, encouraging them to keep a look out for any lumber at Hauptmann's home that might have been used to create Rail 16. He had also suggested a securing of any tools found at the home of the suspect.

He didn't hear back because the investigators were busy pursuing other angles. His Friday *Wisconsin State Journal* explained that detectives had found a significant amount of the ransom money. Detective Sergeant John Wallace was dispatched by Schwarzkopf himself "to make a search of the Hauptmann residence for any ransom money that may be hidden."

Wallace was joined on September 20, the day after Hauptmann was arrested, by three other NJSP troopers, three NYPD detectives, and a Bureau of Investigation agent. After finding nothing in the house, they brought Anna Hauptmann out to the garage, where she advised that "no one else had excess [sic] to the garage."

At 11:40, they found "two packages of gold certificates on the south wall of the garage concealed in a compartment between the second and third upright from the rear end of the garage. These two packages contained 183 gold certificates to the amount of $1850.00 which was wrapped in a *New York Daily News* newspaper of June 25, 1934 and *New York Daily Mirror* of Sept. 6, 1934 (the certificates found were 10 dollar denomination)."

They counted the money in Mrs. Hauptmann's presence and then resumed the search.

They would soon discover even more money.

[NYPD] Detective Murphy found on the south wall underneath the work bench and window a can concealed by a board nailed across the uprights, the said can was supported by two nails driven into the wall to prevent the gallon can (shellac can) from falling to the floor. On examining the can it was found that same can was cut open at the top and on opening the can there was a towel and a large cloth concealing the money in the can. Further examination of the can proved that there were 12 packages of 10 and 20 dollar gold certificates wrapped in both the New York Daily News and Daily Mirror of June 25, 1934 and September 6, 1934. A count of the gold certificates amounted to $11,950.00, making the total amount of bills found $13,750.00.

The authorities back at headquarters advised them to bring in Anna Hauptmann for questioning. She would later be released from custody and taken out to dinner by detectives as they tried to get information from her about her husband. While there, reporters heard patrons at the restaurant insult her and others scream, "Stone her! Hang her!"

She was "spirited out the back way," the UPI reported.

While in the garage—and this was not reported by the newspapers—Wallace also "found a large wooden plane with the blade nicked on the east end of the garage and same was taken by the investigator and kept in his possession and later tagged to be held as evidence, as it was believed that this plane may have been used in the construction of the ladder found at the Lindbergh residence on March 1, 1932."

Meanwhile, Bruno Richard Hauptmann was being held in a cell with a throng of curious onlookers standing outside the Greenwich Street Police Station in New York City trying to get any information about where the case was headed. John F. "Jafsie" Condon was brought in to look at a lineup of twenty men, including Hauptmann, to see if he was "Cemetery John," the man to whom Condon had given the ransom money more than two years earlier.

"The prisoner," the UPI wire service reported, "was a shaken and hesitant figure when he mounted the platform. . . . He was nervous and at times slightly uncertain."

Condon faced New York Police Inspector John J. Lyons and asked if he could proceed with the lineup "by elimination?"

The witness walked straight up to Hauptmann and set him aside with three detectives who were taking part in the lineup. He lined up the four men and asked each of them to say and spell their names. Condon bowed his head and listened intently.

Next he had each man read aloud the following lines, which "Cemetery John" had said in person to him before delivering the ransom: "I always keep my word. If the baby is returned in good health, I will do everything to help you."

The UPI wire service indicated that Hauptmann was "nervous, inclined to tremble."

After having Hauptmann and only Hauptmann read one more statement aloud, Condon asked all four men, "Did you see me before?" Each answered, "No."

The UPI reported, "Condon came as close to Hauptmann as he could. Loudly, directly into his face, he repeated the question, emphasizing 'you.' 'No, I never saw you before,' Hauptmann answered stolidly."

Then, in an unusual twist, Condon asked for and was granted permission to talk to Hauptmann alone. They talked in the corner for a few minutes before Condon turned away without comment. The NYPD would report that he had made a "partial identification" of Hauptmann.

If Condon was hesitant to conclusively identify Hauptmann,

the taxi driver whom the kidnapper had paid one dollar back in March 1932 to deliver one of the ransom notes to Condon's home was not. "That's the man," John Perrone told detectives. "That's the guy who gave me a dollar to take a note to Dr. Jafsie."

Hauptmann, seemingly incredulous, denied ever having seen Perrone before.

"You're the man and there's no doubt about it," the driver replied to Hauptmann.

The suspect was arraigned and held without bail on a charge of "unlawfully receiving the Lindbergh case ransom money," the UPI reported.

"There is no doubt in my mind about this man," NYPD Assistant Chief John J. O'Sullivan told reporters after questioning Hauptmann. "We have a perfect extortion case. The other case, far more serious [the kidnapping and murder] is developing rapidly."

Twenty-four hours later, Arthur Koehler woke up early, eager to hear the latest news. It was a cloudy day in Madison, with a light breeze, high humidity, and highs reaching the mid-fifties. He opened his paper and read about how the warden from the Ohio state penitentiary had released a letter received in early 1932 and allegedly signed by Hauptmann to an inmate that stated, "Will kidnap Lindbergh's baby. Hope for me." A New York detective had been sent to Germany to investigate possible angles there, including Hauptmann's story to the police that he had received the money from his friend Isidor Fisch before Fisch went back to Germany. Fisch had recently died, making the story unprovable, but the authorities were hoping to learn something in Hauptmann's native land.

At the bottom of the page one article, Koehler's attention was piqued at the following line, "Kidnap ladder traced to lumber yard where Hauptmann worked in 1931–32." A page later and buried under another eighteen paragraphs was more on the earlier assertion.

"A new link in the chain of circumstantial evidence, authorities disclosed was the tracing of Hauptmann's past to the lumber yard of the National [Lumber and] Millwork Corp. in the Bronx," the paper read. "The lumber used in the kidnaper's ladder came from this yard. Hauptmann worked in the yard on odd jobs only a few months before the crime."

Koehler exhaled for the first time in what seemed to be minutes. He hadn't realized the impact of his work until now. His research and scientific detective work had led authorities to that lumber yard. He had no doubt that Rails 12 and 13 came from that facility. If only National Lumber and Millwork had kept receipts of whom it had sold lumber to, Koehler could have helped solve the case months earlier.

He had been told back in December in a meeting with Detective Bornmann and Lieutenant Keaten that "National Lumber and Millwork Company at 3541 White Plains Avenue had been investigated and nothing suspicious was found concerning the owners and employees." Apparently they had not looked into past employees.

Koehler turned to page three and discovered a bank of ten photographs in a section called, "Camera Catches Kidnaping Suspect's Tumble Into Police Net." There were images of a young Hauptmann in a German army uniform and a close-up shot of him at the courthouse for his arraignment. There were pictures of his wife, Anna, and their ten-month-old son, Manfred. Other images included a smiling Walter Lyle, the gas station attendant who'd flagged the ten-dollar gold note Hauptmann passed that had led to his arrest, and the hundreds of people crowded outside the police station where he was being held.

However, the pictures that drew Koehler's attention were at the top. The first, on the left, showed Hauptmann's home in the Bronx. The second, next to it, showed his garage with officers inside of it. But it was all the wood in that second image that really piqued Koehler's curiosity.

He immediately got into his Studebaker, drove into work, and crafted a telegram, which he sent by Western Union to Captain Lamb in New Jersey: "Newspaper pictures show garage with scraps of wood and wood brackets on wall and vise stop Vise possibly used for clamping rails together when sawing and may have left mark Suggest guard everything. Arthur Koehler."

He was convinced there were clues there. If only they would let him continue his work. However, the New Jersey State Police, the New York City Police Department, and the Bureau of Investigation were focused on other areas of the investigation: finding more

Newspaper photos of Hauptmann's garage, showing wood scraps everywhere, inspired Koehler to send a telegram to his New Jersey State Police sources encouraging them to "guard everything." (Courtesy: Dr. Regis Miller/Forest Products Laboratory)

of the ransom money, discovering the device that had made the distinctive marks on each of the ransom letters, and uncovering any connection between Hauptmann and his alibi, Isidor Fisch.

The three agencies swarmed over Hauptmann's home to find evidence. After the initial find of ransom money on September 20, three officers from New Jersey and four NYPD detectives went back to 1279 East 222nd Street to turn the place upside down looking for clues.

Sergeant Andrew Zapolsky, one of the New Jersey officers, wrote in his report that he was specifically tasked to find "an instrument which may have [been] used in making the symbols on the Lindbergh Ransom notes." He was also told to search the attic and "pick up anything that we thought was the property of Isidor Fisch and also to be on the lookout for the instrument stated above."

Access to the attic inside Hauptmann's apartment was available only to those of a particular girth. One got in through a narrow closet space about eight feet tall and twenty-two and a half inches wide, and by climbing up four shelves that served as steps, about eighteen inches apart. Getting into the attic actually required an individual to use his hands to pull himself through the small opening.

Zapolsky was the first detective to look inside the attic. He removed an empty suitcase, two pieces of bent pipe, a ruler, a plane blade, and a canvas mason's bag. The evidence was taken to the Bronx County Court House and placed in a closet in the district attorney's office.

The next day, Sunday, September 23, Koehler resorted to getting his information once again from his local paper, still not having heard anything from Lamb or Schwarzkopf. The grand jury was set to meet on Monday to indict Hauptmann on the extortion charges. Koehler also read about Hauptmann's alleged 1932 confession letter to the Ohio prisoner and speculation from Germany that Fisch had not died from natural causes in Germany but had been "murdered, neighbors whispered."

A noteworthy handwriting expert, Albert S. Osborn, whom Koehler coincidentally had met more than a decade earlier when he too was an expert witness in the Magnuson murder trial, concluded "positively" that Hauptmann's writing matched that in the ransom notes. Nothing more was mentioned in the news about the ladder or the National Lumber and Millwork Company.

Koehler had finished reading the paper when his phone rang. It was his boss, Carlisle Winslow, who said he was planning on releasing the lab's involvement in the case and that a newspaper photographer would be taking pictures of Koehler in his lab first thing on Monday morning for a story in that day's *Wisconsin State Journal*. Winslow wanted to be reminded of the details of the investigation for the statement he would provide to the reporter.

The secrecy Koehler had sworn to for the last year and a half was about to be blown up.

The next morning, dressed in his traditional dark suit, dark tie, and white shirt and wearing a stoic face, Koehler posed with a magnifying glass in one hand and the other holding one of the rails used in the kidnap ladder. The page-one headline would read, "Madison Lab Scientist Traces Lindy Kidnap Ladder to Hauptmann's Bronx Lumberyard." A subhead stated, "Arthur Koehler Adds Link to Chain About Suspect After Long Probe at Forest Products Building."

"Lumber in the ladder used by the kidnaper of the Lindbergh baby was traced by the U.S. forest products laboratory here to a Bronx lumberyard where Bruno Hauptmann was employed, Director C. P. Winslow announced today," the story began.

"Early in the case, Col. H. Norman Schwarzkopf, superintendent of the New Jersey police, requested the assistance of the Forest Products laboratory in developing any clues from the wood in the ladder used in the kidnaping of the Lindbergh baby," Winslow stated. "The laboratory at once assigned Mr. Koehler, its leading wood technologist, to work on the case in cooperation with the New Jersey state police.

"Mr. Koehler's intensive technical examination of the wood in the ladder disclosed not only the species of wood but also certain very distinctive and peculiar markings of the wood. With his conclusions as to the cause of these markings as a basis, and working in close cooperation with Col. Schwarzkopf's organization, more than 1,000 lumber mills from New Jersey to Alabama were canvassed and lumber samples from many of the them were intensively examined by him at the Forest Products laboratory.

"From this study, Mr. Koehler and representatives of the New Jersey state police traced to destination and intensively examined many lumber shipments of the species and dimensions used in the ladder until lumber with the identical distinctive markings occurring in the ladder was found at the retail yard of the National Lumber and Millwork co. in the Bronx.

"This is the company where it is now reported that Bruno Hauptmann was sporadically employed shortly before and after the kidnaping," Winslow explained.

Still no word came from New Jersey, but Lamb had read Koehler's note and dispatched the scientist's partner throughout the investigation, Detective Lewis Bornmann, to go to Hauptmann's home for the first time on September 25. Bornmann had been assigned after the arrest to guard duty over the prisoner and to canvass the area around the Lindbergh estate in Hopewell to see if anyone recognized Hauptmann.

Bornmann reported to the State Police Training School that Tuesday morning and later wrote in his report that he was dispatched by Lamb to meet Detective Maurice Tobin and two NYPD carpenters, Anselm Cramer Sr. and Charles Enkler, to "conduct a thorough search of the house and garage and to pay particular attention to any wood that might be of the type that was used in the construction of the ladder."

But even Bornmann was intrigued with the idea of finding more ransom money. On September 25, he found writing on the closet door of the middle room of the four-room apartment, a room that the Hauptmanns had used as a nursery. Near an upper hinge, he discovered a notation: "$500 1928 B-00007162A 1928 B-00009272A."

The detectives looked at the list of bills paid out in the ransom and found that the last four numbers of each notation matched one of the five- and one of the ten-dollar ransom bills.

The left inside part of the closet door revealed, "in what appeared to be Hauptmann's handwriting," the address 2974 Decauter and underneath it the numbers 3-7154. They would prove to be the 1932 home address and phone number of Dr. James F. "Jafsie" Condon, the intermediary between Lindbergh and the kidnappers.

The closet door was removed, and Bornmann took it to the Bronx County Court House for storage.

The next morning at nine, Bornmann met the carpenters and one of the Bronx detectives at Hauptmann's apartment again. They immediately went into the attic.

"Nothing of value was found," Bornmann would later write, "with the exception of several small pieces of wood and shavings and several cut nails that may possibly have a bearing on the case." He collected them so Arthur Koehler could analyze them later.

The carpenters had been tasked with demolishing the garage to see if any more ransom money was hidden, so the group spent only a short time inside the house before heading outside. The garage was roughly fifty feet to the east and rear of the home.

Behind where the workbench had been removed were numerous 2x4-inch pieces of wood used to bolster the garage walls. Bornmann stated in his report that he noticed one of them "showed signs of having been removed and replaced on a previous occasion and upon it being pried loose disclosed on its inner side (that is the side which had been flush against the right wall of the garage) five one and an eighth inch by approximately four inch holes had been bored and inserted in each of these holes were tightly rolled rolls of ten dollar gold certificates."

Bornmann also found a hole in that 2x4 that held a small automatic revolver. At roughly 11:25 AM, Bornmann and his Bronx detective counterpart took the money and the gun to the Bronx district attorney's office. An hour later, they were instructed to remove the money from the holes in the wood, to count it, and to check the serial numbers against the ransom bill list.

Hole number 1 held nineteen ten-dollar bills. Holes 2 and 4 held twenty bills. Hole 3 held fifteen bills, and hole 5 held ten bills. A total of $840 had been secreted away in that 2x4. The serial numbers matched bills given by Lindbergh as part of the ransom.

Bornmann and Tobin headed back to the house to continue their search for material related to the ladder. Immediately they secured "several pieces of ponderosa pine" found inside Hauptmann's garage for Koehler to compare with pieces of the kidnapping ladder.

Then Bornmann, Tobin, and the carpenters went back into the attic. Their first search had been hasty, as everyone involved wanted to get out to the garage where the majority of exposed wood on the property existed. But now Bornmann saw that the flooring in the attic was unfinished. He remembered one of his many conversations with Koehler. He thought of all the interviews they had done with lumber workers, all the mentions of Ponderosa pine and Douglas fir. He and Koehler had heard over and over that the wood used in the uprights of the kidnap ladder, the 1x4 stock, was used for crating on the docks and in big cities for underflooring, roof boards, and attic floors.

As Bornmann would later write in his official report, Hauptmann's attic contained twenty-seven pieces of 1x6 North Carolina pine tongue-and-groove roofing, approximately twenty and a half inches long. The boards crossed the attic from east to west and were nailed to the rafters with cut nails.

"It was noticed the last board of the flooring on the south side was not the same length as the others and further investigation disclosed that a piece of this board approximately 8 foot long had been removed," Bornmann wrote. "A small quantity of sawdust between the joists and also nail holes on the joists and a small saw mark on the adjoining board affirmed the fact that this particular board had been the same length as the others and a piece about 8 ft long had been removed."

Not waiting for the carpenters to do their jobs, Bornmann pulled off another section from the board, about nine feet in length, to look at it more closely.

"Being familiar with the various kinds of wood used in the construction of the ladder and as the flooring appeared to be of the same type wood as one of the rails in the ladder, this particular section was removed to be turned over to Arthur Koehler, Wood Technologist," he continued.

In Hauptmann's attic, the last board of the flooring on the south side was not the same length as the others. Another section of that board was pulled off, so Koehler could study if it matched the wood in Rail 16. (Courtesy: Dr. Regis Miller/Forest Products Laboratory)

Bornmann had one of the carpenters remove the cut nails that had been used to connect the board with the joist to compare them "with the nail holes on rail #16 of the ladder."

Numerous detectives had visited the attic before Bornmann, and none had discovered what he found. But no one else who had been to the house, not Wallace or Zapolsky or any of the other New Jersey State Police officers, had ever worked directly with Koehler. The scientist's contacts at the NJSP had been Lamb and Schwarzkopf at the highest levels and Bornmann and to a far lesser degree DeGaetano at the field level.

Further, the other investigators hadn't been looking for wood; they had been looking for ransom money, the instrument that had made a mark on the ransom notes, and anything connected with Isidor Fisch. They may even have seen what Bornmann finally noticed on the afternoon of September 26, but if so, they did not understand its significance.

Because while the other New Jersey officers may have known about the ladder investigation and Koehler's role in it, no one knew the specifics about Koehler's research like Bornmann did. Those car rides visiting dozens of lumber mills and yards all over the Atlantic seaboard had given Bornmann an insight into Koehler's work that no one else possessed—not even Lamb and Schwarzkopf. Koehler jokingly referred to Bornmann as his "Siamese twin" throughout the investigation.

As for the New York police and the Bureau of Investigation, they didn't even know Koehler existed in this case, since his involvement had been kept secret by Schwarzkopf and his associates, who were worried those agencies would steal the limelight from whatever, if anything, he might discover.

Maybe on the morning of September 25, when Lamb first spoke to Bornmann about heading out to Hauptmann's home, he had told him specifically about Koehler's letter of a few days earlier, imploring them to keep an eye out for Rail 16 or, more specifically, advising them that a "board may have been taken from a local structure accessible to the maker of the ladder." What Bornmann found certainly qualified under that description.

"No one else looked for it except me," Bornmann later said in

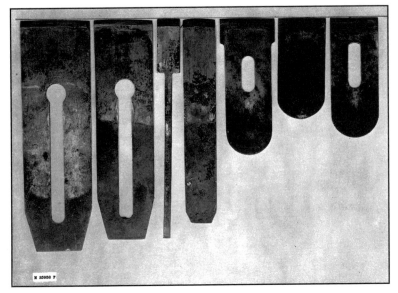

Hauptmann had many planer blades in his garage. Koehler would conclude that one of those blades was used on the 16th Rail as well as the ladder's rungs, linking Hauptmann to the construction of the kidnap instrument. (Courtesy: Dr. Regis Miller/Forest Products Laboratory)

a television interview on the case. "I was interested in the wood from the beginning."

When Bornmann reported back to Lamb about what he and Tobin had found, the next step was obvious.

Schwarzkopf sent an urgent telegram to Winslow at the Forest Products Laboratory in Madison requesting Arthur Koehler immediately return to New Jersey to help with the case. Winslow sent his response at 5:19 PM central time, spelling his own name wrong in his haste: "Koehler will join you Trenton Friday morning. CP Winspow"

Koehler arrived once again at the Trenton Rail Station, on September 28, nine days after Hauptmann had been arrested. This time he didn't immediately go to the State Patrol Training School in West Trenton, where he had done all of his previous work on the case. Instead, he was brought to NJSP departmental headquarters in Trenton, located across from the State Capitol, which faced the Delaware River to the west. As Koehler approached the headquarters, he could see a pack of reporters. Schwarzkopf saw Koehler's visit as an opportunity to get positive press for his agency. The NYPD and Hoover at the bureau had reporters seemingly on retainer to write their view of the case, and the colonel wanted to show the world that the NJSP had been active throughout the investigation and had a scientist on retainer whose work would rival any detective's. The press had already been briefed about his arrival and about his role in the investigation, specifically about his work tracing Rails 12 and 13 to the National Lumber and Millwork facility in the Bronx.

After answering all of their questions, it was time for Koehler to get to work. He was transported back to his old stomping grounds, Troop C Headquarters, to examine first the southern yellow pine that Bornmann had picked up inside Hauptmann's garage.

He could see immediately that the boards weren't the shape of the lumber in the ladder. "Furthermore," he wrote in his report, "this lumber went through a planer with 8 knives in the top and bottom heads at the rate of 0.52" per revolution of the heads which is different than any lumber used in the ladder."

The next day, he gladly suffered the media once more, this time "posing for three different moving picture outfits," before trying out the planes found inside Hauptmann's garage. They had

Some of the tools found in Hauptmann's garage. The accused was an unemployed carpenter at the time of his arrest. (Courtesy: Dr. Regis Miller/Forest Products Laboratory)

been brought in the day before with the rest of Hauptmann's tools to Koehler's temporary work space/laboratory.

He fixed a board of pine in a workbench vise. Then he picked up Hauptmann's biggest plane. The workshop was soon filled with the sounds of blade cutting wood.

It was "a shriek of accusation," he'd later say, "the complete betrayal of the author of the ladder."

His initial examination proved fruitful. "The largest plane, which has a knife 2-½" wide, has numerous nicks in the blade which make marks exactly like those on the pine rungs and rail 16. There is no question but what the rungs and rail were planed with that plane. It had not been sharpened or dulled further since then," he wrote in his September 29 report.

Over the next three days, Koehler itemized, measured, and remeasured all of the tools found in Hauptmann's home and inside his garage. The accused had six planes in addition to the one Koehler believed had been used to fashion Rail 16 and the rungs in the kidnap ladder. The planes contained knives ranging from ¾ inch to the 2½-inch knife in the particular plane that drew his attention.

Hauptmann had wood bits, steel drills, hammers, multiple screwdrivers, and eight different saws (crosscut, rip, circle, and keyhole) with different size blades. Of particular interest were the nails. The four in the package found by Bornmann when he went through the garage on September 26 had a "P on the shank like the nails in the ladder." But more tellingly to Koehler, "the cut nails taken from the attic and garage fit the holes in rail #16 exactly, which indicates that the board probably was removed from some of Hauptmann's previous work either for others or for himself."

Koehler looked at the fifteen pieces of lumber brought in from Hauptmann's garage and cellar, each labeled with a letter of the alphabet. Some of it was the North Carolina pine apparent in the kidnap ladder. Unfortunately for the investigation, most of it had "no apparent connection with the ladder." When it came to sample "O," a triangular bracket found holding up a shelf in the garage, the knife cuts were "nearly the same as on rail #16." Further, "The back edge was planed with a hand plane which made marks exactly like those on rail 16 and the pine rungs."

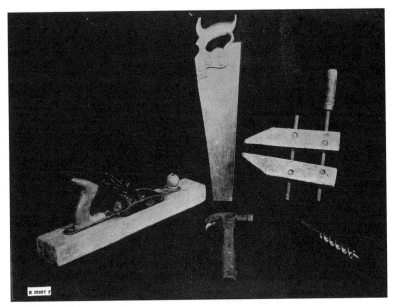

From the beginning, Koehler told Schwarzkopf that the ladder showed poor design and workmanship and that he did not believe its maker to be a "high-grade" carpenter. (Courtesy: Dr. Regis Miller/Forest Products Laboratory)

He also looked at a cigar box marked "Found by Detective Horn in closet in hall." The NYPD envelope in the box held nails, screws, tacks, and keys. Of the six 8-penny nails in the envelope, Koehler found three to have a *P* on the shank. Another envelope labeled "Nails, (Det.) Petrosino (Bag in Garage)" held another twenty-two 8-penny common nails with a *P* on their shank.

Interestingly to Koehler, the cigar box also contained a set of chisels. Aside from the ladder, a ¾-inch chisel was the only physical evidence found at the Lindbergh estate the night of the kidnapping. But "no chisel ¾" or 1" wide was found in the cigar box or tool chest, although the second recess from the bottom up in rail #16 of the ladder shows that a ¾" chisel was used in cutting out the recess," he wrote in his report. This was a different conclusion from his very first report on the ladder back in March 1933, when he had written that it wasn't possible to determine the width of the chisel used in the crime.

There was a ¾-inch and a ⅜-inch cold chisel among Hauptmann's tools, but the cold chisels were made of tempered steel and were used to cut "cold metals," not wood.

After chronicling the items brought to his laboratory, it was time to put some of the tools to work, specifically the saws. In order for Koehler to determine the width of the cuts of the blades in the saws, it was important to use them to cut pine and fir boards similar to those used in the ladder. To the uneducated, the measurements of the saw's knives should have been enough to determine the width of the cuts they'd make, but Koehler knew better than to take that for granted.

In his investigation of the kidnap ladder, he had measured cuts that had been made too deep in the ladder rails and not completely mortised out, 0.033 inch and 0.034 inch in width. Now his goal was to use each of the saws to see if anything matched. The crosscut saws were for cutting across the grain of wood, while the ripsaws were for ripping or cutting with the grain.

He tried the relatively new Disston ripsaw with the 25½-inch blade first. The condition of the saw's teeth was good, but it cut the pine to a width of 0.043 inch and the fir to a width of 0.045 inch. That was close, but in Koehler's world, a difference of 0.010 was too much to prove anything.

The next three biggest saws all cut the pine and fir to widths between 0.045 and 0.057, so he ruled them out.

Next he shifted to an Atkins crosscut saw with a 22-inch blade. Its teeth were dull, but it cut both the pine and fir to a width of 0.035 inch. Another Disston crosscut saw with a 16-inch blade was also pretty new. Its tip was bent, but the condition of its teeth was good. It cut both boards to a width of 0.033 inch.

"This shows," he concluded, "that Hauptmann had two saws with which the cuts might have been made."

He then segued to "parallel, shallow, [and] oblique cuts" that were found on Rungs 1, 2, and 4. Three independent measurements determined they had been made by an 11-point saw of which Hauptmann had two: maybe not coincidentally the Atkins crosscut with a 22-inch blade and the Disston crosscut saw with the 16-inch blade.

"The marks evidently were made by drawing the side of the board across the side of the saw or vice versa," Koehler wrote. "The saw must have been very sharp, judging by the feather-edged cuts and a microscopic examination of cross sections of the cuts. It is highly probable, therefore, that if one of the two 11-point saws in Hauptmann's tool chest was used in constructing the ladder, it was the shorter (16") saw because it still has sharp teeth while the other one is dull. This saw also appears relative new. Why Hauptmann got a new, short 11 point saw when he already had one equally fine although 6" longer is an open question."

Koehler theorized in his report to Lamb and Schwarzkopf that the shorter saw may have been specially purchased to make the ladder away from Hauptmann's garage. The shorter saw was easily transportable, in a suitcase, for example. With it, a plane, a ¾-inch auger and brace, chisel, hammer, and clamp, one could make a ladder. He mentioned that Rails 14 and 15 clearly had been clamped together because "the saw cuts match perfectly as to spacing, direction and depth."

There were no marks on either rails or rungs to indicate they had been cinched into either a vise or clamp, but one of the clamps found in Hauptmann's garage was a wooden carpenter's clamp that Koehler figured "would leave no mark."

However, that led to another unanswered question: "If Haupt- mann made the ladder away from home why did he use the largest plane he had when the next smaller one might have done just as well," he wondered.

Possibly the ripping and planing were done in Hauptmann's garage but the notching of the rails and cross cutting the rungs to proper length (which would be a give away if someone had noticed it and remembered it later) together with the ladder assembly were carried out elsewhere.

It seems logical that some secluded spot outside of the resi- dential district where the ladder could be assembled full length and tried out without being seen would be chosen for that pur- pose. That would also explain why the hand plane marks on the side of the ladder, which undoubtedly were made when it was found that the top section fitted too tightly with the middle one, do not match with the plane marks on the edges or with any made by Hauptmann's planes. Did Hauptmann take a smaller plane along, which was later resharpened or did someone else furnish the plane?

New Jersey authorities, specifically Attorney General David Wilentz, were beyond the point of speculation. They didn't want conjecture, they wanted a conviction, and to get it they would need concrete evidence to extradite Hauptmann to New Jersey on murder charges. And they weren't the only ones. The country demanded justice and the dozen or so years in prison that Haupt- mann was facing as a result of the New York extortion charges was simply not enough.

Wilentz knew that under New Jersey law only a killing com- mitted during a burglary, robbery, arson, or what was called a "straight law" felony would result in a punishment of either life in prison or death. Kidnapping was not one of those types of felonies in the New Jersey statues. In other words, if the murder indictment was based on a kidnapping charge, the death penalty would not be possible. So prosecutors resolved to call the kidnapping a burglary, so they would be in a position to ask for the death penalty even if the jury determined Charles A. Lindbergh Jr. had been killed accidentally in the commission of the crime.

They found themselves in a hurry to get their evidence ready, as a judge in the Bronx did not want to wait for the New Jersey authorities to build their case. He had ordered the convening of a panel of 150 people to serve as a jury pool in an extortion trial against Hauptmann to begin on October 11, less than a month after he was arrested.

"I am convinced that the Bronx case against Hauptmann will result in a conviction," Bronx District Attorney Samuel J. Foley told reporters, including one from the Associated Press, on October 6. He had been telling the media for the last week that he was in perfect concert with New Jersey authorities on how to proceed, but in this weekend briefing he "would not say, however, whether the case would be adjourned to permit the German carpenter's extradition to New Jersey."

Wilentz, meanwhile, was rushing to get together material to present a murder case against Hauptmann to a grand jury on Monday, October 8, at the Hunterdon County Courthouse in Flemington, New Jersey, near where the Lindbergh estate was located and thus where the crime was committed.

Wilentz had been appointed New Jersey's top law enforcement official, even though the case he hoped to prosecute would be his first ever in criminal court. He was born in Latvia at the end of the nineteenth century and immigrated to the United States with his parents around 1900. He lived the quintessential American success story, graduating from public school, working at a local newspaper after college, coaching a local basketball team, and traveling to Manhattan at night to attend New York University Law School.

He enlisted in the army during World War I as a private, and at the end of the war he was a lieutenant. That was when he completed law school, opened up his own law firm, and became active in Democratic politics.

Wilentz was described by a *New York Times* reporter covering the trial as a "short, wiry man [who] dressed nattily and spoke with a sharp, satirical tongue."

Koehler found himself on the other end of that tongue that

first weekend of October as the attorney general wanted to know what the scientist could testify to in front of the grand jury. Could he say Hauptmann built the ladder? Could he prove that fact?

Not yet, said Koehler, but he could speak to the tracing of the wood in Rails 12 and 13 back to the National Lumber and Mill-work Company, and considering the fact Hauptmann used to work there, that was compelling. He could discuss how the nails taken from the board in Hauptmann's attic fit perfectly into the holes in Rail Number 16.

But maybe the best piece of evidence Koehler could provide was his conclusion that the largest plane found at Hauptmann's, the Disston with the knife 2½ inches wide, had numerous nicks in the blade that made marks exactly like those on the pine rungs and Rail 16.

"There is no question," he told Wilentz, "the rungs and rail were planed with that plane."

First thing Monday morning, Koehler put on his best dark suit, white shirt, and dark tie and glanced at the front page of the local paper, with its blaring headline of the impending murder indictment being sought by New Jersey prosecutors. He had been told by prosecutors that the courtroom would be full because "all the grand jury people are telling their friends not to miss the wood expert."

Koehler held in his hand an official subpoena to testify. So did Colonel Lindbergh, Bureau of Investigation agents, New York police detectives, eyewitnesses, and other experts. When Koehler arrived at the historic Hunterdon County Courthouse in Flemington, New Jersey, a crowd of two hundred or more were waiting on the steps and milling about the lawn. They had been there since an hour before the grand jurors arrived, but not before numerous cameras had been set up on the courthouse portico.

The twenty-three grand jurors, twenty men and three women, posed for pictures for nearly twenty minutes before filing into the courthouse. Those who entered seventy-one-year-old Justice Thomas Whitaker Trenchard's courtroom were about to hear evidence unlike any in the peaceful county's 149-year history.

"Ladies and gentlemen of the Grand Jury," Justice Trenchard began with his instructions, you have been convened today at the United request of the Attorney General of the State of New Jersey and of the Prosecutor of the Place of this County.

Their purpose is to lay before you evidence they state tends to show that one Hauptmann murdered Charles A. Lindbergh, Jr. in this County on March 1, 1932.

The State's representatives definitely state to the Court that they will ask you to return only an indictment for murder at the present time.

They have stated to the Court that the evidence to be presented will tend to show that Hauptmann, the accused in this county, in the course of a burglary of the dwelling house of Colonel Lindbergh done for the purpose of committing a battery upon and stealing the infant son, Charles A. Lindbergh, Jr. and its clothing, caused such child to be stricken and injured as a result of which he died; or that, in any event the evidence will show that the child was killed as the result of a blow or stroke closely connected with the burglary and which was inflicted by the accused in this County.

After stating "the pertinent principles of law" for the grand jurors, Trenchard continued,

If, then, the evidence presented to you in the Grand Jury room reasonably tends to show that the child was feloniously stricken in Hunterdon County by Hauptmann and afterwards died as a result thereof, and that the stroke causing death was inflicted in pursuance of the perpetration of a burglary and had an intimate and close connection therewith and was naturally consequent thereto, you should find an indictment for murder, regardless of whether the stroke and injury was accidentally or was intentionally inflicted.

But even if you should not find that the stroke which resulted in death was inflicted in the perpetration of a burglary, if you nevertheless find that the evidence presented to you in the Grand Jury room reasonably tends to show that the stroke which caused death was caused or delivered by the accused in Hunterdon County with intent to do serious bodily harm to the child while the accused was carrying away the stolen child and its clothing, you should return an indictment for murder.

If you return an indictment for murder, the grade or degree of the crime will be determined by the trial jury, if they find the accused guilty.

You may now retire and proceed with consideration of the matter at your convenience.

At 10:30 AM, the grand jurors proceeded into the grand jury room to hear the evidence presented by Wilentz and Hunterdon County Prosecutor Anthony Hauck. Dr. Charles H. Mitchell, the neighboring Mercer County physician, who performed the autopsy on the baby boy, was the first witness to testify. He told the grand jurors the baby's death was caused by a "blow to the head."

Next, two handwriting witnesses shared their common belief that the writing on the ransom notes matched the writing that Hauptmann had provided on the forms to register his car.

By that time, several hundred people were outside the courthouse waiting for Lindbergh. His car arrived at 11:30 in a convoy with three New Jersey state troopers on motorcycles. Dressed in a gray suit, blue shirt and tie, and brown shoes, Lindbergh was greeted by Schwarzkopf and Hunterdon County Sheriff John H. Curtiss, and they walked through the crowd on a path carved out by other troopers and entered the courthouse.

Lindbergh waited just a few minutes in the grand jury's anteroom before being called in. His testimony took only six minutes, but in that time he identified the original ransom note, a photo of his son's body when it was discovered two and a half months after he disappeared, and most importantly for the purposes of the case, the voice of Bruno Hauptmann as the one he had heard from afar when Condon paid the $50,000 ransom to the kidnappers.

Roughly fifteen minutes after he arrived, Lindbergh departed. A flurry of eyewitnesses followed his testimony, placing Hauptmann with ransom money, with the ladder, and in the vicinity of the Lindbergh estate at Hopewell.

After an hour lunch break, finally it was Koehler's turn. He answered questions for almost fifteen minutes, providing what *The*

New York Times called "technical testimony," chronicling the construction of the ladder and where the lumber to build it came from. Schwarzkopf later told him that he had made a good impression on the grand jury.

Just after 3 PM, with all of the testimony completed, Hauck abruptly burst out of the grand jury room to learn the score of Game 6 of the 1934 World Series. It had been a tight series up to that point, with the Detroit Tigers up three games to two over the St. Louis Cardinals, who were vying for their third championship in nine years. "The grand jurors want to know how the ball game is getting along," he said.

Hauck learned that future Hall of Fame first baseman Hank Greenberg had just hit a single in the bottom of the sixth inning, scoring another future Hall of Famer, Charlie Gehringer, to tie the game at 3 apiece. If he had stayed out of the grand jury room just a few more minutes, he would have heard the Cardinals retake the lead in the top of the seventh, but an indictment was more important to Hauck than a baseball game.

After hearing from twenty-four witnesses, the grand jury deliberated for an hour before foreman George N. Robinson instructed Hunterdon County Clerk C. Lloyd Fell that the group had a verdict. It was handed to Justice Trenchard and officially entered into the record.

"The Grand Inquest for the State of New Jersey in and for the Body of the County of Hunterdon," it read, "upon their respective oaths present that Bruno Richard Hauptmann on the first day of March in the year of Our Lord, One Thousand Nine Hundred and Thirty-two, with force and arms, at the Township of East Amwell in the County of Hunterdon aforesaid and within the jurisdiction of this Court, did willfully feloniously and of his malice aforethought kill and murder Charles A. Lindbergh Jr. contrary to the form of the statute in such case made and provided against the peace of this state, the government and dignity of the same."

Wilentz told Koehler that the indictment was not the end of his work. The scientist wanted to see Hauptmann's home firsthand, to witness what Bornmann had witnessed. So the two men went first thing the next morning out to the Bronx. Koehler hoped to sift through the wood from the now torn-down garage. He wanted to climb into the attic. He needed to make sure the detectives hadn't missed anything.

Looking first at the lumber from the old garage and in the basement, he found none that resembled the lumber or had plane marks like those in the ladder. In the kitchen, he found an unpainted wooden platform that had been planed by hand, but the marks did not correspond to the Disson 25½-inch planer that had been used on the ladder.

Koehler and Bornmann headed up to the attic, accompanied by Cramer and Enkler, the two police carpenters who had been present when Bornmann discovered the missing board two weeks earlier.

"On this day," Koehler wrote in his official report of the visit, "we took back the piece taken up in the attic and replaced it, driving the cut nails partly back into their original position." He continued,

> At that end of this board which was near the middle of the attic there was sawdust on the lath and plaster below; and in direct line with the end there was a short saw cut into the adjacent board. Both of these facts indicated that a piece had been cut off from the board right there in the attic. Furthermore, the joists beyond the end of this board had cut nail holes in them from which the nails had been removed, all of which indicated that part of the board had been removed at some previous date.
>
> I had in my pocket note book measurements of the distances between the four nail holes in rail #16 and Detective Bornmann and I compared those distances with distances between nail holes in the joists and found that four of those in the joists corresponded exactly with those in the rail.

Bornmann called Captain Lamb with Koehler's findings and was ordered back to headquarters in Trenton to immediately give a verbal briefing to Colonel Schwarzkopf. Schwarzkopf instructed the men to return to Hauptmann's home the next day and to bring Rail 16 with them.

"Take pictures," he suggested, "to show [Rail 16's] relationship to the remaining length of flooring and its original position on the attic joist."

First thing the next morning, the scientist, detective, and two carpenters were joined in the attic by Detective Tobin. They looked at one another with trepidation. Koehler laid Rail 16 on the joists where the wood was missing. He took the cut nails that had been in the board Bornmann pulled up and placed them in the holes of Rail 16.

He took a deep breath and began tapping lightly on the first nail with a hammer. Cramer followed suit on another nail. By the time they had finished, there were smiles all around.

The nails fit into the joists perfectly. Their angle and depth was spot on. Their size and spacing matched.

"This rail [16] had been a part of that particular piece which still remained in the flooring of the attic," Bornmann wrote in his report.

Even more bluntly put, Rail 16 and the attic floor had once been attached.

They took pictures from all angles and brought the negatives back to headquarters to be developed.

"It was a wonderful detective stunt," Koehler later wrote. "Such a result simply could not happen as a mere coincidence."

To scientists like Koehler, coincidences were taunts or dares that lead to further calculations with a goal of finding certainties.

"I worked it out that nails of such size could be driven into 10,000 places in the surface of that board without duplicating holes," he said.

By the laws of chance it would take a world much vaster than our own to provide a coincidence of those four nail holes matching accidentally four other nail holes with which they had no connection.

The way you work that out is this: Let us say no chance involves the first nail hole and a suspected mate, but let us further say that the chance that a second nail hole likewise would fit directly to another is as one in 10,000. The third nail hole to match has but once chance in 10,000 times 10,000 less three—the spaces occupied by the three nail holes, but let's not

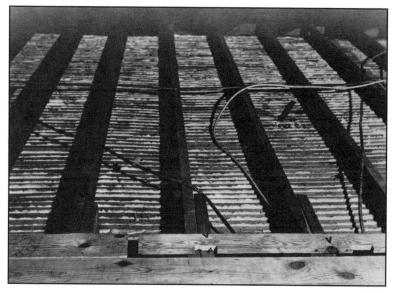

Koehler took the 16th Rail into Hauptmann's attic and discovered its nails fit into the joists perfectly. Rail 16 and the attic floor had once been attached; Koehler called it "a wonderful detective stunt." (Courtesy: Dr. Regis Miller/Forest Products Laboratory)

quibble—and so the fourth, if it should be linked together with another in conjunction with its mated companions, well that would be the product of another 10,000 minus four.

Moreover, only one board in 10,000 would have cut nails of that size in it. The chance of being wrong about the identity in such a case of circumstantial evidence might be written so: $\frac{1}{10,000,000,000,000,000}$.

What a lawyer would call circumstantial, Koehler called proof. "There simply is not such a chance in human experience," he said.

The next day, he was back in his temporary lab studying and comparing the grain and planer marks on the board from Hauptmann's attic with those on Rail 16. He was looking at tree rings found on every piece of wood.

"Any country boy who ever saw a stump knows fairly well how to count the rings and figure out an approximation of the age of the tree that once stood there," he later said.

Every tree within itself has written all its history. The growth in spring shows white and pithy, but in the summer the slower growth becomes, in most trees, darker tissue. This is repeated year by year, and that is why these rings seem double and confuse those who try to say a tree is such and such an age. Count the band of white and black as one year's growth.

The board end of the piece of flooring that had been robbed to make a ladder showed its rings quite clear, and so did the ladder rail. A gap of one and three-eighth inches had been trimmed off, yet the rings matched.

They had the same curvature and the same width. "Striking similarity," he said. Further, he deduced that three adjacent rings located on the same place in each are narrower than the rest. Subsequent study would lead to more proof.

"A board is cut lengthwise of a tree so that the rings of small stuff of second growth are curved and several rings expose their edges along a board in what we call the grain. It is a pattern that is always varied and yet the pattern of the grain in ladder rail and

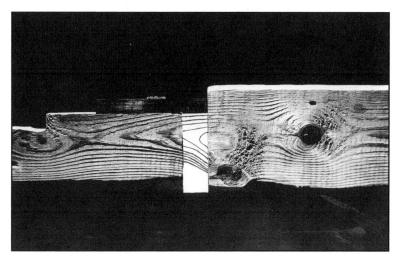

The growth rings on the board from the attic matched the growth rings on the 16th Rail. They came from the same board. As Koehler would later say, "A tree never lies." (Courtesy: Dr. Regis Miller/Forest Products Laboratory)

floor board matched as perfectly as if the interrupted curving lines they plotted years ago had been etched within the tree just to be a trap for anyone who dared so to misuse wood as to form it into a kidnap ladder," he would later tell a reporter.

His official report was more direct: "Since it can be said that no two pieces of wood are the same, it is evident that these two came from the same piece."

He planned to elaborate before the jury in the murder trial of Bruno Richard Hauptmann. He told Wilentz that he intended to tell jurors there was "no doubt that the board from the attic floor and the ladder rail were at one time one piece, which was nailed down in the attic as part of the floor and that part of it was cut off, removed and used for the ladder rail."

9

Milton and Eva Apgar stood at the door with their mouths wide open, staring at the man who would be sleeping at their house for at least the next month. Their guest had the most stature of anyone to ever visit their home, so they had assumed he'd be taller.

But the lean, wiry writer standing on their doorstep sported size 5½ shoes and weighed 140 pounds after a steak and potato dinner. He hoped, though, that his attire would set him apart. He liked to say the clothes he picked out each morning were "the first sentence of his day's story."

On this day, he wore a fifty-dollar blue suit from Nat Lewis's on Broadway and a pure silk shirt from Charvet et Fils on East 53rd Street with his initials, DR, stitched in red on both the lapel and the inside of the cuffs.

Damon Runyon had a cigarette in his mouth, two bags in his hands, and round, wire-framed glasses covering his pale blue eyes. As he always said to those who mocked people with glasses, "Napoleon gets taken out in Russia because he cannot see when they give him the weather report."

Speaking of weather, he would have much preferred to be at his house in south Florida, spending days watching his racehorses at the Hialeah track and his nights on the veranda with temperatures far warmer than the mercury would rise to here in Flemington, New Jersey. But his best filly, Angelic, needed significant medical care, and so the nation's most famous sportswriter couldn't turn down an assignment to the nation's most widely anticipated trial.

In fact, he never turned down an assignment—mainly because he couldn't count on another one being offered if he did. And with the high life he lived, he needed that next assignment. After all, another of his regular sayings was, "The payroll is a more important document than the Bible."

So here he was at the home of Milton, a dentist, and Eva, a public school teacher, on Mine Street in Flemington, New Jersey. By the time he had been tasked with writing about the upcoming trial of Bruno Richard Hauptmann, all of the rooms at the Union Hotel, the only hotel in town, had been spoken for. Located directly across from the courthouse, the hotel had received more than nine hundred requests to inhabit its fifty rooms. Even with cots in the hallways—and Runyon was too big a deal for that—there was simply no space.

So the residents of Flemington were pressed into service. Numerous members of the community allowed reporters, actors, and athletes to stay in their homes during what H. L. Mencken described as "the greatest story since the Resurrection." That came from a reporter who had covered as dramatic a fight over religion as the country had recently seen in Tennessee in the so-called Scopes Monkey trial, featuring legendary lawyers Clarence Darrow and William Jennings Bryan.

Runyon's hosts were ebullient to have him in their humble abode, and it was humble compared with his usual Parc Vendome ninth-floor apartment on West 57th Street, just steps from New York's Central Park. There, his living room featured a two-story-high ceiling, parquet floors covered with Persian rugs, and polished Queen Anne wood chests. His temporary Flemington residence was far more quaint, but he wouldn't be there often, as he planned to crank out up to five thousand words per day at the trial.

Nevertheless, Runyon was unfailingly polite to the Apgars, as he didn't want to be what he would call one of the "clunks," or in other words, a dullard. There were certainly numerous things the couple wanted to talk about with their guest. After all, Arthur Brisbane, who was staying with a Mrs. Johnson at her place at 4 Main Street, had called Runyon the best reporter of the era as he traveled easily between prize fighters and gangsters. Two of Runyon's short stories had recently been made into films, the second of which, *Little Miss Marker,* starred a young actress named Shirley

Temple. The movie would launch her past Greta Garbo as the nation's biggest film draw of the year.

Runyon wasn't the only journalist staying at the Apgar's home, but he certainly was the highest profile. Lou Wittimer, who was helping longtime Hearst reporter Jim Kilgallen with the International News, had a smaller bedroom in the Apgar home. Kilgallen's daughter, Dorothy, who wrote for the *New York Evening Journal*, was also in Flemington to cover the trial. Other reporters were scattered around town as well. Still others, like Walter Winchell, chose to commute daily to Flemington from hotels in Trenton, about forty-five minutes away.

Flemington had been, simply put, overrun. In an effort to support the two-plus million words set to be written about the trial every day, large swaths of the sky were blacked out by the extra telegraph wire put up by Western Union and Postal Telegraph companies to transmit the stories worldwide. It was the biggest wire setup in history.

As the members of the criminal law section of the American Bar Association later described the scene,

> The statement made that there were in Flemington during the trial 700 newspaper men, including 129 cameramen, was probably not an exaggeration. Motor, plane, telegraph and telephone raced with each other to get the first copy to metropolitan New York for world-wide distribution.
>
> This little town, ordinarily with one telegraph operator, had forty-five direct wires, a special teletype machine connected directly with London, a direct wire to Halifax, quick service to Paris, Berlin, Buenos Aires, Shanghai, Melbourne and other capitals of the world.

Another press report stated that 180 telegraph wires had been installed. Special parking places had been established, "with special prices," *The New York Times* reported. The paper also reported that food prices went up at restaurants and markets around town, but Mame Pedrick, who helped operate the Union Hotel later told a Knight Newspapers writer, "We didn't raise our prices at all. It was a $1 meal to everybody, the same as always."

Runyon expensed his meals these days. The fifty-five-year-old, who was born in Manhattan, Kansas, had made his reputation covering not just sports, but also the more famous Manhattan and the "guys and dolls" that inhabited that part of New York. He grew up in Colorado the son of a newspaperman, and after fighting in the Spanish-American War, he tried to start a baseball league. He failed and headed to work as a sportswriter for one of the Hearst papers in New York.

He had gained such a following that stories were being written about him. In one academic work published by a University of Wisconsin researcher, Svend Riemer, Runyon's humor was described as "cosmopolitan, bohemian, smart-alecky or whatever other expression we want to use."

"Runyon's genius," Riemer wrote, "derives from a natural fusion of form and content. His style is in close affinity to the mood that predominates in his narrative, and the plot of his stories furthermore underlines the sociopsychological attitude that he wants to get across, or, better, in the attitude which he exploits and upon which he elaborates."

Runyon would have called that description bunk. He was just a guy who told other guys and dolls stories. There were lots of those forthcoming in Flemington.

His first column written from Flemington, though, wasn't about Hauptmann or Lindbergh at all; it was about the result of the Rose Bowl played on New Year's Day between Alabama and Stanford.

"The writer refrains from comment on the Alabama-Stanford Rose Bowl football game other than to say he told you so," he wrote. "He received 1718 letters from the Pacific coast when he predicted that Alabama would win the game, a somewhat larger number than he received a year ago when he stated that Columbia would defeat Stanford.

"Some of these letters were of a high personal nature. The authors do not seem to realize that, in imparting this advance information on football games, the writer is merely endeavoring to be helpful to his readers, hoping that he may dissuade them from betting on the wrong team."

His gloating about Alabama's 29–13 victory would be his last lighthearted prose for weeks.

Hauptmann's legal team had changed since his early court hearings. His original counsel, James M. Fawcett from the Bronx, had not been successful in a two-day hearing to fight the extradition charges from New York. He had allowed Hauptmann to take the witness stand to defend himself and to bolster the testimony of his wife and two friends who gave him an alibi for the night of the kidnapping. However, Hauptmann had had trouble containing his emotions, shouting his denial of the crime as Attorney General Wilentz questioned him.

"At the previous proceedings," *The New York Times* reported, "he had shown complete mastery of himself, but never was he more self-possessed than during his court room fight to stay clear of New Jersey."

Fawcett told reporters he planned to appeal the Bronx County judge's ruling to allow Hauptmann to be sent to New Jersey to face murder charges, but *The New York Times* reported that Fawcett said, "There may not be enough money in the defense funds to make possible an appeal to the United States Supreme Court."

Fawcett would appear one more time with Hauptmann, at the arraignment in Flemington on October 24. An hour before the arraignment began, the court was packed, with every fixed seat occupied and some set-out folding chairs filled as well.

Handcuffed to a Hunterdon County deputy sheriff, Hauptmann, dressed in a gray suit and dark tie, sat down at the defense table before immediately rising to stand before Justice Trenchard to hear and respond to the indictment.

"Bruno Richard Hauptmann," the prosecutor said, "you have been indicted by the Hunterdon County Grand Jury . . . on the charge of murder. . . . How do you plead, guilty or not guilty?"

"I plead not guilty," Hauptmann said.

A trial date of January 2, 1935, had been set—in theory to accommodate Fawcett, but also, Wilentz said, to prevent jurors from having to serve over the holidays. If money was a concern for Fawcett, it was not for his new lawyer, Edward J. Reilly, who came on board at the beginning of November. He would be paid by the Hearst newspapers in exchange for Anna Hauptmann agreeing to interviews and photographs throughout the trial. Fawcett did not seem skilled nor sophisticated enough for Anna Hauptmann.

"[Fawcett]'s out," Reilly told reporters. "I'm in. Mrs. Hauptmann was thoroughly explicit."

Reilly's reputation and nickname was "Big Ed," and at six feet and two hundred pounds with a baritone voice that never missed the chance to talk into a microphone, he fit the description. The *New York World Telegram* described him near the end of 1934 as looking like a "retired policeman with a flair for clothes."

He had represented defendants in many of the most sensational murder cases to come through the Brooklyn area over the last couple of decades and had earned another nickname, the "Bull of Brooklyn," for his gruff and aggressive trial tactics. The case that had attracted the attention of Anna Hauptmann involved nineteen-year-old Cecelia McCormick, who had faced first-degree murder charges in 1933 for smuggling a gun into a local jail to her husband, who was an inmate. He shot and killed the jail keeper before shooting himself, committing suicide. Reilly got her off by claiming that the state was trying to "whitewash" the case and pin the whole mess on "this little girl."

His reputation had been cemented roughly a decade earlier, though, when he defended a spurned nurse from Cincinnati who followed her former beau to Brooklyn, where she shot and killed him in broad daylight. He'd produced a "scientist" in that case to show that the defendant was an honorable woman who'd suffered a "brain explosion" under stress. Women showered the defendant with flowers when she was found not guilty.

He had some failures through the years as well, and the family members of those defendants called him by yet another nickname, "Death House" Reilly. The Hauptmanns were unaware of that nickname when they brought him on board.

While he never missed an interview or an opportunity for a free drink, he did miss much of the elaborate preparation the prosecution was dedicating to the case. If Reilly's strategy was to excel in bombast and hyperbole, he would find a worthy foil in the scientific witnesses of the prosecution, who based their conclusions and opinions on research.

For example, Koehler spent the two-plus months before the trial measuring and remeasuring all of his earlier findings. He also continued to try to trace the Douglas fir found in Rails 14, 15, and 17, which didn't match the 1x4 taken from the fence in back of Hauptmann's home.

He and Bornmann tried to trace the Ponderosa pine found in the ladder's rungs, visiting lumber mills and yards in New York, Massachusetts, Rhode Island, and Pennsylvania. They were hoping to replicate the results they'd had in tracing Rails 12 and 13.

They drove to Philadelphia to track the history of Hauptmann's 11-point saw with the 16-inch blade. There, the folks at Henry Disston & Sons looked at the blade through a reading glass and determined, as Koehler would write in his report, that "it had been filed but not set since it left the factory. . . . [They] were of the opinion that the last filing was done by an expert saw filer."

Koehler and Bornmann took more pictures of Hauptmann's attic, and they reinterviewed Max Rauch, the son of the Hauptmann home's owner, for the third time, and he swore again that the flooring in the attic had been intact when he inspected it roughly two weeks before Hauptmann rented the apartment.

Koehler went back to Madison over the Thanksgiving holiday, to see family but also to catch up on his day job, "since the work [had] piled up" at the Forest Products Laboratory. "Furthermore," he wrote Schwarzkopf, "we had to make our estimates this week for a large increase in federal relief appropriations which may or may not materialize."

The colonel wanted Koehler back at the very beginning of December for the duration of the trial, but Koehler was hoping to be in Madison for Christmas.

Koehler and his colleague Edward Davis arrived in New Jersey on Wednesday morning, December 5. Davis was prepared to testify about the planer marks found on Rail 16 as well as those on Rails 12 and 13 if prosecutors needed him to. Immediately they went to work at the state police barracks, studying the number of knives in the planer that had dressed Rails 12 and 13 and recalculating the rate of feed of the planer per revolution of cutter heads, all to ensure that the wood in those rails had, in fact, come from

Senator Dorn's lumber yard down in South Carolina.

Then they continued the process Koehler had started a year earlier, comparing under the microscope the samples from the National Lumber and Millwork Company against Rails 12 and 13 to ensure that the peculiar machinery defect on both was consistent.

Next they turned their attention to Koehler's more recent discovery that Hauptmann's 2½-inch wood block plane was the one that had made the marks on Rungs 1 through 10 and on Rail 16. And Davis analyzed Koehler's deduction that Rail 16 had come from Hauptmann's attic.

The World War I veteran found his Forest Products Laboratory superior to have been accurate on all counts. Further, the two scientists actually discovered two new pieces of information that they would note on their joint report as "significant."

First, they found that a ¼-inch chisel found at Hauptmann's was of the same make and model as the ¾-inch chisel found at the scene of the crime. "It will be recalled that the mark of a ¾" chisel was found on one of the ladder rails and that no chisel of that size was among Hauptmann's tools," they wrote. Again, this differed from Koehler's original report on the ladder, in which he had stated that he couldn't tell what size chisel had made a mark carving out the mortises on the ladder. When that belief changed is not reflected in any of his reports.

Second, they found more information to bolster the connection between Rail 16 and the floor board from Hauptmann's attic. Besides confirming that the growth rings matched, they discovered that "there was rather extreme torn grain on corresponding sides of all knots in both pieces. Also there was a pronounced degree of raised grain on corresponding sides of several dips and irregularities of grain in both pieces."

Koehler believed evidence like that had never before been offered in a courtroom anywhere in the world.

The two men did their own woodworking next. It was as if Koehler was in his own basement using his "smooth plane," a popular tool in seventeenth- and eighteenth-century northern Europe that likely came to America with his grandfather in 1852, to work on the sides of a short board.

"The rungs of the ladder (middle and top sections) were set in recesses cut out of the rails," they wrote. "In making these recesses or mortises deeper saw cuts than necessary had been made in several places. These deep saw cuts sometimes extended into the rails as much as ³⁄₁₆" beyond the bottoms of the mortises making it possible to measure the width of the cut and so determine whether any of Hauptmann's saws could have been used in the ladder's construction."

So they used each of Hauptmann's nine saws to make two cuts about 1⅛ inch deep across the grain of both a piece of North Carolina pine and a piece of Douglas fir. They then measured the width of each cut "with a machinist's thickness gauge," or, in other words, to the thousandth of an inch.

The experiment reaffirmed Koehler's earlier thought that Hauptmann's 11-point Atkins saw or his 11-point Disston saw could have been used, and that since the Disston was the newer, sharper one of the two, it was more likely to have been the tool used.

Koehler and Davis next created diagrams and models and labeled the photographs to be used at trial.

Finally, after a year and a half working on this case, Koehler would acknowledge it in his turn writing the Dutchman letter to his brothers on December 14, 1934. On State of New Jersey Department of State Police stationery, he wrote, "You may have seen something in the papers about me recently. Some of the things that I found out leaked out in a mysterious way although the newspapers had things so badly mixed up that it sounded questionable. I will have to appear as a witness at the trial and by the time some of you get this the whole story may be out in the papers. . . . I will have to be there throughout the whole trial so that if anything in my line comes up I can call it to the attention of the attorneys."

He asked his brothers, Alfred in California in particular, to pick up newspapers that included mentions of him. His parents would later tell a reporter that "Our letters from Arthur say little about the Hauptmann case. Maybe [they] don't allow him to discuss the case."

After nearly two full weeks of work, Koehler and Davis spent all of December 18 briefing Attorney General Wilentz, his staff, and officers with the New Jersey State Police in person. From 11:30 AM to 4:30 PM, with a short break for lunch, Wilentz and his staff peppered Koehler with questions, trying to make sure his story had no holes and that he'd be ready for an attacking defense.

Koehler wrote his brothers afterward that Schwarzkopf came to him following the "dress rehearsal" and said that if Koehler wanted "to write a book on science in crime detection, he will write the preface for me."

Wilentz left this meeting feeling far more secure about his wood expert than he had going into the grand jury. That's because no longer was he just dealing with the tracking of Rails 12 and 13.

Now he could use Rail 16, as he would say later to reporters, to "wrap the kidnap ladder right around Hauptmann's neck. I mean it. That's exactly what we're going to do."

At one point, Koehler worried about keeping what he was working on secret. Schwarzkopf had said reporters were hounding him to tell them who the "star witness" was going to be. "I'm not telling them, it's you," he told Koehler. "We are going to keep that secret."

So when Koehler heard directly from reporters about a note in Walter Winchell's column saying that the wood expert had "definitely" traced a piece of wood in the kidnap ladder to Hauptmann's home, Koehler panicked at the same time he was listening carefully to the reporters' questions.

Specifically, Winchell had reported one of the ladder rungs was identical to a piece of wood nailed to a ceiling in Hauptmann's home.

"There is absolutely no truth in the matter," Koehler told reporters looking for verification of the story. To the nonscientists, this might have seemed a stretch of the truth, but Koehler dealt with details. First, he had not traced one of the ladder *rungs* back to Hauptmann's home, but one of the ladder *rails*. Second, it had not been nailed to a ceiling, but rather to the attic floor.

Semantics, maybe, but to Koehler it wasn't lying when he said, "there is absolutely no truth" to the reporters seeking comment on those specific details. The premise of Winchell's story, though, was entirely accurate. Koehler had linked the ladder to Hauptmann's home.

For his part, Wilentz had dealt with reporters enough to simply say he had not received a report yet from Koehler and that he expected one the next day. He may not have had the report in hand yet, but he knew exactly what Koehler had found. Even though he had never prosecuted a case before, he knew enough to know he wasn't going to tip his hand or share whatever he had with the defense before he absolutely had to.

Koehler and Davis headed back to Madison for the Christmas holiday. They would return to New Jersey for the start of the trial on January 2, 1935. Naïve as to how crazed the NJSP would be on that day, Koehler suggested to Captain Lamb that "if a car is available, you might send one to the depot at that time."

On his way back to New Jersey, Koehler stopped off at Pittsburgh, where his brother Walter, studying at the University of West Virginia in Morgantown, came to pick him up to spend the New Year together. While there he gave an autograph, his first, to his nephew, Walter Jr., and gave his second to a neighbor boy.

During his nearly two weeks back at the lab over the Christmas holiday, Koehler had sketched out a thirty-page question-and-answer guide for Wilentz and his staff to follow. He had also put together suggested testimony for Senator Dorn that the prosecutors could review. The prosecution would appreciate the help, as January 2 brought a spectacle unlike any witnessed before in an American courtroom.

In theory Justice Trenchard's courtroom, used to handling the routine legal affairs of a rural county, held 260 people. On January 2, a panel of 150 jurors had been summoned. Lawyers, attendants, and witnesses represented dozens more. Then there were the 135 newspaper reporters—more, it was speculated, than the number that had covered World War I—each of whom wanted a place to sit and write. And that doesn't even mention the radio producers, the movie stars, and the star athletes.

Finally, there was the crowd of spectators who wanted to get in. What started the first day of the trial as just an aggressive group of hundreds that brushed aside the one state trooper guarding the front door of the courthouse, breaking one of the glass panels in the front door in the process, would become a crowd of roughly twenty thousand on the day Hauptmann testified.

People stood in the aisles. They sat on the window sills. They clogged the aisles.

"The Bronx subway was never like the court house here," the New York tabloid *Daily Mirror* wrote during the trial under the headline "Court Jam." "So many spectators were crowded into the chamber where Hauptmann is on trial that one woman, caught in the milling during the noon recess today, narrowly escaped falling through a side window which broke, fragments of glass showering a dozen other women below in the street."

One random woman pleaded with Koehler to help her get in. "Please take me in with you," she said. "They will let me in if I am with you."

Koehler said she could try but cautioned, "I can't make any plea for you." She walked in right after him without any questioning from the police.

Another part of the problem was subpoenas, which were supposed to be handed to witnesses but instead had been given to friends of the lawyers on both sides, creating a mockery of the legal requirement to appear in court. On one day during the trial, there were more than one hundred such "subpoenas" issued.

Writer Edna Ferber described the court room as a "shambles . . . planned to accommodate perhaps a hundred, it was jammed with what seemed at least a thousand, seated, standing, leaning, perched on window sills, craning over balcony rails, peering through doorways."

Ethelyn Koehler, too, was interested in attending the trial when her husband testified. So was Carlisle Winslow. Captain Lamb said he would get them in "but couldn't guarantee a seat."

On the courthouse lawn were the gawkers and the hawkers. They sold flag pins and pins commemorating Lindbergh's successful flight over the Atlantic. They sold pennies that had a picture of the courthouse on the back for a dime. One man sold pennies with the Lord's Prayer on the back. Other vendors sold so-called "Lindy hats," or the aviator/bomber hats with large ear flaps and a short brim in front turned up to show the fur lining.

Two eight-year-olds, Abram Case Parker and Charles Ryman Herr Jr., came out with their own newspaper, *The Hauptmannville News*, carrying their handwritten stories of the latest events in the trial. They charged two cents per copy.

But the most popular souvenir was a replica ladder.

One Flemington resident, six or seven years old at the time, made three hundred dollars—at the height of the Depression—selling the eight-inch ladders. As he would later tell the *Princeton Recollector*, "That was money to me. . . . I couldn't tell you how many I sold but I'd sell 'em for a dime and I had a bigger one for a quarter. We sold a lot; couldn't keep up. My father made 'em, my father and my brothers—my mother, too. . . . I'll be honest with you, they couldn't make the damn things fast enough."

One of the defense lawyers tried to get the replica ladders removed from the grounds, saying they were prejudiced against his client. He failed.

The American Bar Association committee that later studied the trial called the marketing of souvenir ladders "morbid" and "pathetic." It quoted one magazine writer's impression of the trial: "What hit hardest at Flemington? Those ghastly souvenir ladders. . . . Once America despised ruthless greed, held life and law sacred, now greed is smart—and life and law are cheap. . . . When a people who once bowed before a cross snicker at a kidnap ladder—look out."

The Saturday Evening Post summarized the whole trial atmosphere in contempt. "Among the lows we have reached in the depression is the new one in good taste, good manners and good policy accomplished at Flemington," the magazine wrote. "Our criminal trials are apt to be public circuses, the more sensational the trial the more outrageous the circus."

The circus was covered by media outlets worldwide. "The trial promises to be a long affair, although the swiftness of 'Jersey Justice' is proverbial," wrote *The London Times* on the day the trial began. "While Mr. Justice Trenchard is known not to tolerate unnecessary delays, the prosecution alone has 180 witnesses to call, and the defence has perhaps half as many more."

Wilentz's opening statement was full of fire, displaying an open hostility toward the accused. "He broke into and entered at night the Lindbergh home with the intent to commit a battery upon that child, and with the intent to steal the child and its clothing. And he did," he said in his forty-five-minute oratory. He described how the baby died when Hauptmann fell carrying him down the ladder. The motive for the crime, he told the jurors, was a timeless one: greed.

"He wanted money, money, money, lots of money," Wilentz railed. He alluded to the importance of Koehler's evidence even if he didn't quite understand it, referring to a rung when he meant a rail.

"One rung of that ladder, one side of that ladder comes right from his attic, put on there with his tools and we will prove it to you, no matter how difficult it may sound—we will prove it to you so that there will be no doubt about it."

He concluded by stating the obvious.

"We will be asking you to impose the death penalty; it is the only suitable punishment in this case."

Reilly immediately asked for a mistrial, alleging that the prosecutor had unjustly prejudiced the jury against his client. Justice Trenchard denied, but he did remind the jurors to listen to all the evidence before making up their minds.

The first prosecution witness following those who testified to the location of the Lindbergh estate (using a billiard cue to point at numerous maps pinned to the wall) was Anne Morrow Lindbergh. Never before had she spoken publicly about the murder of her first-born child. Any shifting in the chairs that took place during the earlier technical testimony quickly ceased. One reporter described the scene after her name was called by the attorney general as "an excited hum, and then sudden hushed silence." The world had been waiting nearly three years to hear the Lindberghs' testimony.

"I have seen one of the most magnificent exhibitions of human courage possible to imagine," commentator Boake Carter told his radio audience that night.

> I have seen a young mother, robbed of her first-born son, finger the tattered remnants of the clothes he wore the night of his murder, bite furiously on her lower lip to keep back the tears, and then proudly lift her head and tell without a quiver what a mother feels when she discovers that her child has been stolen from the crib in which, but a few hours before, she had bidden him good night.

And the emotional effort that it cost Mrs. Anne Lindbergh to recite for the first time for the world's benefit what happened that fateful night of March 1st was so plain that the tension of almost every man and woman in New Jersey's old Flemington courthouse was terrific for the entire duration of her softly spoken story. Had the story ended there and then when she stepped down from the witness stand, there would have been no need for the jury to leave the jury box to come to an opinion. . . .

Wistfulness marked every line of the almost severely dressed Anne, as she sat with hands folded in her lap. The nakedness of tragedy came when Attorney General Wilentz, in charge of the prosecution of Bruno Richard Hauptmann, handed Mrs. Lindbergh the tattered and torn remains of what had been her son's night clothes and asked her to look at them carefully and identify them. The deliberate summoning of all her courage to do what he asked and the little upward thrust of a small, pointed chin, as though the action automatically choked off whatever may have been her inner feelings from the gaze of a curious and hushed public, left many a veteran newspaperman, cynical from years of contact with human nature, utterly silent in genuine admiration. . . .

The scene cannot be described in words. Not if one had a hundred thousand in which to say it. It was an exhibition of superhuman courage—for it was done not in the heat of the moment, but in the cold light of day, before the gaze of hundreds of curious pairs of eyes. It was courage one seldom sees.

The "Bull of Brooklyn," rumored to spare no prosecution witness, demurred. "The defense feels that Mrs. Lindbergh has suffered enough anguish as it is and so it has no desire to cross-examine her," Reilly said.

The next witness was the world's most famous man himself. While his wife was emotional, Charles A. Lindbergh was matter-of-fact. Onlookers noticed a bulge in his coat pocket and surmised he was carrying a gun in a shoulder holster.

For two days, the famous aviator walked the prosecutor and then Reilly through the night of March 1, 1932, as well as what happened afterward. He spoke about finding his son missing and seeing a crib that "was in such condition that I felt it was impossible for the baby to have gotten out himself." He described the initial ransom note and the others that had followed.

The next morning delivered the fireworks the media and a blood-thirsty crowd outside the courthouse had waited for. Lindbergh described going with John Condon to drop off the ransom money at St. Raymond's Cemetery in the Bronx.

"I heard very clearly a voice coming from the cemetery, to the best of my belief calling Dr. Condon," Lindbergh said.

"What were the words?" Wilentz inquired.

"In a foreign accent, 'Hey, Doctor.'"

"How many times?"

"I heard that voice once."

After some questions about what happened next came Wilentz's hammer.

"Since that time have you heard the same voice?"

"Yes, I have."

"Whose voice was it, Colonel, that you heard in the vicinity of St. Raymond's Cemetery that night, saying, 'Hey, Doctor?'"

"That was Hauptmann's voice," Lindbergh said with conviction.

An audible gasp went up in the courtroom. Some reporters later speculated the trial ostensibly ended at that moment. If Lindy was convinced it was Hauptmann, they figured the jury would be convinced as well.

Reilly tried to cast aspersions on other possible suspects, ranging from Lindbergh's neighbors to his servants, but Lindbergh never wavered. The resolve he had shown to fly across the Atlantic was fully on display in the Flemington courtroom. Lindbergh believed Hauptmann was guilty.

Koehler wanted to hear Lindbergh's testimony himself, but he did not attend the first few days of the trial for a couple of reasons, the first being, as he said in a letter to Ethelyn, "the courtroom is so crowded that there is not room for all the witnesses." The second reason was that he wanted to give Edward Davis a chance to be in the courtroom and "take a good look around himself," in case he would be called to back up Koehler.

On the fourth day of testimony, after the prosecution had established the baby was kidnapped and murdered, it was time to enter the ladder into evidence. It had been in numerous hands since March 1, 1932, and Wilentz knew he needed to provide a timeline and concrete evidence detailing where and in whose hands the ladder had been in order for it to be admitted into evidence.

Koehler, Davis, and Bornmann went in the back door of the courthouse carrying the ladder and were chased by photographers trying to get whatever image they could. The courtroom was so crowded they all had to stand through the entire proceedings. Koehler borrowed the seat of one young lady as she stretched during a recess simply to rest his own legs.

Wilentz started with Detective Bornmann, who had responded to the call to the Lindberghs' home the night of the crime and had found the ladder about seventy feet away from the house. He had brought it inside the home before turning it over to Trooper Frank A. Kelly, the New Jersey State Police's fingerprint expert. Kelly was in possession of the ladder before it went to Captain Lamb, who released it back to Kelly in the summer of 1932 to take to Washington for an initial inspection. Then it went back to Lamb before pieces were sent to Madison for a detailed study by Arthur Koehler.

Each of those individuals were called to testify, albeit briefly, as Wilentz sought to have the ladder put into evidence. Many would be re-called for further testimony later in the trial, but for his present purposes, Wilentz needed to establish a chain of custody for his evidence. As the last one to have handled the ladder, Koehler went last.

"You live where, Mr. Koehler?" Wilentz began.

"In Madison, Wisconsin."

"And you are connected with the United States Government in what capacity?"

"I am wood technologist in the forest service which is part of the U.S. Department of Agriculture."

"Now on various occasions since this Lindbergh case, have you had, have you received from Captain Lamb this ladder?"

"I have."

"And by the way, will you tell us what is this cut that has been pointed out on No. 2 on section marked No. 1 with this little thumb-tack? I notice a cut there. Did you make that cut?"

"I did."

"This piece of what appears to be a new piece of wood as compared with the other, did you have that affixed?"

"Yes."

"And when you got through with it, did you return it to Captain Lamb?"

"I did."

Koehler's cross-examination was a bit more detailed, as the defense sought to preclude the ladder from being admitted into evidence.

"Where that light portion of wood is fastened to the side of the section of the ladder, you say you put that on there?" asked Frederick Pope, one of Big Ed Reilly's assistant counsels.

"I helped in putting it on."

"Why did you put it on there?"

"That rail was cut in two, and it was put on to bring them back into their original position."

"Who cut it in two?"

"I don't know."

"Was it cut in two when it was brought to you?"

"Not the first time, but subsequently it was."

"Was it cut in two while it was in your possession?"

"No."

"Or in your department?"

"No," replied Koehler.

For another five minutes, Pope continued to prod at Koehler, extracting details of how he had dismantled other parts of the ladder.

"While the ladder was in your possession, did you remove any of the nails?"

"Yes."

"And did you remove any of the cleats?"

"Yes."

"Did you take the ladders apart?"

"Yes."

After Pope had completed his cross-examination, Wilentz moved to have the ladder admitted as evidence. Pope objected immediately.

"The ladder," he said, "is not in the same condition that it was or in approximately the same condition, and it is not shown to be in the same condition it was when it was discovered, as is testified here, on the Lindbergh estate." He continued,

> It has been taken apart, put together again. . . .
>
> There is still another reason and a very great reason, a very strong reason—there is absolutely no connection, either by circumstance or by direct evidence between this ladder and the accused, and until this ladder has been placed in the possession of the accused, or until there is some evidence in this case which would tend to show or which would be sufficient to go to the jury, to have them consider whether or not the ladder was ever in the possession of the accused, this ladder is not evidential against this accused.
>
> It may be admitted for identification until that proof is complete, but until there is something in this case to show that Mr. Hauptmann, the defendant, was in some way either directly, immediately or remotely connected with this ladder, it is not evidential and should not be admitted in evidence.

He became even more passionate as he rebutted Wilentz's argument that the government had established the chain of custody for the ladder.

"We are here defending a man for his life and his every right must be and will be protected by this Court," Pope said. "And we insist that this ladder shall not be admitted in evidence in this case as evidence against him until he is shown to have been connected with it in some way."

Koehler smiled to himself as he sat on the witness chair listening to the lawyer. If Pope wanted a connection between the ladder and Hauptmann, he'd be glad to give him more than one.

It just wouldn't happen for another two and a half weeks.

10

160 steps.

Liscom C. Case and the other Hauptmann trial jurors knew that number by heart.

Five times per day, they climbed and descended sets of stairs, at breakfast, lunch, and dinner plus two times during breaks in the court action. From their rooms at the Union Hotel to where they ate their meals were forty steps. They trudged up forty-six more steps to wash up before the trial started for the day. They headed back down those forty-six steps to get out of the hotel and then, guarded by state troopers, walked through the gauntlet of thousands of onlookers across the street to the Hunterdon County Courthouse, where they hiked the final twenty-eight steps into Justice Trenchard's courtroom.

Their compensation, besides stronger leg muscles, was three dollars a day.

For the eleven other jurors this was merely a workout, more strenuous for some than others. However, for the sixty-four-year-old Case, it led to chest pains and shortness of breath. Heart trouble had led to an early retirement a decade earlier from the Leigh Valley Railroad, where he had served as the foreman of carpenters. And heart trouble would lead to him being treated by a physician throughout the latter half of the trial.

Press reports speculated on the possibility of a mistrial if Case couldn't continue, as there were no alternate jurors. On multiple occasions, Justice Trenchard specifically and pointedly asked him if he was okay. Case would eventually take his meals in his room to cut down on the some of the stair climbing and exertion.

Case lived in the hills of Hunterdon County, in Franklin Township where he grew up. He and his wife, Ellen, ten years his senior, had shared three years at home together before she passed away in the spring of 1928, not long after their thirtieth wedding anniversary. They had no children.

He lived near his former employer's spur line that connected the town of Clinton with Landsdown and the south branch of the Raritan River. His home was a simple two-story, painted white with dark trim around the windows, but since Ellen died, he spent most of his time "out behind his house in a white-washed little woodshed," where he kept his carpentry shop.

Like 149 of his fellow Hunterdon County citizens, Case had been summoned in November 1934 to appear at the courthouse the day after New Year's Day for jury duty. The jury pool had been chosen by Jury Commissioner Charles Holcombe and Sheriff John Curtiss.

Case watched as the prosecution and defense went to work on January 2. Their questions followed a pattern. Prosecutors wanted to know mainly if prospective jurors had religious convictions that would preclude them from issuing a death sentence and if they would "be able to render a verdict based solely on the evidence" they would hear at trial. Defense counsel focused on what, if anything, potential jurors had read in the papers or heard on the radio about the case and, specifically, about the defendant. Further, Lloyd Fisher, who handled the defense's jury selection, wanted to know if they understood the rule of law that the accused is presumed innocent.

Charles Walton Sr., a machinist and former semi-pro baseball player, was the first Hunterdon County citizen agreed upon by both the prosecution and defense to serve, and thus became the foreman of the jury.

Juror number 2 was Rosie Pill, a widowed housekeeper who lived with her son, his wife, and their three kids. When she wasn't caring for her grandchildren, she was doing beadwork.

Juror number 3 was Verna Cole Snyder, a housewife married to a blacksmith. She was devoted to their seven-year-old adopted son and to her Methodist faith.

Juror number 4, Charles F. Snyder (no relation to Verna Snyder), was a farmer and had served on three previous juries deliberating murder cases.

Juror number 5 was Ethel Morgan Stockton. She was married to a machinist at the Milford Paper Mill and had a seven-year-old son. Her husband and brother-in-law were in the jury pool as well, but both were dismissed.

Juror number 6 was Elmer Smith, who had only recently returned with his wife and son to New Jersey after spending a year in California. He was a former justice of the peace and an insurance salesman.

Juror number 7, Robert Cravatt, was a schoolteacher who also worked with a local Civilian Conservation Corps camp and as the treasurer of his hometown basketball team. At twenty-eight, he would be the youngest member of the jury.

Juror number 8 was Philip Hockenbury, who worked as a track inspector for the Central Rail Road of New Jersey. He had been fixing switches on the rails since 1920.

Juror number 9 was George Voorhees, who, like Charles Snyder, was a farmer in Hunterdon County. He was married with two grown children.

Juror number 10, May F. Brelsford, was the only native of Flemington on the panel. Her husband was an electrician, and she helped care for her two stepchildren.

After Brelsford was selected, the lawyers and Justice Trenchard adjourned for the night. In all, fifty-seven prospective jurors had been screened. Prosecutors used seven of their twelve peremptory challenges and the defense used fifteen of its twenty. More than two dozen others were disqualified for reasons ranging from illness to prejudging the case.

There were still two members of the jury to be selected, so Case would have to wear his Sunday best, a light brown suit, again on Thursday, January 3. He showed up first thing that morning and once again sat in the courtroom near dozens of others who'd also been summoned. Earlier concerns from the jury commissioner that he would need to find more potential jurors had faded, as both sides were running out of challenges.

Just before Daisy Emmons's name was called, there was a stir in the courtroom as Anne Morrow Lindbergh entered. She was set to be the first prosecution witness, leading those in attendance to anticipate that the jury selection would wrap up soon. But then the defense rejected Emmons.

"Liscom C. Case," Sheriff Curtiss called out. The mild-mannered carpenter walked up to the chair next to the judge and was "sworn in on voir dire"—an old French legal phrase meaning to speak truthfully. After ascertaining where specifically in Franklin Township, Case lived, Fisher began to question him.

"Have you formed any opinion as to the guilt or innocence of the accused in this case?"

"I can't say that I have," said Case.

"None at all?"

"None at all."

"Have you discussed the case with anyone?"

"Well, I have spoke of it, not to discuss it."

"In your discussions did you express an opinion as to the guilt or innocence of the accused?"

"No," Case replied. "To the best of my knowledge I never have."

He told Fisher he'd read about the case in the paper and heard about it on the radio over the last couple of nights, but still had no opinion on Hauptmann.

"If you are permitted to sit on this jury, would you be guided by the evidence that you hear from the witness chair in the course of the case in arriving at your verdict?"

"The only thing I could do."

"You would not be influenced by anything that has gone before?"

"No, I wouldn't say that I would."

"But solely by the evidence that you hear here?"

"That is the way I understand; that is the evidence I should go by."

"And that is the evidence you would go by, sir, is that right?"

"That is the evidence I would go by," Case said, wondering why he'd been asked roughly the same question several times in a row.

Fisher said he had no challenge for Case. After learning the prospective juror had no "conscientious or religious scruples against capital punishment" and that he would follow the evidence, the prosecution had no challenge for him either.

"We are content, your Honor, with this juror," Fisher said.

"The State is content," the prosecutor said.

And with that, Case became juror number 11.

Shortly after that, Howard V. Biggs, an unemployed accountant who used to be the county assessor, became juror number 12. Married with two sons, he had never spent any significant time away from his wife in the nearly twenty-seven years they had been together.

"Not one of us was great," jury foreman Walton would tell reporters after the trial, "but no dunces were in the box. None of us had had such a stuffing of education that we had lost our common sense."

Common sense could have predicted how the jurors' lives would be turned upside down in that kind of media environment. Reporters scoured their personal lives, telling their stories in sometimes cruel fashion.

They regularly mocked Verna Snyder for her weight, writing the words "261 pounds," in every sentence about her. One reporter put her weight at 278 pounds in a story midway through the trial. Rosie Pill was ridiculed for seemingly falling asleep during testimony. Robert Cravatt was tweaked in the media for insisting on having his eggs basted at breakfast every morning.

"After dinner, in the early days of the trial, we were taken for walks," Cravatt would later recount. "These expeditions had a sort of circus parade air, with us as the circus. Everyone turned out.

"We were looked at, gawked at, gazed at, smiled at, laughed at, photographed and shouted at, so that when we got back to the hotel we were glad. State troopers were before us and behind us and all around us."

Liscom Case, known to his fellow jurors as "Silent Cal," was not spared the sharp critique of the media. Reporters seemed fixated on his "munching his mustache" and on the fact that he was a "little man" who had to cup his hand to his ear to hear every word at the trial as he sat in the second row of the jury box.

The press called him the Mystery Juror, as he was always covering his face with a handkerchief or dropping his eyes to the floor when they sought to take his picture. The Middletown, New York, *Times Herald* ran a photo of him, handkerchief blanketing all but his forehead with a caption that read, "[Here] he is shown fooling the photographer again." Another newspaper ran the same picture with the caption "Peek-a-boo in the jury box."

Three weeks into the trial, Liscom Case was exhausted. Besides the stress of the trial, the steps were taking its toll on his heart. He was going more and more slowly, bogging down his fellow jurors, who had to wait for him, as they were required to travel as one everywhere they went.

He was tired of being confined. He was tired of reading censored newspapers and no magazines at all and being offered Shakespeare and Dickens by the officers in charge of their seclusion. Mainly he was tired of not being able to work in his carpentry shop. He missed his tools.

But now, finally, there was a line of questioning that piqued his curiosity. In the first three weeks of the trial, Case had listened intently to the testimony of John Condon, the retired educator who became an intermediary between the kidnapper and the Lindberghs. He had followed the money trail with the respective federal, New Jersey, and NYPD authorities who had found more than $14,000 of the ransom money in Hauptmann's garage. He had heard the witnesses who tied Hauptmann to New Jersey for the crime and to New York for the collection of the ransom. And he had sat quietly, hand covering his brow, during the numerous handwriting experts who linked the writing on the ransom notes with Hauptmann.

But all the while, as a carpenter himself, he was intrigued by the ladder. He saw it in the courtroom every day. Dozens of witnesses had come and gone since prosecutors had first tried to introduce it as evidence only to have Trenchard reserve judgment.

Wilentz would try again on January 22 to have the ladder admitted into evidence by re-calling Detective Lewis Bornmann to the stand. The defense objected immediately.

"We submit," defense counsel Pope said, "that the history of this ladder has not been told. . . . No one has ever suggested that this defendant had anything to do with this ladder."

Wilentz knew that Koehler could and would do just that. He also knew Koehler's testimony would not be allowed if the ladder was not officially accepted as evidence. He rose to address the court again, to stress once more that the chain of custody of the ladder had been accounted for and that, with few exceptions, "it is as it was found when brought up Lindy's lane the night of the kidnaping." Before he could speak, Justice Trenchard intervened.

"I wonder whether Mr. Pope recalls the testimony of an old gentleman that on March 1st I think it was that he saw a ladder in the defendant's car," Trenchard said, referring to eighty-seven-year-old Amandus Hochmuth, who earlier had told jurors that he had seen Hauptmann in the vicinity of the Lindbergh estate on the day of the crime.

Trenchard heard brief arguments from both sides before issuing his ruling.

"I feel constrained to admit this ladder in evidence," he said. "It will be admitted."

"It was a distinct victory for the state," the Associated Press reported, "for the defense during the past three weeks had been able to block the exhibit each time the ladder was offered." The ladder was given the number Exhibit S-211. The chisel found on the grounds of the estate soon followed into evidence.

With the ladder officially in evidence, Wilentz and his team would do exactly what the defense feared: tie the ladder directly to Hauptmann. This was the testimony Liscom C. Case, an avid carpenter, had been waiting to hear.

The prosecutors began to set the stage for the tracing of the wood evidence. They called Max Rauch, Hauptmann's landlord, who swore the attic had no boards missing when he rented the upper apartment to the Hauptmanns. Senator J. J. Dorn flew in from South Carolina to detail his "one by fours" and the visit Koehler had made to his lumber yard. At one point he was speaking so softly, he was asked to pretend that he was at the State Capitol, after which his booming voice could be heard by everyone in attendance. Then they called a representative from the Long Island wholesaler who had bought the lumber in question from Dorn. And the prosecution brought in the co-owner and an employee of the National Lumber and Millwork Company in the Bronx, who swore that they had received the lumber in question and further that Hauptmann had worked there off and on in the early 1930s and had purchased wood from the yard a couple of months before the kidnapping.

Next the prosecution sought to recreate the scene in Hauptmann's attic by re-calling Bornmann and then each of the NYPD carpenters who had joined the detective and Koehler when they were tracing Rail 16. The prosecutors brought the piece of wood Bornmann had ripped up from the attic to compare to the ladder rail. It was introduced into evidence and labeled S-226.

The carpenters were the final witnesses of the day, setting the stage for the prosecution's eighty-seventh witness in the trial.

Former judge George K. Large, who was aiding the prosecution during the trial, told *The New York Times* what to expect from Koehler's testimony. "The long strip that was brought into the courtroom," Large declared, "is a part of the board that Hauptmann used to make the right upright of the largest section of the ladder. It has been set right down on the floor in the attic of Hauptmann's home and even the nail holes fit perfectly."

Whether Large was intentionally being deceptive is unclear, but Rail 16 was the upper left-hand rail in the kidnap ladder, not the upper right-hand rail. His rhetoric didn't stop there, as he told the reporter that "Mr. Koehler started from scratch and sent out 40,000 circulars to lumber mills over the country" to help trace the wood in the ladder. That was about 38,500 more than he really sent out, but it sent the message to the newspaper audience that Koehler was credible.

Large concluded, "In some respects Mr. Koehler's testimony will be the most interesting in the trial because of his achievements. He had placed that wood right in the lumber yard in the Bronx before anybody had ever heard of Hauptmann. When Hauptmann was arrested, we could trace him from that yard."

Koehler had spent his time between appearances on the stand as an interested bystander at the trial. He told Ethelyn that one day he "was the most photographed man in Flemington" when he ended up in the backseat of the same car as the Lindbergh's nanny,

Betty Gow. As for the famous aviator, Koehler was star struck and had "made up my mind I wouldn't speak to him first."

Lindbergh would break the ice, coming up to Koehler, shaking his hand, and beginning a conversation about their shared admiration for Madison. Lindbergh called it "one of the nicest cities in the country." Koehler wrote Ethelyn that "as would be expected, Lindbergh is just like any other fellow when you talk to him."

Ethelyn would join her husband in New Jersey the weekend before he was set to testify, and as she wrote the children, she was "excited." She told them she was feeling confident she'd get into the courtroom because "[t]he head jailer at Flemington asked Papa for his autograph which Papa gave and he told the jailer that in return, he should get me in to the trial which he agreed to do."

She was so nervous for her husband she became absentminded, leaving her galoshes in Grand Central Station. When she went back to New York City to try to find them, the porter asked her, "Is your husband that wood expert? I read about him." She wrote her children that "he was ready to stand on his head to be of service to me, but he could not find my galoshes."

A second concern for Ethelyn was the lovely turkey dinner she ate on Sunday night that "did not digest and about 7:30, I started vomiting. I kept it up every hour all night," she wrote to her kids.

She wasn't going to miss the trial, though. On Monday, she boarded a bus for witnesses and members of the media to head to the courthouse. Initially, the reporters objected to wives riding along, but there was enough room for everyone. However, sitting there waiting for the bus to go, Ethelyn "got sicker and sicker. I did not know whether I was going to faint or vomit, but either one would have made a spectacle so I clambered out again. Papa and a state trooper helped me over to the hotel. Of course we had to face every camera in the place."

Koehler tried to cover his wife with a newspaper, to prevent her from the embarrassment of being sick in front of others, but she figured they got thirty or forty pictures. She was mortified in addition to being sick. He got her a doctor, and after sleeping all afternoon, she felt much better.

The next day was the day before Koehler was set to testify. He and Ethelyn posed for pictures at the request of the Associated Press on the courthouse steps, and reporters swarmed him at the end of court that day, leading to some stress. His anxiety had been building since Wilentz told him he "was going to use him for his 'big shot.'"

He had trouble sleeping that night. He told Ethelyn about the "home runs" he planned to deliver. She smiled and suggested they both try to get some rest.

Tens of thousands of people descended on Flemington on January 23, 1935, in anticipation of the prosecution wrapping up and Hauptmann taking the stand in his own defense. At one point over the past week, the Associated Press had reported that sixteen thousand cars and sixty-four thousand visitors had converged on or passed through Flemington. Those arriving on the sixteenth day of the trial would have to deal with a driving snowstorm that made traffic conditions especially difficult.

"Manitowoc Man Helps in Bruno Prosecution," read the headline in Arthur Koehler's hometown newspaper that day. The story gave him another middle initial he didn't have, "Arthur J. Koehler," and spoke of him as "the No. 1 wood technologist in the government service."

When Koehler approached the stand at midmorning, dressed in a three-piece gray suit with a dark tie and a white handkerchief in the breast pocket, he expected this stint to certainly be longer than his first time in the witness chair.

Ethelyn sat in the front row, a reassuring presence. Next to her was one of the US senators from New Jersey. She sat two chairs away from Lindbergh and directly in front of the reporters.

As Koehler placed his left hand on the Bible and swore to tell the whole truth and nothing but the truth, Liscom C. Case perked up. He had been sitting just under the American flag, head against the wall and his legs stretched out comfortably. When Koehler took the stand, reporters noticed that he "sat on the edge of his chair" and seemed prepared to become "an absorbed listener."

"Mr. Koehler, will you please tell us where you live and what your business is?" Wilentz began.

"I live at Madison, Wisconsin and I am employed there at the United States Forest Products Laboratory."

"Do you mean that you are employed by the United States Government?"

"I am."

"And what does the Forest Products Laboratory work consist of?"

"The work of the Forest Products Laboratory consists of making tests and investigations on wood."

"Tell me whether or not you are the wood expert of the United States Government?"

"I am the expert on the identification of wood for the Government," Koehler gently corrected his questioner.

"Are you in charge of the Department?"

"I am."

"Now, in that connection, for how many years have you done this work?"

"21 years."

"How many pieces of wood do you examine a year for the Government?"

"Each year there are submitted from 2,000 to 3,000 samples of wood for identification which I handle."

Despite all of his preparation leading up to this point, Koehler was surprised that Wilentz was examining him. He had been prepped all along by Wilentz's assistant, Robert Peacock, and had assumed he'd be the one asking questions. But the attorney general was not about to delegate his star witness.

Koehler proceeded to explain the cases he had testified in before, including the Magnuson murder trial, giving details regarding the bomb he had helped trace by the wood in its casing.

"In addition to your experience in the manner you have just indicated," Wilentz continued, "have you had experience as a carpenter?"

"Why, I have worked on a number of carpenter jobs. My father was a carpenter by trade, had a large assortment of tools, and I have worked on the construction and repair of buildings and on cabinet work."

From there, Wilentz steered him toward Rail 16.

"Did you take off this rail 16, a part of Exhibit S-211, for the purpose of investigation in the attic of the Hauptmann home?

"I did."

"When did you do that?"

"I made that investigation on October 9, 1934, the first time."

"Having taken off this section rail 16, what did you find?"

"I found that the nail holes in it corresponded exactly with four nail holes in the joists in that attic and the grain of the wood in that rail corresponded exactly with the grain of wood of the board next to it."

Wilentz was ready for the big question, the one that would, as he had promised, "wrap the kidnap ladder" around the neck of Bruno Richard Hauptmann.

Wilentz began, "Tell me whether or not there is any relationship, in your opinion, between rail 16 and exhibit S—what is the number?"

"I object to the question," Pope said before the conversation went any further. "I object to the expression 'in your opinion' by the witness."

Trenchard asked Koehler not to answer until the judge had heard Pope's full objection. The defense lawyer, who like several others involved with this case loved woodworking, had been selected to tangle with the evidence surrounding the ladder and the witness set to deliver it.

"The witness cannot say whether there is any relationship except by expressing his opinion, and we say that this witness is not qualified to express an opinion regarding wood," Pope declared.

Trenchard looked surprised and said, "Do you say that he is not qualified as an expert on wood?"

"We say that there is no such animal known among men as an expert on wood," Pope responded. "That it is not a science that has been recognized by the courts; that it is not in a class with handwriting experts, with fingerprint experts or with ballistic experts. That has been reduced to a science and is known and recognized by the courts.

"The witness probably may testify as an experienced carpenter or something like that," Pope continued, "but when he attempts to qualify and express opinions as a wood expert, that is quite different."

"Well, of course, the term 'wood expert' is a broad term," Trenchard responded. "It might very well be limited so far as this case is concerned. What I am trying to find out is the basis of your objection. Do you object to his qualifying as an examiner of wood and to finding out the history of that wood? Do you object to that?"

"Yes, certainly we do, and that he is not qualified to express an opinion," Pope replied. He continued,

> For instance a physician examines a patient and he finds certain symptoms, he expresses an opinion. He is qualified because he represents a science. A fingerprint expert examines finger prints, he makes measurements and comparisons. He expresses an opinion because that has been reduced to a science and has been recognized by the courts, but this is no science. This is just merely a man who has had a lot of experience in examining trees, who knows the barks on trees and a few things like that.
>
> He may come into court and he may tell what he did and what he saw, but when it comes to expressing an opinion as an expert or as a scientist, why that is quite different indeed. We say that the opinion of the jurors is just as good as his opinion, that they are just as qualified to judge whether there is any relationship between those two pieces of board as this man of experience as he terms himself.

In response, Justice Trenchard said that he was inclined to view Koehler as an expert but would give Pope time to cross-examine him to determine the extent of his credentials.

Wilentz chose that moment to weigh in.

"If your Honor please, may I suggest now, of course I have no objection to cross examination as to qualifications at this time."

Before Pope could begin his questioning, Trenchard adjourned the court for lunch at 12:27, to reconvene at 1:45 p.m. At that point the scientist who rarely expressed a temper likely uttered a few "Ding bust its," the closest he would come to profanity. He smiled a quick smile at Ethelyn before leaving the courtroom with the prosecutors to discuss their next strategy.

"He and Wilentz conferred on how they could put the defense down the hardest," Ethelyn would write home.

For once, Case couldn't wait to take those 160 steps. He didn't hold the group up this time on the walk back to the courthouse from lunch. His enthusiasm for the afternoon session was palpable.

When court reconvened, the strategy Wilentz, Koehler, and the others on the prosecution team had devised over the lunch hour was fully on display. Its brilliance lay in its simplicity.

"Mr. Pope, I will make an effort to qualify Mr. Koehler, if there is any question about it," Wilentz began. "Mr. Koehler, are you a graduate of any university?"

"Yes."

"Will you tell us what university, when you graduated, and the course you pursued there?"

"I graduated from the University of Michigan in 1911 where I pursued the course in forestry," Koehler calmly replied. "Later on I took some post-graduate work at the University of Wisconsin in forest products and received the degree of Master of Science at the University of Wisconsin in 1928."

"Have you devoted your entire adult life to this work?"

"I have."

"Are you the author of any papers on the subject and books?"

"Yes, I have written a number of government bulletins and a book."

"Have you some of these bulletins and books here?"

"I have."

"Will you please get them for us?"

"Yes. I have here a number of bulletins, reprints, a book and a list of publications other than these."

"You are giving to me then a book published by the McGraw, Hill Book Company entitled, 'The Properties and Uses of Wood' and this Koehler referred to here is yourself, is that so?"

"Yes."

Case and the jury were fascinated. The defense table was beginning to see the path this would take, yet Pope had inadvertently laid its foundation. After Wilentz offered the book into evidence, the rest of their plan played out.

"Can you read for us the list of publications of which you are the author so as to avoid the necessity of presenting all the papers

Koehler would serve as the final prosecution witness in what H. L. Mencken called "the greatest story since the Resurrection." His testimony would earn him comparisons to Sherlock Holmes. He was so convincing, Hauptmann's lead lawyer said, "I have never heard more damaging testimony or seen a more enthralling demonstration than that presented in the courtroom today by Arthur Koehler." (Courtesy: Dr. Regis Miller/Forest Products Laboratory)

for the defense?" Wilentz said without the hint of a smile.

"There are a large number here, 52 altogether," said Koehler simply.

"All right," Wilentz could barely contain himself now, knowing he was about to score a major victory. "Tell us all of them."

"'An Improved Method of Infiltrating Wood with Celloidin,' 'Our National Forests,' 'How Taste of Wood Affects its Use,' 'How the Odor of Wood Affects its Use,' 'What Makes Wood Float,' 'The Burning of Wood,' 'How a Tree Grows,' 'Forest Trees as Sources of Food,' 'What Wood is Made of.'"

Mouths were starting to open. Reporters noted that Case "perked his ears." Pope could do nothing.

"'A Visual Method of Distinguishing Long Leaf Pine,' 'Identification of Oak Woods,' 'Woods Older than the Hills,' 'Native Woods as a Passable Substitute for Boxwood,' 'Guide Book for the Identification of Woods used for Ties and Timbers,' 'A Plea for a Closer Discrimination in the use of the words Grain and Texture with Respect to Wood,' 'How to Distinguish Douglas Fir from Sitka Spruce.'"

Koehler's voice continued consistently, matter-of-factly.

"'Information for Inspectors of Air Plane Wood,' 'The Grain of Wood, With Special Reference to Direction of its Fibres,' Also part of the 'Inspection Manual of Aircraft Production,' 'American Substitutes for Boxwood,' 'Relation of Moisture Content and Drying Rate of Wood to the Humidity of the Atmosphere,' 'Factors Affecting the Strength of Wood Members,' 'Selecting Wood for Airplanes.'"

In the front row, Damon Runyon couldn't keep up with his pen and legal pad. The reporter who loved finding the extraordinary in his stories would write a column for certain about this "bald-headed, mild looking middle-aged man from the woods of Wisconsin."

"'How to Tell Birch, Beech and Maple Apart,' 'Shrinking and Swelling of Wood,' 'Identification of Mahogany,' 'Defects Found in Lumber,' 'Handbook of Box and Crate Construction,' of which I wrote the part on Identification. 'Lumber used in Motor Vehicle Manufacture,' 'Distinguishing Characteristics of Mahogany,' 'The Identification of Tree Mahogany and Certain So-Called

Mahoganies,' 'Identification of Pulp Woods,' 'Identification of Douglas Fir Wood,' 'What Makes Lumber Sell.'"

"Let me interrupt for a moment," Justice Trenchard interjected after Koehler had read thirty-four of the fifty-two titles. "Mr. Pope, do you still want to question this witness as to his expert qualities?"

Koehler could not have planned it any better.

But Pope, Reilly, and Fisher had not expected this. "Just a second, sir," Pope said. "Will you allow us to confer?"

"May we preserve our rights to this extent," Reilly said, "and have the Court pass upon the witness's qualifications, as to whether the Court thinks he is qualified or not."

"Yes," Trenchard said. "I would say to counsel now that I deem this witness to be qualified as an expert."

Reilly asked for an exception, to preserve the legal point for a possible appeal, and Trenchard granted it.

Wilentz continued on, cementing Koehler's reputation by allowing him to describe his duties at the Forest Products Lab.

"Am I to understand then that if there is some dispute with reference to wood that is sent to the United States Government, whether it is sent to Washington or some other point, it comes to you for disposition?"

"Yes."

"All right, sir, is that the situation with reference to 2,000 or 3,000 samples you testified to this morning?"

"Yes."

"What ordinarily causes the submission to you of these pieces of wood?"

"Why, we receive samples from the public for a great variety of reasons. There may be a dispute between buyer and seller as to the identity of a car load of lumber."

"When you say 'the identity' I take it you mean whether or not it is one type of wood or another?"

"Yes."

"Or one quality of wood or another?"

"Yes."

"What else?" queried Wilentz, who had been equally in the

dark about this science and this laboratory until Colonel Schwarz-kopf clued him in when Hauptmann was arrested.

"A manufacturer gets hold of a piece of wood which he likes particularly, but he doesn't know what kind it is, and he sends it in to the laboratory at Madison to have it identified," Koehler explained. "Once in a while a piece of wood goes wrong in services, gives trouble, and they want to know what kind of wood it is. That is one of the first requirements. In the case of old surveys it has been customary to mark witness trees and those witness trees have died and even decayed partly, but maybe part of the stump or root is left and they want to know whether that is the same tree as was originally marked as a witness tree."

They talked about identifying stumps and testifying in lawsuits for the purposes of identifying wood or passing judgment as to its quality before Wilentz came back to what had caused Pope's embarrassing objection earlier.

"All right, sir. Now, let me ask you again sir. I show you State's Exhibit S-226 and I show you rail 16 of State's Exhibit S-211, and I ask you what, if any, is the relationship between that rail and the exhibit just referred to?"

"As a result of a careful study of the two," Koehler said, "I have come to the conclusion that those two pieces at one time were one piece. They have been cut in two."

To hammer home the point, Wilentz and Koehler believed a demonstration in front of the jury would be effective.

"Now, will you please come down here and show the jury just about where it is your opinion they were cut. Take all the time you want to, Mr. Koehler, that is necessary."

Koehler asked Wilentz to hold a part of the board for him.

"Is this the right end?" Wilentz asked.

"Yes. These two pieces of wood at one time were one piece. A little gap has been cut out. That was about their relative position in the original piece," he said as he gestured with a pointer to the boards.

"Why do you say that they are the same piece, they were originally the same piece, and have been separated?"

"Well there are a number of points of similarity between the two that make me believe that they were one, were one piece."

Koehler resumed his seat in the witness chair.

"Can you better show them with some photographs taken by yourself?" Wilentz asked.

Koehler produced the easel he and Davis had brought from Madison and one of the enlarged photographs he had overseen. The first image showed the nail holes in Rail 16. It was a blown-up image of the same rail that Koehler now held in his hand.

He described how he had taken the nails from the board Bornmann ripped out of the attic and placed them into the holes in Rail 16.

"Those nails fit perfectly," he said.

"Let me understand. You mean you took nails out of a part of the floor?"

"Yes."

"Which is here in evidence, S-226?"

"Yes."

"Those very nails?"

"Yes."

"And you put them into those holes in this rail here, known as 16?"

"Yes."

"Tell us about that then."

"Well, they fit in there perfectly. Then with those nails in those holes and projecting from the lower side, I took that rail and laid it over the joists in this portion of the picture shown in this Exhibit S-215 [a photograph of the attic]."

"When you say laid them on the joists, you mean just as they were there as a part of the floor?"

"Yes."

"Go ahead."

"There were nail holes in these joists along the south side of the floor and the west half of the floor and I found that these protruding nails stuck into this rail fit exactly in the four nail holes which were in those joists. Now that indicated to me without any doubt—"

Pope interrupted futilely.

"I object to what is indicated to the gentleman. He may testify as to what he found, what he saw, and the jury will determine what it indicated."

"He may testify as to his opinion," Trenchard said. "He may be asked as to his opinion."

"All right," Wilentz chimed in, taking his cue. "Tell us what your opinion is?

"In my opinion," Koehler offered, after the defense was granted another exception, "that rail had at one time been nailed down there on those joists because it would be inconceivable to think—"

Pope tried again.

"That is argumentative," he pleaded. "We object to it."

"Well, what is your reason for the opinion?" Wilentz interjected. "Give us your reason for the opinion?"

"He has a right to," Trenchard ruled definitively. Pope sat down again.

"All right, let's have it," Wilentz encouraged.

"There are four nail holes a certain distance apart and a certain direction from each other and in my opinion, it wouldn't be possible that there would have been another board somewhere with cut nail holes in them, spaced exactly like these nail holes are in the joists, the same distance apart, the same direction from each other," Koehler said.

As if the point weren't made, Wilentz pressed on, asking for more detail. Koehler was happy to oblige.

"Now, let me ask you, Mr. Koehler, the distance between the nail holes on rail 16, between hole No. 1, as you have indicated it, and hole No. 2, is it the same distance between 1 and 2, and 2 and 3, and 3 and 4, or are they different distances?"

"They are different."

"Are they in different directions?"

"Yes."

"That is, as my finger goes from No. 1 to 2, across there?" Wilentz gestured to the board in Koehler's hand.

"Yes."

"And then down here to No. 3, and across to No. 4, as you call it?"

"Yes."

"And is that the same way that the holes were in the joist that you have talked about?"

"Exactly," Koehler said emphatically.

"Did it require any manipulation at all, or did they fit perfectly?"

"They fit perfectly."

He continued to describe how when laid down next to one another the boards were perfectly parallel, proving further that they had once been one piece of lumber. As the demonstration linking the two pieces of wood continued, Pope continued to object to the introduction of nearly every photograph, including one that showed the magnified ends of the piece ripped from the attic and Rail No. 16 on top of one another.

"Our objection," he tried again, "is, and we distinguish, if your Honor please, between a photograph of a natural condition, which of course is always admissible evidence, if it is testified that it truly represents the condition as the witness found it or as it existed at the time. And a photograph of a maneuvered or a manipulated condition, which has been manufactured, so to speak by a witness for showing certain things which he wants to show. One is a natural photograph of a natural condition and one is a photograph of an unnatural condition."

After hearing from Koehler that while he hadn't taken the pictures himself, he had supervised it being taken, Trenchard allowed the photo.

Case strained to see the photograph. He was fascinated.

So too was Lindbergh. Ethelyn wrote that "he leaned forward so far in his chair, he nearly fell out. His mouth was open, eyes intense, hands on his knees or chin in his palms. Was he interested?"

"Will you explain to us further now as you see it there," Wilentz asked, "why you have stated that the two upper boards representing S-226 to my left and the ladder rail referred to in there as rail 16, were at one time together in one board?"

"Well, I object to that," Pope tried again, "because manifestly that is a matter of speculation and a pure guess on the part of the witness. It can't be otherwise. I don't know that his guess is any better than the guess of the jury."

Trenchard asked for the court reporter to repeat the question before once again, rejecting Pope.

"He may answer the question," the jurist said.

Koehler walked the jury through how he had found a saw cut at the end of the board in the attic and sawdust on the lath and plaster of the ceiling before he segued into the uniqueness of trees. He would show Pope that the equivalent of a tree's fingerprints were scientific in nature.

"By matching up the grain in this board in the floor and this rail from the ladder, I find that the grain matches practically perfectly, considering the gap that is between the two," he said.

"Unbelievable," said the reporter sitting behind Ethelyn. "Never heard anything like that," said another. Each time she heard a compliment, she wrote home to the kids that she "was so proud, I nearly bursted: I wanted to get up and shout, 'He's mine.'"

Wilentz introduced as evidence another photograph, showing the markings between the board and Rail 16. The picture also showed two other pieces of lumber unrelated to the ladder or the attic.

"Is it necessary to have these comparisons in order to intelligently explain the connection between the ladder rail and the board from the attic floor?" Wilentz asked.

"It is in my opinion," Koehler responded.

As if on cue, Pope rose from the defense table.

"We have no objection to the General using any photograph which he says will help him show the identity of the grain in the end of the ladder rail and in the end of the board taken from the attic floor, but we do most strenuously object to his showing photographs of other pieces of lumber entirely unconnected with this case, which were not taken from this attic, which were not taken from the ladder and which had no connection whatever, either with the house or the ladder or the kidnapping or anything else, and introducing something entirely foreign to this case . . . because we submit that there can be no such thing as a comparison of a piece of lumber that was taken from that attic floor or from that ladder, with a piece of lumber that was found out in Michigan or some other place in the United States until it is identified as a part of the same board."

Trenchard's curiosity here was piqued. "What do you say about that?" he asked Wilentz.

"If your Honor please," he started, "I think nearly every exhibit has some identity because of a comparison—a man is shorter than other man, or he is taller, or he is heavier or he is lighter; a shoe is larger or it is smaller, it is wider or otherwise; one piece of wood is darker or lighter—and everything, it seems to me is identified only because there may be a comparison. . . .

"It cannot at all prejudice the defendant or defense counsel," the prosecutor continued. "As a matter of fact, it will help them. Now if your Honor should conclude that this is more helpful as we very respectfully submit to you, since it is explained, it has no other purpose except for comparison, so that this witness may be able to tell the real significance of the grains in the ladder rail and the attic floor, just as the handwriting expert can come down and say, 'This is the 'e' on the note and this is a different 'e' for comparison—since it can only serve a helpful and useful purpose, if your Honor please, we submit it is admissible."

Trenchard was unmoved, allowing only for the photo to be marked for identification at that particular time. So Wilentz relented and put up a different photo, this one featuring only the grain of the ladder and of the attic board in question.

"Tell us the relationship between the two," he asked Koehler.

"That lower picture is a photograph of this end of the floor board and you can see this big streak that is on the board on the picture, and you can see, I think, that the grain curves with the convex side up. And we have the same thing there."

To show how much of a mismatch in terms of wood knowledge was apparent, Pope asked "on the record exactly what that means, the convex referring to the bottom picture on the board."

"All right," Wilentz said. "Now, you started to tell us about the grain and the convex what?"

"The convex side of the annual rings is up here," Koehler said.

"Proceed with your description."

"In order to get a picture of the two adjoining ends it was necessary to tip the rail back and over."

"Which rail?"

"Rail 16."

"The ladder rail?"

"Yes."

"Just refer to it as the ladder rail," Wilentz suggested to his witness.

"The ladder rail, to turn it back over on top of the floor board so that they could take a picture of the two at the same time, and that accounts for the fact that the rings seem to curve in the other direction in this ladder rail, but that is just because it has been turned over on its back."

"Yes, sir."

"Now, I want to point out the similarity between those two photographs, that is the photograph of the ladder rail, the end of the ladder rail, and the end of the floor board. you will notice that in general, these curved lines here, those are the annual rings."

"Annual, do you call them?"

School was in session now. Koehler, who often helped greet the public for tours of the Forest Products Laboratory, was in his element. Case leaned over to whisper something to juror 12, Howard V. Biggs, who sat next to him.

"Annual rings," Koehler began to explain. "A tree each year produces a layer of wood under the bark and those are known as the annual rings, and it is by means of those rings that the rate of growth and the age of the tree can be determined, and that is, naturally they have to be curved because they go around the tree. There are the same number of annual rings in the floor board, counting it across in the most direct manner as there are in the rail."

"That man is a genius," said a reporter sitting behind Ethelyn.

"Does that indicate that the two boards are of the same age?" asked Wilentz, who like most others in the room was learning as he went along.

"That indicates that it took the same number of years to produce that much growth. Furthermore than that," Koehler continued, "the variation in the width of the rings is the same. You will notice that there are three narrow rings right from in here where I point with my pencil—I will mark them," he said as he put small pencil marks on the picture, "and toward the lower side, the next two are heavier and on the upper side the next two are heavier. Now, in this other picture of the end of the rail, we also have three narrow annual rings following each other and the next two rings on the convex side in the bottom in this case, and is in the top on the floor board are wider. And the two rings on the other side or concave side of the narrow ones are wider again, just as we have in this floor board.

"There is one apparent inconsistency," he noted. "In this portion of the floor board to the right, the rings are wider and distorted than they are in this piece, this end of the ladder rail, but that is due to a knot."

"Just wait a minute," Wilentz cautioned. He offered the next photo into evidence, showing a blown-up version of the knot in question.

"Proceed from there, please," he said after it was accepted by the court.

"Knots distort the grain and the closer you get to the knot, the more the grain is distorted, hence the grain is greatly distorted in this corner of the floor board," Koehler said. "You will notice however that the annual rings on this corresponding corner of the rail are also wider, showing that there was some factor influencing their growth right there. Now that in my opinion is the influence of this knot extended over into the end of the rail, but the grain is not distorted so much in the rail, because it was farther away from the knot there.

"I can make this a little clearer if you want me to," he said as another photo was introduced into evidence of the grain in the two boards being compared.

"I want you to," Wilentz said. "Please don't let me hurry you. If I miss something I want you to tell me about it."

"To bring out more clearly the similarity between the growth rings in the rail and in the floor board, I will take another photograph, which is a duplicate of that, made of the same negative to the same scale and show you that that can be matched up with this one perfectly."

"Why do you need two?" asked Wilentz.

"I want to superimpose part of one over the other," Koehler replied.

"You are not going to destroy the exhibit, are you, by cutting it?" Pope popped up, somewhat mystified by what was being proposed.

"I have to do that for this purpose," Koehler said, preparing a pair of scissors for his courtroom experiment. "I want to cut off a piece of this picture and superimpose it on that."

Pope remained standing but did not object, as he wasn't sure what Koehler wanted to do.

"I will take this picture of the end of the rail and cut it through the middle," Koehler said. "Now, I will take a portion of this picture and superimpose it upon the floor board."

"Take your time," said Wilentz as his witness looked around, apparently in need of something. "What do you want?"

"Thumbtacks," he replied.

One of the court staff handed him some. He posted the pictures on the easel.

"Now by taking these three narrow rings on this picture of the rail and superimposing them over the three narrow rings of the picture of the floor board, you will see there is a practically perfect match."

"Can your Honor see this?" Wilentz asked the judge.

"Yes, I see it," Trenchard replied.

"Now that to my mind in itself proves conclusively that these two pieces of wood were at one time one piece on account of the practically perfect match you can get between the two," Koehler said.

Wilentz asked him to use his pencil, to trace what he considered to be the perfect match of the grain.

"Here are the three narrow annual rings in the floor board that I referred to," he said, pointing. "These are the corresponding annual rings that I have marked over here. Now you can see how not only the curvature but the width of the rings follow right through from one to the other. You can see how these two wider rings below these three narrow ones are also found in the ladder rail."

"How do you explain the difference in color?" Wilentz asked about how the ladder rail was darker than the attic sample. "There seems to be a difference in color."

"This ladder rail," explained Koehler, "had been processed for finger prints and some of the liquid ran into the end grain of the wood."

"Have you completed your comparison of the grain, the following of the grain of one into the other or do you want to proceed further?"

"I now will show you how that same grain connects up on the top surface of these two boards. As I said before, there was a piece missing between the two, about an inch and a quarter wide, but I can connect up the corresponding grain."

Pope finally found a reason to have remained standing.

"I object to this unless the gentleman saw the missing piece that was about an inch and a quarter wide or can account for it," he said. "I object to his testifying that there is any matching of the grain between these two boards. It seems quite obvious that you could take almost any piece of North Carolina pine showing that general grain and draw them far enough apart and together and manipulate them so you might get a comparative continuity of grain. It is that missing piece, sir, that we object to."

"My suggestion is that the witness may be interrogated as to whether or not he knows that there was a missing link there originally," Trenchard ruled after some back and forth between the rival lawyers.

"From your experience, from your investigation and examination of these pieces of lumber," Wilentz asked, "what have you to say as to whether or not there isn't a piece missing that originally connected the two pieces?"

"These three narrow annual rings in the two end views of these two boards . . . in my mind are a means of showing which rings were originally connected because there is a series of three narrow rings in both of them."

"Yes."

"Now, those rings do not run out to the surface. Therefore, I cannot connect them up on the surface. So I will count out from there to the fifth ring beyond. It is one, two, three, four, five," he said, once again pointing at the exhibit on the easel. "That one runs out to the surface. And I will do the same on the other one; I will do that on this one. One, two, three, four, five. That is the one there.

"Now, I will mark those same rings on here. This ring right here is the fifth one out from this rail."

"That is the fifth ring then on S-233 [a picture of the end grain of the attic board]?"

"That is the fifth one."

"Yes sir," Wilentz said.

"And on this board, this ring right here is the fifth one out from those three narrow ones," Koehler said pointing to the ladder rail.

"All right."

"I will connect those up," he said. "Now they are the corresponding rings. Now that same ring goes around here on the other side, over here, and on the floor board, that fifth ring out is over there. I connect them up. Now I connect up the rest of the rings because they must follow. This ring makes no connection over here. It just makes a loop there. And the others have to follow in sequence."

All eyes in the courtroom followed his pencil as he traced a connect-the-dots-like path between growth rings in the two samples. The link was clear.

"Now that in my opinion shows a perfectly logical connection, looks perfectly natural. There is nothing inconsistent about that between those two boards," he concluded.

Sensing he was on a roll, Wilentz moved on to what would be Koehler's next experiment in Trenchard's courtroom.

"I notice that the ladder rail is not as wide as the attic boards. Will you explain that, if you can tell from an examination of the two?"

"In examining the ladder rail, I noticed that both edges were planed with a hand plane. The plane was not in very good condition and left little ridges, and also these ridges were wobbly over the end, showing that both edges were planed with a hand plane."

"I want to show you an exhibit in this case. S-177," Wilentz said, referring to the plane removed from Hauptmann's garage. "Can you tell whether or not S-177 is the plane that was used in planing the ladder rail?"

"It was," Koehler replied.

"Is there any question in your mind about it?"

"Not the least."

"Now let me ask you this: why do you say it, will you explain it?"

"Because on the ladder rail there are a number of ridges of different size and when I plane a piece of wood with that plane it makes similar ridges of the same size and same spacing apart as is found on the ladder rail."

"Would any other plane in your opinion make those ridges and marks?"

"No, that would be out of the question."

"Why, will you take a piece of wood—have you got an extra piece of wood here not connected with this case at all?"

"Yes."

"And take this plane, plane that piece of wood and show the jury the marks that it shows on that piece."

"Yes."

Before Koehler could put blade to wood, Pope was out of his seat again, objecting to the impending woodworking exhibition and stating that Koehler's testimony should suffice. Justice Trenchard overruled that objection.

"I will take a piece of wood which has previously been planed by a machine planer and is practically smooth," Koehler told the jury. "Now I will plane that with this hand plane and then make an impression of the marks made by that plane and also an impression of similar marks on the rail or some of the rungs of this ladder and show their similarity."

Pope again objected, asking what type of wood Koehler was going to use. When he found out it was Ponderosa pine and not North Carolina pine as found in Rail 16, he suggested that unless the latter could be provided, a fair comparison could not be made.

Wilentz was stumped. Koehler didn't have another piece of North Carolina pine on hand, but he did have an idea. As the attorneys bickered back and forth before the judge, Koehler offered to plane the Ponderosa pine and compare it to the marks on the rungs "of this ladder and they are made of Ponderosa pine."

"And that is exactly the same type of wood as you have here?" Wilentz asked.

"Yes."

Pope was unmoved, wanting more information.

"Is the piece of wood upon which you propose to make the

demonstration the same type, the same quality of wood that makes up these rungs of the ladder?"

"Yes."

"No different," Wilentz pressed.

"No."

"No trick about this, is there?"

"No."

"The same type of wood?"

"Yes."

"The same type of grain?"

"Yes."

"The same strength?"

"Approximately." Koehler remained a stickler for the truth, and he could not say absolutely without measurement whether the wood for his demonstration would be the same strength as the ladder rungs.

"Of course you don't know whether it came as a part of the same tree, do you?"

"No, not of the same tree."

"Ponderosa pine, it is, isn't it?"

"Yes."

"The rungs in the ladder are part of Ponderosa pine?" Wilentz was firing questions quickly at Koehler now.

"Yes."

"Will a demonstration of the plane upon the piece which you propose to use have the same force and effect as if you used it upon the very rungs of the ladder?"

"It will."

"Have you the plane and will you give us a demonstration?"

"Yes. In order to make an impression of those plane marks, I employ a very simple method that I learned when I was a youngster. I used to put a piece of paper over a coin and rub a pencil back and forth over the paper and get an impression of the coin on the paper. I can do that same thing but putting a piece of paper over the plane surface, rubbing a pencil back and forth, and getting an impression of these marks made by the hand plane. Before I do that however I will take this piece of wood before I plane it and see what we get so as to have something for comparison.

"Now I will mark this piece of paper before planing in court."
Wilentz suggested the court stenographer mark it, and Koehler
agreed before turning to Justice Trenchard with a most unusual
request.

"If it is all right, your Honor, I would like to make the demonstration here," he said pointing to the judge's bench. "This seems to
be a substantial thing to work on."

Trenchard shrugged his shoulders and said, "All right, so far
as I am concerned."

"Now before planing the top edge of this piece of wood, I
will make some marks on there with a pencil to be sure that we
can see that the plane takes something off," Koehler said, before
putting his weight into the plane and lodging the board against
Trenchard's bench for balance.

"On this one and you can see that all the blue marks have been
removed. That means that the planer took off a complete shaving
all the way across the piece of wood." He was directly talking to
the jury, and Case nodded knowingly. "I will now proceed to make
an impression of the marks made at that point."

Reporters noted that Case's face showed "approval" as Koehler
turned the judge's bench into an improvised workshop. Hauptmann, meanwhile, "watching him intently with his sunken eyes,
gives an audible snort that is akin to laughing out loud."

With a blue pencil, Koehler rubbed the paper he'd put over the
edge of the board, to gain a visible imprint. Then he showed the
jury the difference between the two pieces of paper, the before-
and-after demonstration.

"Now I will next proceed to make a similar impression of the
hand plane marks on one of the rungs of the ladder."

He picked Rung 10, even though he could have used any of
the rungs in the kidnap ladder. All had been planed with the same
planer. He completed the first part of his experiment, and it was
time for Wilentz once again to ask questions.

"Now as I understand it, then, you have these three pieces; one
is S-234, that is the impression of the piece of wood you used for
demonstration purposes. The next is S-235, the impression from the
same piece of wood after it had been planed by the plane in evidence."

"Yes," Koehler said.

"Now, S-237, the impression from the rung of the ladder."

"Yes."

"Now will you please proceed with your explanation and demonstration."

"Now I have those three impressions fastened to one card," he said. "This white portion here was made on the block of wood before planing. This piece in the middle was made on the piece of wood after I planed it here and this impression was taken off from one of the rungs of the ladder, rung Number 10.

"Now if you will look along there, right along there," he continued, using the blue pencil to guide the jurors' eyes, "you can see a number of lines on this impression from the ladder rung which coincide exactly with similar lines of these impressions made on the wood which I have planed. Look along it in a diagonal manner that way."

"How far do they correspond?" Wilentz asked about the samples of the board planed in court and the one from the ladder rung.

"All the way."

The pre-plane sample of Ponderosa pine showed no similarities.

Pope once again rose to object, "unless it be shown that the Ponderosa pine used in the demonstration came from the same forest or the same section of the country that the Ponderosa pine which is in the ladder."

At that, Koehler interjected, not waiting for his lawyer or the judge.

"Well, it undoubtedly—" he started before catching himself. "Shall I answer that?"

"Did they come from the same section?" asked Wilentz.

"It undoubtedly came from the section where Ponderosa pine grows."

"Where does Ponderosa pine grow?"

"It grows in the Western States."

"None in the Eastern States?"

"No."

"None in the Southern States?"

"No."

"What States do you call the Western States?"

"From the Great Plains westward."

"Tell us something about Ponderosa pine."

"Ponderosa pine is one of the most common species of pine—in fact, it is the most common species of pine in this country. It grows throughout the forested area from the Great Plains westward to the Pacific Ocean. It is a relatively soft grade of pine and is used extensively in the East and all through the country for a great many purposes."

A few questions and answers later, Trenchard interjected.

"Do you desire to press it any further, Mr. Pope?"

When defense counsel answered yes, Trenchard promptly overruled his objection.

From there, Wilentz and Koehler walked the jury through how the marks from Hauptmann's plane did not just match Rung 10. There were identical markings on Rail 16 and Rung 8 as well. They produced photos to show the jurors those markings.

When the court called for a five-minute recess, the New Jersey senator got up and Koehler went over to sit next to Ethelyn. He reached over and held her hand.

"It was not at all like him to do anything like that in public but I was glad I was there for he seemed to feel the need of something to hold," Ethelyn wrote home. "Of course no reporters bothered him while he was talking to his wife."

When court reconvened, Wilentz wrapped up that line of questioning.

"Tell me please, what plane it was that was used to plane the rungs 8 and 10 and rail number 16."

"This plane here," Koehler said, pointing to the one taken from Hauptmann's garage.

When Wilentz asked Koehler to identify which plane was then used on a piece of wood found in Hauptmann's garage, Pope rose again.

"He can't do that," he said. "He can only guess at it."

"He can't guess at it," Wilentz quickly replied. "He gives us his expert knowledge."

"Unless he was there and saw or knew he can't do anything

but guess at it," Pope said exasperated. "He may give an opinion, that is all."

One more time, Trenchard shot him down. "That is what he is giving," the judge said.

The prosecution then moved to the chisel, State's Exhibit S-210, found at the kidnap scene and the lack of a similar instrument found in Hauptmann's tool chest.

"Can you tell whether or not that chisel was used in the construction of the ladder, which is in evidence as S-2111, and, if you can, will you tell us about it."

"I can tell whether that size was used," Koehler responded carefully.

"Whether that size?" Wilentz asked.

"Yes."

"All right. Tell us what size chisel was used in the construction of that ladder and what part of a chisel of that size was used, if it was."

Pope continued to stand up from his chair for his objections as he had throughout the testimony. "If he wants to express his opinion as to whether this identical chisel was used, why, perhaps his opinion may be expressed, but to say that an ordinary three-quarter inch chisel was used to make the ladder doesn't connect it with this chisel in any way," he said.

"Well, it may be a circumstance for the consideration of the jury," Trenchard weighed in.

"Well, if this chisel were found in Hauptmann's garage it might be a circumstance, but it was found some forty miles away from there," Pope continued to press on.

"Yes," Trenchard said. "And it was found, was it not, under the southwest window of this nursery?"

"Somewhere on the Lindbergh property, I don't remember where," Pope pleaded. "It is an ordinary three-quarter inch chisel."

"Where the ransom note was left, which has been traced to this defendant," Trenchard said, growing weary with Pope's insistence.

"We don't agree to that," Pope asserted.

"I know you don't," Trenchard said, "but I am telling you what the evidence tends to show. Therefore I think that these pieces of circumstances must be given over to the jury to consider. That is my ruling in the matter."

"What sized chisel was used in the construction of this ladder, if you know?" Wilentz started again.

"A three-quarter inch chisel was used in chiseling out recesses for the rungs."

Wilentz called for someone with the court to open Hauptmann's tool chest before continuing his questioning. He asked Koehler if he knew what size chisels should be found in a carpenter's chest.

"As a rule a good carpenter's tool chest should contain a quarter inch chisel, half inch chisel, three quarter inch chisel, one inch and one and a half, and possibly two-inch chisel."

"Tell us what size chisels there are there?" Wilentz asked in reference to Hauptmann's tool chest.

"There is a quarter inch chisel, a half inch chisel, and an inch and a half chisel."

Wilentz had one more point to make, a circumstantial one, but one he hoped would leave an impression with the jury.

"Will you take a look at the quarter inch chisel which is a part of the exhibit heretofore entered and take a look at the three quarter inch and let me know whether or not they are the same make, same type of chisels."

"Yes, they are," replied Koehler.

"What kind of chisels are they?"

"They are Buck chisels, so-called Buck chisels made by Buck Brothers and the pattern is the same on the two. The milling on the ferrule is identical on the two, the general pattern is the same."

"Between the quarter-inch chisel and the three-quarter inch chisel?"

"Yes."

Point made.

"All right sir. Now you told us, I think, that a three-quarter inch chisel was used to construct this ladder?"

"Yes sir," Koehler replied, at which point he broke out more photographs.

"This is the picture of one of the recesses for the rungs in this rail 16," Koehler walked slowly along the jury box to show the members after the first photo was introduced as evidence. He explained what they were looking at:

> These recesses were chiseled out and this shows a mark made by the chisel, one side of the chisel went down there and then there is a right angle turn here. Here is a parallel line on this side. This is the corner of the recess right here, so the line extends, or the mark made by the chisel extends from almost the middle of the rung, not quite the middle of the recess, I mean, over to the very edge of the recess. Now I superimposed a chisel on there of approximately, that seemed to be approximately that size, I took a three-quarter inch chisel, by superimposing that over that mark and this picture shows it better than the other one and this mark right here, one side you see of the chisel lines up with this edge of the cut and this other side lines up with the edge of it or the corner of the recess. It couldn't have been a wider chisel. Now, this corner of the recess would have prevented that. That three-quarter of an inch chisel, in other words, fits perfectly into that mark made by that chisel.

"Of course, you don't know what three-quarter inch chisel made the mark?"

"No."

"Your testimony is that a three-quarter inch chisel did it?"

"Yes."

Then Wilentz asked Koehler to use the chisel as he held the ladder to show the jurors up close what he was talking about.

"I want you to walk along nice and slowly and indicate to each juror, I will hold it, now one at a time, and I wish you jurors in back would please lean forward," Wilentz said as he held the ladder.

Case jumped up and leaned over juror number 2, Rosie Pill, to see how the chisel matched the grooves in question.

The demonstration completed, Wilentz turned to Koehler's tracking of Rails 12 and 13. He had Koehler explain how he had become involved in the case and how he had tracked some of the wood in the kidnap ladder to the National Lumber and Millwork Company in the Bronx months before Hauptmann was ever arrested.

"Will you tell us how you traced it?"

"I traced it by means of the planer marks made on the lumber when it was planed at the planing mill."

"You mean the machine planer marks?"

"Yes." He described how he'd visited Senator Dorn in McCormick, South Carolina, and traced one of the company's shipments to the Bronx yard.

"How did you know, how could you know and how did you know that the defect which was shown on the ladder and which defect you say you also found in lumber in the Bronx lumber yard," Wilentz said, voicing the thought of the entire courtroom at that moment. "How did you know that these planer marks were made by the planer you found in the Dorn Company mill?"

"That is a long story," Koehler said.

"We want the long story. Let's have it."

"I think I had better explain to the jury first what I mean by planer marks," Koehler said.

"Yes sir."

"I have some drawings here which illustrate how a planer makes marks as it dresses lumber," he began. "I believe the jury is not familiar with the way these machine planers work, so I have a diagrammatic drawing here of certain essential features of a machine planer. This shows," he said as he began pointing once again to an exhibit, "a piece of lumber in here which is being planed. Above this board there is a cutter head, which has knives set into it. There are eight knives shown in this cutter head. Some have six, some four, ten, even twelve. That cutter head revolves as the lumber goes through it, and these knives come around and cut a shaving off the surface of the lumber. There is another cutter head on the lower side with knives set in it, and as that cutter head revolves these knives plane the bottom side of the lumber."

"How many knives in that?" Wilentz wanted to know.

"There are eight knives in that one," Koehler answered, "but that is not necessary in every case. There may be more or less. These two rollers are called the feed rollers. The lumber goes through between these rollers, and is shoved through the machine by them, and the speed at which these feed rollers revolve determines the speed at which the lumber goes through the planer. Now on most planers the speed of the feed rollers can be changed, to a high speed or medium or low speed, to different rates of speed, but the speed of these cutter heads is always the same."

After officially entering the diagrams into evidence, the "long story" continued:

> Since those knives go around in a circle, each knife makes a circular cut out of the board. Those cutters are so small we don't ordinarily notice that, but yet that is the case, and as a result, a board which is planed by a machine planer has a wavy appearance. Now if those knives are all in good condition and functioning properly, each one, all of those waves are of the same size.
>
> Suppose one of the knives has a defect in it, like is shown here in knife No. 7, a nick every time that knife comes around it makes a mark there where that nick is. The other knives don't have such a nick in them, so we can tell how often that knife comes around and below this cutter head I have a diagrammatic drawing of a piece of lumber which shows the circular cuts on the surface and also shows a mark in every cut, marked No. 7, that is, each time this defect comes around. There are eight cuts from one to the other. Here is one, two, three, four, five, six, seven, eight—in other words, every eighth cut like that shows that defect."

Case nodded his head knowingly as Koehler continued.

> Once in a while a knife may not be lined up properly with the rest of them, as is shown here for knife No. 5. As a consequence when it comes around it doesn't make as heavy a cut as the other knives, it makes a narrower cut and I have shown that here with cut No. 5. You will see cut No. 5 is narrower in each case. And there are eight cuts from one to the other, one, two, three, four, five, six, seven, eight. In other words, every eighth cut is a narrowed cut in that case. Therefore, by examining the surface of a piece of lumber, it usually is possible to tell how many knives there were in the cutter head that dressed the lumber because

as a rule there is something wrong with a knife somewhere, maybe a little nick in it or the knife may be out of line and so it is possible by examining the surface of a piece of planed lumber in most cases to determine how many knives there were in the cutter head that dressed the lumber.

In addition to these cutter heads planing the top and bottom of a board as it goes through the planer, there are similar cutter heads standing vertically on the two sides of the board and plane the edges of the board as it goes through the planer, so that all four sides of a board are planed as it goes through the planer. . . .

Now the number of knives in those cutter heads that plane the edges may be the same as in the top and bottom cutter heads, but usually they are less. Very often if there are eight knives in the top and bottom cutter heads, there will be six in the side heads, as they are called, or if there are six knives in the top and bottom cutter heads, there will be four in the side heads.

Now here I show a photograph of rail number 13 of this ladder, that is one of the rails of the bottom section of the ladder. This is a photograph of a portion of the side of one of those rails. You will notice that there is a periodic mark occurring at regular intervals. That is due to one of the knives not protruding as far as it ought to and every time it came around it didn't make as wide a cut as it should. Consequently I can tell how far that lumber moved through the planer per revolution of these cutter heads. The cutter head dressed the surface. I find in measuring that distance on the lumber itself that that distance is regularly 93 hundredths of an inch.

Hauptmann and the rest of the defense table did not move. The defendant sat with his arms folded and his legs crossed.

Koehler proceeded to walk the jury through his detective work: the discovery of the type of machine planer used, the canvassing of lumber mills from New York City to Alabama, the collection of samples from those that held the right kind of machine, and eventually the visit to McCormick and Senator Dorn's lumber yard.

"I visited their mill to see if I could definitely determine whether they had dressed this lumber," Koehler said. "And I found that when they ran lumber through their planer with a certain sized feed pulley on that planer it made revolution marks exactly like on that ladder rail."

Then he testified about studying sales slips to find the car loads of 1x4-inch North Carolina pine shipped north, traveling with Bornmann to the mills that had received that lumber, and how because planer knives would be sharpened from time to time, not all of those carloads would have the distinguishing mark in question.

"Knowing that, you started to trace it further. Tell us about it," Wilentz asked.

"I would like to show what that distinguishing mark looks like. Here is an edge of the bottom rail of the ladder and here is the edge of a board which I obtained from the National Lumber and Millwork Company. You will notice these waves in there, periodic waves, they are spaced exactly the same distance apart in the two," he said, once again using a pencil to point to places on a picture of the lumber. "The thing I have in mind particularly is a little shallow groove, a little difficult to see perhaps, but you see it in some places, here, which occurs every so often. In fact, they are 86-hundredths of an inch apart. That was due to some irregularity in the edge of one knife, and I knew if I could find a shipment in which that irregularity showed up, I could locate the shipment from which these ladder rails were made."

He described going to the Bronx lumber yard and what he had found there. "A sample of lumber at the yard . . . showed exactly the same defect in the planing on one edge as occurred on the ladder rail; and I also found that there was a defect on the face of the board," he said as he pointed to another photo. "There is a periodic defect in the knife that shows up near one edge in both pieces, also due to a defect in the knife that dressed that lumber.

"Therefore, having a defect in the planing on one edge and also on one face of this lumber from the National Lumber & Millwork Company, which corresponds exactly with that similar defect in the ladder rail, I was convinced that I had found the yard from which this ladder, these ladder rails were obtained."

"Sounds like a fairy tale," Ethelyn heard a reporter say.

Wilentz now moved on to an exhibit that showed a photo of Rails 14 and 15, from the middle section of the ladder. Koehler had deduced that if the two were placed alongside each other, the saw cuts made for their recesses matched up perfectly, which showed that those two pieces had been clamped together when they were cut.

Hauptmann had owned clamps, already introduced into evidence as State's Exhibit 196.

"Can you tell whether or not those were the clamps, or were they similar clamps?" Wilentz wanted to know.

"I can't tell. The clamp did not leave any mark on the wood, but neither would that clamp," Koehler replied. "Any one of those could have been used."

Koehler was next shown photographs magnifying the excess saw cuts used to make the recesses on Rails 16 and 17 from the top section of the kidnap ladder. He described how he had measured the width of the saw cuts made in cutting out the recesses, ranging from 35 to 37-thousandths of an inch.

"Was there a saw in Hauptmann's tool chest that is in evidence that made a similar size cut?"

"Yes," Koehler said. "I tried out all the saws and found two saws in that tool chest that will make cuts of that width."

Before they went any further, Wilentz's attention was drawn back to two earlier exhibits showing the cutter head knives from the Dorn lumber yard. He asked what they were intended to show.

"In examining this ladder," Koehler explained, "I tried to find out as far as I could what sized lumber was used in its construction. Now these Ponderosa pine rungs are two and three-quarter inches wide and they were planed on one edge. That means that they originally were wider. Now, the only way I could determine how wide the board was from which those rungs were made was to see if they would match together in any way, and I found that the four rungs of the bottom section of the ladder, and the four rungs of the middle section of the ladder . . . could be matched together, end to end and side to side, by means of their grain, so as to show without any doubt, that those eight rungs were cut from one board, so-called one by six Ponderosa pine. The board was first stripped lengthwise, and then the edges were planed, because the hand plane marks ran consecutively from one rung to the next one on those edges; and after they were planed, then the strips were cut into four pieces of the proper length."

Since they were on the topic of the width of wood, Wilentz asked Koehler about the attic board that he had testified had at one time been connected with Rail 16. Both prosecutor and witness were thorough.

"Please look at [Rail 16] and then tell us why it is if the rail of the ladder was a piece of [the attic board], why is it that one is wider than the other?"

"All the other rails of the ladder are so-called one by four stock, and this one was dressed down the same width which is also indicated by the fact that both edges are hand planed; in other words, it is ripped down from a wider board so as to be the same width as the other rails in the ladder."

It was getting late. Wilentz encouraged Koehler to sit back down in the witness box, as he would just ask a few more questions until court would adjourn at 4:30. He asked about Koehler's first trip into Hauptmann's attic. This testimony was anticlimactic considering the ground they'd covered earlier, but it gave the reporters a fighting chance to write their pieces in time to make their evening deadlines.

Wilentz asked the judge if he could bring back Koehler to the stand the next morning as he had "surely overlooked one or two things." But there certainly was nothing major left to cover. As Koehler was leaving the courtroom that day, Lindbergh clutched his arm, leaned toward him, and said he was "absolutely amazing" and that he'd "never heard anything like it before."

Arthur turned to Ethelyn and smiled.

"I'm so proud of you," she said.

"It's the greatest day of my life," he responded with a gentle clasp of her hand, "except the day I got married."

A prosecuting attorney told the *Chicago Daily Tribune* that "Koehler was a pretty good witness" and that the state was satisfied with its case.

Maybe more tellingly, as the defense lawyers left the courtroom they were surrounded by reporters asking about the day's events and in particular about the so-called wood wizard, as one reporter would call him.

"What'd you think of Koehler's testimony?" the reporters all cried out.

"There has been nothing better than it," said a frustrated Pope, who had tried continuously and unsuccessfully to stop Koehler's demonstrations. "It is perfect."

The Universal Service reporter copiously took notes on Reilly's answer to the question. "I have never heard more damaging testimony or seen a more enthralling demonstration than that presented in the courtroom today by Arthur Koehler," he said. "I wouldn't say that we have had anything better than it, but we are going to break it down on cross-examination."

11

By the time Arthur Koehler returned to the witness stand on the seventeenth day of the Hauptmann trial, he was known around the country.

Newspaper headlines crowed with above-the-fold, bold-face praise.

"Science and Justice," screamed the *Washington Evening Star*.

"Highlight of the Trial," declared the *Boston Herald*.

"Sherlock Holmes in Witness Box," read the headline in the Wheeling, West Virginia, paper.

Koehler's testimony was praised from coast to coast in the syndicated prose of Damon Runyon. "One of the most astonishing tales of scientific detective work ever related as fact or fiction is poured into the ears of the amazed jurors in the Lindbergh baby murder trial of Bruno Richard Hauptmann today, as the state of New Jersey practically closes its case by apparently keeping its promise to 'wrap the kidnap ladder around Hauptmann's neck,'" he began.

> What Hauptmann can say in his own defense, how he will attempt to alibi out of the damaging evidence of the ladder made with tools said to be his own and including a piece of board from his attic, will come to light tomorrow at noon when Hauptmann, by agreement between defense and prosecution, will take the stand himself.
>
> The tale of scientific wood and tool detection, told today by a bald-headed, mild looking middle-aged man from the woods of Wisconsin, an expert for the government of the U.S. named

Arthur Koehler, puts the greatest fictional exploits of Sherlock Holmes in the shade.

Carlisle Winslow, director of the Forest Products Lab, would immediately send Runyon a copy of the architects' drawing of the lab with a note saying that "this is the back woods where Koehler works."

Other reporters were equally effusive in their praise.

Arthur B. Reeve with *The New York Post* wrote, "After hearing the testimony of Arthur Koehler, Hauptmann is finished."

The Reading, Pennsylvania, *Times* called him "the only real detective (in the case)."

The Columbia, South Carolina, newspaper, *The State,* labeled him a "woodsman Sherlock Holmes."

They weren't the only ones to make the comparison to the fictional sleuth. *The New York Times* said Koehler testified "in the role of a modern Sherlock Holmes while Attorney General Wilentz played the part of Dr. Watson by asking questions now and then to draw him out. . . . The jurors followed the testimony with signs of intense interest, leaning forward in their chairs and following every word closely. . . . Liscom Case, Juror No. 12 [sic], a retired carpenter showed special interest, calling for several of the photographic exhibits while Mr. Koehler testified and apparently discussing this evidence with the juror sitting next to him."

Under the headline, "Adventure on Prosaic Roads," the Marietta, Georgia, *Times* wrote, "Today, there was revealed before a court room jammed almost beyond human endurance a drama so vivid and stirring that the least imaginative of the spectators could see, in their mind's eye, a tall, gaunt German carpenter sawing, planing, chiseling and hammering upon a strange three-section ladder. The medium of this drama was annual rings, pitch marks and knots, ridges and depressions, nail holes and saw cuts in pieces of South Carolina [sic] and ponderosa pine."

Willard Edwards from the *Chicago Tribune* called Koehler's work "an amazing piece of detective work" and described the Wisconsin man as "a hard-working, plugging detective with astonishing qualities of perseverance."

The New York Post, realizing the importance of Koehler's testimony, presciently wrote: "The Hauptmann trial may go down in legal history less as the most sensational case of its time than as the case which brought legal recognition to the wood expert on a par with handwriting, fingerprint and ballistic experts."

The Associated Press said he delivered a "smashing blow" to the defense.

He was called a "super scientist detective," a "bloodhound," a "relentless tracker" who told a tale "more engrossing, more breathtaking than any detective story ever heard in court or written in type."

Maybe the most complimentary comment came from a Brit, Ford Madox Ford, an English novelist, poet, critic, and editor who sat through the trial and contributed to the *New York World Telegram* on occasion. Koehler's testimony provided one of those occasions, underneath the headline "Destiny's Role Given Koehler."

"A little, baldish, shining, implacable man with an amazingly clear vocal organ, he was like the instrument of a blind and atrociously menacing destiny," Ford wrote.

> You shuddered at the thought of what might happen to you if such a mind and such an inconceivable industry should get to work upon your own remote past . . . a man who searched 1,900 factories for traces of the scratches of a plane on a piece of wood, it was fantastic and horrifying.
>
> I have never—and in my time I have seen some things— imagined that any moment could be so shockingly moving as when with the air of a conjurer producing a rabbit from a top hat, he brought out from invisibility a common plane and proceeded, utterly matter of fact, to plane a piece of plank, producing exactly the grooves and scratches that are to be found on the ladder that is the principal item of the State's evidence. You felt that if the motionless—and always motionless—prisoner sits in the end motionless in the electric chair, that little sleuth, with the implacability of a weasel hunting by scent an invisible prey, will be the man who will have sent him there.

Ford was more definitive in a conversation with a reporter from the *Chicago Daily Tribune* as he told him that Koehler's testimony "is going to send Hauptmann to the [electric] chair."

The superlatives flowed in person as well.

Walter Winchell told Koehler after his testimony, "You're the tops, Koehler."

Adela Rogers St. Johns, a prominent New York journalist with the Hearst papers, pulled Koehler aside and said to him, "My father was a criminal lawyer and tried over 170 cases of which I heard a great deal and I have been in the Hearst service for 30 years, but yours was the most impressive testimony I ever heard."

The court stenographer, Charlton Shell, told Koehler, "I have had 19 years' experience as a court reporter, but your testimony was the cleverest and most convincing I ever heard."

The Western Union lady at his hotel gasped audibly when he came to send a telegram, asking, "Are you *the* man?!" After he said yes, she said, "I am glad I saw you. Now, I can go home and brag to my family."

Speaking of family, Arthur's brother Ben wrote him that his "picture has been published in all the newspapers of the land, I think. . . . [Your testimony was] just as interesting as any detective story ever written and it is not a novel."

At 10:27 on January 24, Koehler once again faced Attorney General Wilentz. In answer to Wilentz's questions, he made clear that the only parts of the kidnap ladder that came from South Carolina were Rails 12 and 13 and that the Forest Products Laboratory was the only one of its kind covering "all kinds of research on wood" in the country.

The two men had one more critical point they wished to convey to the jury. Wilentz introduced State's Exhibit S-251, a photo of Hauptmann's car taken on the day he was arrested.

"Did you take this ladder, Exhibit S-211, and attempt to fit it into that car?"

"I did," Koehler responded.

"Did it fit in the car?"

"Yes. When I took the three sections assembled and nested together, they fit in on top of the front and rear seats, and there were several inches to spare."

"Do you mean that when you put them together like this," Wilentz said, breaking down the ladder from being extended, "put the three sections together?"

"Yes."

"That is, one within the other?"

"Yes."

With that, Wilentz said, "Take the witness," and defense attorney Pope began his efforts to fulfill Reilly's earlier promise to the media that they would "break down" Koehler's testimony. He began where Wilentz left off, asking about whether a bystander could have seen the ladder inside Hauptmann's car.

"Yes," Koehler answered, "unless it was covered up."

"Unless it was covered up," Pope repeated, letting it hover with the jury.

He segued to Koehler's other courtroom appearances, parrying, searching for a hole to poke open further. He drew from the scientist the fact that he'd been on the witness stand in civil trials as well as the Magnuson criminal case, but he did not pursue the one case Koehler mentioned that he had lost. Koehler later wrote in his notebook, "I was skating on thin ice when Pope asked about other lawsuits and I mentioned the Cincinnati case in which I lost out."

After reestablishing Koehler's tenure of twenty-one years with the Madison lab, Pope found an area to explore.

"Now, you have never undertaken to identify chisel marks or plane marks upon lumber in court before, have you?"

"In court? No."

"This is the first time you have been called upon to testify to that?"

Koehler nodded.

"You are shaking your head. Would you mind saying yes or no? I want it on the record, that is the reason."

"Yes," said Koehler.

"Now you demonstrated to the jury yesterday that one of the notches in the rail, notch recessed for the purpose of allowing the rung to be put in there, after being sawed down on the side had been cut out with a three-quarter inch chisel?"

"Yes."

"Please, so we get it on the record. The notch referred to on the rail of the ladder could well have been made by any standard three-quarter inch chisel, couldn't it?"

"Yes."

"In other words, a three-quarter inch chisel is not only a common chisel, but it is one of the standard sizes, is it not?"

"Yes."

"And whether it be a chisel made by the Stanley Company, by the Goodell, Pratt Company or one of the common cheap cast steel chisels, it is the same size and functions in the same manner?"

"Yes."

"Were you shown the set of Stanley chisels belonging to Mr. Hauptmann and which were in his garage at the time of his arrest?"

"A set of Stanley chisels?" Koehler asked.

"Yes," said Pope.

"No."

"So you don't know then whether among the set of Stanley chisels there was a three-quarter inch chisel?"

"No I don't."

He then shifted to Koehler's entry into the case.

"You came into this case first in the month of May, 1932, did you not?"

"Yes."

"That was nearly three months after the ladder was found?"

"Yes."

"And of course you are depending entirely on what somebody else told you as to the conditions of the ladder at the time it was found?"

"Yes."

"And its condition at the time it was first shown to you?"

"That I observed myself."

"You do not know whether the ladder, when it was originally found, contained a piece of Douglas fir or not, in the place of the North Carolina pine?"

"I didn't see it when it was originally found."

"Would you mind showing me the rails [other than Rail 16] that are made up of North Carolina pine?" Pope asked

Koehler stepped down from the stand to highlight the rails on the bottom section of the ladder, Rails 12 and 13.

"It is a different quality, is it not, from the board that was found in the attic floor?"

"It is a common grade of lumber, they are all three of them a common grade of lumber."

"I didn't mean that, Mr. Koehler. I just asked you if it isn't a different quality or a better quality?"

"What do you mean by quality then, if you don't mean the grade?" Koehler replied.

"I think you lumber men do call it 'grade' that is the term you use. It is a better grade, isn't it?"

"It has no knots in it, if that is what you mean, or just a small knot, whereas the other piece has several knots in it."

Pope was getting frustrated.

"Mr. Koehler, I suppose that when a man accustomed to dealing with lumber speaks of the grade or quality of the lumber that he usually has reference to its quality and its grade the same as you would if you were speak of silk or plush or wool or anything else. Now I am asking you, is not the railing that you have just shown me of a better grade of North Carolina lumber than the grade of lumber that was found on the attic floor?"

"I will have to explain that because—," Koehler began to answer before Pope cut him off.

"Can't you answer yes or no?"

"No, I can't because I don't know what you mean by quality."

Justice Trenchard had to step in to referee this dispute as Wilentz defended his witness, encouraging Pope to let Koehler explain, and Pope demanding a yes or no answer. Counter to what Pope wanted, Koehler was given the chance to show further knowledge.

"That word 'quality' covers a number of things," he said, turning to the jury as often as he did toward Pope. "It might cover the appearance, so far as being beautiful or not is concerned, it might cover the strength of the wood, it might cover its ability to keep from warping and a number of other things. Now, the word 'grade' usually refers to the presence or absence of defects in the lumber, such as knots and pitch streaks and such."

Pope tried again to make his point. "Now, speaking as a man, for instance, who was engaged in the carpenter business and the building trade—if he went to a lumber yard and he found the two grades of lumber which you have produced here from the lumber yard, the one, the North Carolina pine flooring, underflooring, or whatever—roofers, and the North Carolina pine railing in there. Would the lumber dealer charge him more for the one grade than the other?"

"In that case not."

"In that case not?" a dumbfounded Pope repeated.

"Because they would be classified the same, although there is a variation in a grade."

"So that you think that the grade of North Carolina pine that you have referred to in the other rails of ladder equals to the grade of North Carolina pine that was found on the attic floor?"

"Yes," said Koehler, "speaking commercially."

"I just simply want you to tell the jury the difference in the quality," an exasperated Pope said.

"I can't answer that question unless it is specific."

"Is there no difference in your judgment in the quality of the two pieces of lumber?"

"In some respects there is and in some there isn't."

"In any respect?"

"Yes."

"Then tell us what those differences are."

"The two bottom rails of the ladder do not contain as large knots as the rail cut—as the North Carolina pine rail in the top section of the ladder."

"And in that respect it is better quality?"

"For certain purposes it would be considered better when it is free from knots."

"Well, it is better for any purpose, isn't it, if it is free from knots?"

"I will have to explain again, to answer that question."

Koehler proved a formidable foe for a defense counsel whose hobby was woodworking. As he tried to score with the jury, Pope must have felt like a Sunday softball player trying to strike out a major league baseball player. The gap in their knowledge of the topic was dramatic.

The intellectual thrust and parry continued until Pope finally changed the subject. "Taking the structure of this ladder as a whole would you say that that was built by a mechanic or by an amateur or even less?"

"Do you mean by 'mechanic' a carpenter or a machinist?"

"Well, I didn't know that machinists built ladders, sir, so of course I am referring to a man who attempted to build a piece of, a structure out of wood and I don't refer to a jeweler or machinist as a mechanic who would attempt to use wood," he said. "What I want to know is do you think it was built by a mechanic?"

"No."

"From your knowledge of wood, would you think that a ladder constructed as this one is, or referring specifically to this particular ladder, would hold the weight of a man 175 to 180 pounds?"

"Yes, I think it would."

"And could he go up and down readily without the ladder breaking?"

"He might."

"He might? The nearer the [rungs] are together, the stronger the ladder and the less likely to break under use, is that correct?"

"No. I wouldn't say that the distance between the rungs affects the ladder except possibly that when a man makes a long step it gives more of a jerk."

Next Pope tried to make hay with Koehler's saw cut measurements.

"The normal width of an ordinary cross cut saw before there is any set in the teeth is what?"

"I don't know."

"You never measured it?"

"I never saw a saw like that."

"Well, how thick is the saw blade?"

"I don't know. It varies, of course, with different saws and it varies from front to back."

Pope began asking about Hauptmann's specific saws and measurements to the thousandths of an inch that Koehler had found on one of the ladder's recesses.

"Now, when you speak of 35,000[ths] of an inch you are speaking of a width slightly less than a thirty-second of an inch?"

"A great deal less."

Pope was throwing everything he had at this and couldn't find an opening. After some discussion of why Koehler couldn't trace the Douglas fir rails in the ladder as definitively as he did Rails 12 and 13, he tried to infer that Hauptmann, a carpenter by trade, couldn't have created what Koehler had called an inferior product.

"Did you find any hammer marks on the ladder over the nails, did you notice any?"

"There were a few on the rungs."

"Just a few on the rungs?"

"Yes."

"From your experience, a good carpenter doesn't leave hammer marks on his work, does he?"

"No."

"He drives the nail down practically flush with the work and then he uses his nail set to set it in."

"He wouldn't use a nail set on 8 penny nails, as a rule, he would drive them flush and leave them there."

The two then sparred over the birch dowels that connected the sections of the ladder. "Now a three-quarter inch dowel pin is not a usual size, is it?" Pope asked.

"Yes."

"It is sort of unusual, isn't it, in size?"

"No, you can buy them in most lumber yards and in some hardware stores."

"Well, you can buy them, certainly but a three-quarter inch is not a size that is frequently used, is it?"

"Yes, it is frequently used for mop handles."

"You mean short mop handles for little sink mops?"

"No, regular long mop handles."

If Pope's goal was to fluster Koehler or break open his story, he failed. Instead, he gave the scientist the opportunity to prove even more scholarly as the cross examination continued.

On the topic of annual growth rings, Koehler later said he was worried that "when he asked whether weather conditions didn't determine width of rings, I thought he was going to get me to say that different trees would be affected similarly."

However, he didn't. The science was new enough, it's likely Pope was learning on the fly, throwing anything he could think of against the wall and hoping it would stick.

Instead, Koehler was able to steer the conversation to the idea that wider rings in wood indicated favorable growth and narrower rings constituted adverse growing conditions such as crowding, not just weather.

With nothing to be gained there, Pope turned to the machine planer marks Koehler had tracked to South Carolina and Dorn's lumber mill.

"If a board is run across a planer head moving with eight knives at approximately 21 to 22,000 revolutions per minute—"

Koehler cut him off. "No, not revolutions per minute, cuts per minute."

"Cuts per minute, I stand corrected," Pope said. "Thank you. 21 or 22,000 cuts per minute if it is moved at a fairly rapid rate of speed, the result will be a perfectly smooth finish on the board, won't it?"

"Not perfectly smooth," Koehler said, "because of all of those cuts."

"Well, if it is run across the knives fast enough it will be absolutely smooth, won't it?"

"No. The faster it is run, the rougher the work it does."

"The faster, the rougher?"

"Yes."

"Well, in order to be rougher, the speed of the board running across the knives would have to be a little faster than the whirl of the knives and the cut, wouldn't it?"

"Oh, it never is that fast."

"Isn't it the slow motion of a board across the planer head that causes the ridges or ripples to show on the bottom of the board?"

"No," Koehler instructed. "The slow motion brings them close together and makes them inconspicuous."

And with that final correction, Pope had had enough. He thanked Koehler and sat back down, having accomplished little, except to point out that a ¾-inch chisel was common and that the kind of testimony Koehler had offered was new to him. The wood scientist's findings and his conclusions were unchallenged.

In his redirect, Wilentz came back to the line of questioning about whether a "good carpenter" built the ladder. "Is this the work of a carpenter of some sort or other?" he asked Koehler.

"It might be a very rough carpenter," Koehler said.

"Well, a jeweler wouldn't make this ladder, would he?"

"No."

"It would have to be somebody that knew something about carpentry, isn't that it?"

"Well, something about it, yes."

He had Koehler once again look over Hauptmann's tool chest to see if any Stanley chisels were there. He found none. They discussed the distance between the rungs of the ladder and how, for Hauptmann, at five-foot-nine or five-foot-ten, it would not be much of an imposition.

And then Wilentz came back to where he started the day before: the definitive piece of evidence to "wrap the ladder" around Hauptmann's neck.

"Are you still of the opinion, Mr. Koehler that this [board from the attic] and Rail 16 of the ladder were at one time one and the same piece of wood?"

"I am," Koehler said, even as Pope rose to object.

"And in answering that last question of the Attorney General, you are expressing your opinion, aren't you?" Pope said on re-cross examination.

"Yes."

"And that is all?"

"Yes."

He tried again to direct attention away from Hauptmann.

"This type of ladder, I mean this general, shall I call it plan of construction of ladder, is a general plan and type of ladder that is used quite extensively in the South in the fruit industry, is it not?"

"Not to my knowledge. I never saw a ladder like that before."

"You never saw one like that before?"

"No."

"Have you ever paid any attention to the type of extension ladder or sectional ladders that are used in the fruit picking areas of the South, of [the] southern United States?"

"I didn't know they used sectional ladders."

"You never noticed that?"

"No."

After a few more questions about where and when Koehler began inspecting the kidnap ladder, both attorneys had completed their questioning. Wilentz conferred with his colleagues before stating plainly, "The State rests."

A commotion broke out in the courtroom. Trenchard tried to gavel it down, but he'd been trying to quiet down the capacity crowds since the beginning and not with a great amount of success. He had threatened to clear the courtroom early in the trial and admonished the officers stationed throughout the room to remove those laughing, scoffing, or talking through the proceedings.

The defense immediately moved for an acquittal. Trenchard refused.

Lloyd Fisher, another of Hauptmann's attorneys, subsequently delivered the opening statement on behalf of the defense. "I am fully cognizant of the grave importance of this indictment," he began. "I shall humbly and in language as simple as I can command give you briefly the facts and the circumstances upon which we rely to gain for the defendant, Bruno Richard Hauptmann, an acquittal at your hands. That is now our responsibility. The fair presentation of all the facts and circumstances attendant to the trial of this indictment which we shall contend will preserve the life and liberty of this defendant."

He spoke about the alibi Hauptmann would provide, backed up by eyewitnesses, about how he was a frugal and hardworking man, and about how the defense's own expert handwriting witnesses would reject the notion his client had written the ransom notes. Further, he listed by name the prosecution's eyewitnesses and said the defense would highlight problems with each of their testimony.

One individual the defense did not mention, nor criticize in the slightest, was Arthur Koehler. Still, Fisher did take aim at the integrity of the ladder.

"I want to come down for a minute, if I may, to the manner of the conduct of the police in this case," he said. "I want to show you what we will prove about it. We believe we will be able to show you that no case in all history was as badly handled or as badly mangled as this case. . . .

"The ladder, we will prove to you has been torn apart, put together and replaced and torn down again. The nails have been drawn and were drawn and put back again. That ladder, we believe will show clearly, is in no more the condition than it was the day it was found on the Lindbergh estate than that chair is in the condition the ladder is now," he said, pointing at a chair in the courtroom. "Now, if we prove those facts, ladies and gentlemen, they are essential facts in this case. If we show you that that ladder has been so handled that it would be impossible now to identify it accurately as the one which was found in the hills, then we shall expect you to disregard all this testimony about the ladder."

After complaining that the defense would be "terribly handicapped by a total lack of the funds" compared with the prosecution, Fisher summed up simply, "We will hide nothing and produce everything and, when you have heard all the testimony, we trust that if you are not already satisfied that the State of New Jersey has utterly failed to make out a case against Bruno Richard Hauptmann, we are quite sure you will be convinced, after you have heard such testimony related as we will present."

With that, the court took a twelve-minute recess, after which Big Ed Reilly called the defendant, Bruno Richard Hauptmann, to the stand. The world had been waiting for this moment since March 1, 1932.

Hauptmann's testimony unfolded over a period of four days and featured numerous denials from the accused regarding whether he had ever seen Charles A. Lindbergh Jr., whether he had kidnapped and murdered the boy, and whether he had made the ladder that helped the perpetrator of the crime.

There it stood, over his shoulder and propped up against a wall, during the duration of his testimony.

"Now, how many years, Bruno, have you been a carpenter?" Reilly asked him.

"About ten years."

"You have seen this ladder here in court, haven't you?"

"Yes."

"Did you build that ladder?"

"I am a carpenter," he said while openly laughing.

"Did you build that ladder?" Reilly asked again.

"Certainly not."

"Come down and look at it, please."

"Looks like a music instrument," Hauptmann said after descending from the witness stand to examine it.

"In your opinion," said Reilly, "does it look like a well made ladder?"

"To me it doesn't look like a ladder at all. I don't know how a man can step up."

"Now did you take this ladder in your automobile or any automobile from the Bronx and convey it to Hopewell, New Jersey?"

"I never transported a ladder in my car."

He went on to deny having anything to do with the construction of the ladder as Wilentz cross-examined him, with Wilentz even raising his voice numerous times in an effort to rattle the accused.

"The first time you built a ladder, you don't build a good one, do you?" he asked bluntly.

"I never build a ladder," Hauptmann replied, refusing to buckle.

During his opportunity to address his client again, Reilly discussed the plane and chisel evidence put forth by Koehler. "Now they have brought into court here and exhibited a large plane. Is this your plane?"

"That's my plane."

"How long before your arrest had you used this plane?"

"This plane was never used since [19]'28."

"And are there any chisels missing from this [tool] box?"

"There are three Stanley chisels missing, them chisels they are no good at all, they were laying in the garage. But the Stanley set, good chisels, but I see it disappeared."

"When did you last see them in that box?"

"I would say a couple days before I get arrested."

Wilentz's cross-examination was ruthless, with the lawyer at times shouting at Hauptmann in an effort to break him. In one moment, he showed Hauptmann sketches of a ladder and window in the defendant's own notebook. Hauptmann denied he had drawn them and yelled back at Wilentz, "Stop that!" as the attorney general pressed on witheringly.

The defense team knew somehow they had to poke holes in the ladder evidence, and to get there they would have to create doubt in Koehler. They had their work cut out for them. The wood scientist's testimony had made him a celebrity. He was the subject of a *Ripley's Believe or Not* strip that focused on how his name was thirteen letters just like David T. Wilentz, Edward J. Reilly, Lindbergh baby, and Hauptmann Case. He was the focus of a *New York Evening Journal* cartoon showing him with a 2x4 and the caption, "You can get by as a big shot here in Flemington now just by carrying around a chunk of wood and a serious look."

Pope pulled Koehler aside on February 1, before putting any witnesses on the stand to challenge him directly, and said, "I don't want to flatter you, but in my 30 years of experience, [your testimony] is the best piece of work I ever saw."

Still, they had a client to defend. They first called Erastus Mead Hudson, who had done the fingerprint analysis on the ladder and found none matching Hauptmann. However, more importantly for the defendant, Hudson also testified that when he was testing the ladder for prints, he did not remember there being four nail holes in Rail 16. He testified that to the best of his knowledge, there had been only one nail hole in that rail.

The implication was that the evidence had been planted by police, the original Rail 16 replaced by one that matched a board from the attic. However, on cross-examination, Wilentz would get Hudson to acknowledge the rail he was studying in court, number 16, was the same one he had originally inspected for fingerprints, not a different board altogether. Pope objected, saying Wilentz had "confused the witness with a shrewd question," but Trenchard overruled him.

The next defense witness designed to poke a hole in Koehler's testimony was Stanley Seal, a wood pattern maker for the Foran Foundry in Flemington. He was called to discuss nicks and marks a plane can make depending on the angle at which it is held. He was not as well versed on the topic as Pope would have liked.

"Now, from your experience as a woodworker, is it possible to recognize with any degree of certainty the markings of a plane bit upon a piece of wood?" Pope asked him.

"I don't know," Seal replied.

"And trace it from the wood to that particular plane bit?"

"I don't know," he answered again.

Once again turning Trenchard's bench into an improvised workshop, Seal planed a board's edge, first using the plane "parallel with the edge of the board" and then running it "on an angle." The side planed on an angle was labeled with an *A* and the one planed straight with an *S*.

There was a difference in the markings on each side. Pope's point was to show that planer marks are not as distinctive as human fingerprints.

Defense witness Charles DeBisschop came from Waterbury, Connecticut, because he was convinced Koehler was talking nonsense. He'd been around trees and lumber in some capacity or another for thirty years, since William McKinley was president at the end of the nineteenth century. He told the court that he hadn't read any books on the topic of wood identification, but he subscribed to *Farm & Forestry* magazine.

He said he had spent "about pretty nearly every night and Sunday," matching up grains of birch, bird's eye maple, and North Carolina pine for cabinetmakers and others.

"There isn't hardly a day gone by but what somebody wants a piece of wood to match something that they broke," he told the court.

He showed the jury two boards, one purportedly from Connecticut and the other from Massachusetts, and showed that despite the fact they were from different trees, he believed the grain in the two pieces of lumber matched. He testified that one was forty-seven years old and the other was eight years old and yet, in his view, they matched.

Wilentz and Pope fought over whether DeBisschop should be considered an expert witness.

"We don't say that the gentlemen hasn't handled and dealt

with lumber and that he doesn't deal in lumber pretty nearly every day," Wilentz said, "but we feel that he hasn't the technical knowledge to qualify as an expert."

Pope countered, "Well, that depends upon what you mean by 'as an expert.' I didn't think that even the State's great witness qualified as an expert." Even though he had expressed his admiration privately to Koehler, publicly he had a job to do that required defending his client to the best of his abilities.

They settled on calling DeBisschop a "practical man," rather than a technical expert. Pope had him on the stand because DeBisschop said that, practically speaking, there was no way the attic board matched Rail 16 from the kidnap ladder.

"I would say they are [from] an entirely different board," he testified.

His testimony fell somewhat flat, though, when he was asked more about the two boards matching and looked over at Koehler, who was sitting at the prosecution table, and asked him, "This is the way it is supposed to be matched isn't it? Is that the way they are supposed to be matched? Which is the top? Which is the top here?"

Trenchard admonished the defense witness not to ask questions. "He ought to answer questions," the judge said. Reporters noted that juror number 2, Rosie Pill, "shook with mirth" after that exchange.

Koehler said later to his wife that the practical lumberman "seemed willing to say anything." But he wondered, "Just the same, the question is or was, what effect will the testimony of this 'practical man' have with a jury composed of ordinary, country village folk?"

Fisher told reporters afterward that Hauptmann was more impressed with DeBisschop than he was with Koehler. The defendant told Fisher, "any man who works for thirty years in the wood business has got more brains in his head than a man from Washington."

The final defense witness related to the ladder was Ewald Mielk, who had been a carpenter and millwright by trade for more than forty years. He too described himself as a practical lumber man without formal training in wood identification.

Mielk was called to dispute the notion that State's Exhibit S-226, the board from the attic, and Rail 16 were the same board. He explained that he believed this because S-226 was far darker than the upright from the kidnap ladder, and thus it showed more life than Rail 16.

"Look at these boards and in view of the fact that you have stated that there is more life in the one board, known as the attic board, than there is in the board known as the ladder rail, that there is a difference in the kind, the size and the spacing of the knots and there is a difference in the grain colors, can you as a practical wood man, tell this jury whether they ever were, in fact, a part of the same board?" Pope asked.

"They are not," he answered.

Under cross-examination from Wilentz, Mielk conceded the extent of his investigation of the ladder and S-226 consisted of "possibly five minutes" spent looking at the two pieces of wood the day before. Further, he acknowledged he did not know the impact of the chemicals used in fingerprint gathering on wood. Koehler had testified that the silver nitrate had stained the wood in question.

Koehler was called as a rebuttal witness and resumed the oath he'd taken earlier. He methodically and, as James Kilgallen from the International News Service reported, "in his cool, unemotional way" went to work debunking the defense's claims.

First, in relation to Seal, the man who had planed the board straight up and down and at an angle for the jury, Koehler said the markings from the edge marked S were "identical to marks found in the wood of the kidnap ladder."

Second, he said the two pieces of wood DeBisschop had brought, allegedly from Massachusetts and Connecticut and of vastly different ages, were once part of the same board.

"Those two boards were at one time part of the same board for a number of reasons," he said as DeBisschop "twisted nervously" in his seat, reporters noted. "In the first place the pattern or the groove produced in the middle of these two boards is in identically the same place and of the same depth and width as can be demonstrated very simply by putting these two boards together, one on top of the other with the edges corresponding and then that center bead corresponds exactly.

"Having the edges of the two boards parallel," he said, once again demonstrating before the jury, "you can see that the center bead in the two boards is in exactly the same place; also the middle bead is in exactly the same place and you can see that better by close inspection."

He went on to point out that DeBisschop had said a board had five annual growth rings in it when in reality it had six. He also stated that wood defined by the Connecticut lumberman as "yellow pine" was actually white pine.

As it related to the number of nail holes in Rail 16, Koehler said there were four nail holes in the ladder upright and that he had measured the distance between them and marked it down in his notebook more than a year before Hauptmann was arrested.

Finally, Wilentz asked bluntly once again, "Do you still say that the attic board and the rail were once the same board?"

"Yes."

On Saturday, February 9, the twenty-ninth day of the trial of the century, both the defense and the prosecution would rest. Between them they had called 146 witnesses. Closing statements would be given the following Monday in front of a courtroom as crowded as it had ever been throughout the trial. Reilly had a crew in from Brooklyn sitting in special seats to the left of Trenchard.

Koehler ended up on the windowsill to the right of the jury.

Hunterdon County Prosecutor Hauck delivered the initial message for the state, complimenting in the process the wood scientist whom he said had delivered "the most wonderful" testimony he'd ever heard.

"A year and a half before anyone had ever heard of Bruno Richard Hauptmann," he said, "Koehler traced the kidnap ladder lumber to a lumber yard in the Bronx where Hauptmann worked. And after Hauptmann was arrested he found that one of the ladder rails came from the very attic of the house where Hauptmann lived.

"But that wasn't all he showed you. He showed you that this defendant Bruno Richard Hauptmann had a plane and that he planed the rungs of the ladder with that plane. He showed you that the chisel used in making the ladder was the same size chisel that was missing from the tool chest of Bruno Richard Hauptmann."

He concluded by shouting and pointing his finger at Hauptmann, "Oh, there is plenty of evidence here that cries Hauptmann, Hauptmann, Hauptmann. Plenty of evidence to justify my request that you convict Bruno Richard Hauptmann of first degree murder."

If Reilly had been "a heavy, listless lawyer" throughout the trial, as some in the media had alleged, he morphed into a "brilliant advocate in the midst of the legal battle of his life" during his closing statement. Speaking from midmorning until dusk and without consulting notes, documents, or testimony transcript, he never once "groped for a word or a fact," according to reporters.

He began with a copy of the Bible in his hand. Walking over to the jury box, he said conversationally,

> I want to give you a text. It is "Judge not lest ye be judged."
>
> Perhaps after hearing the distinguished prosecutor, you feel that this defendant must prove his innocence. That is not the case. The State must prove his guilt and I want you to carry that thought with you into the sanctity of your jury room.
>
> You are big enough not to be swayed by the wealth and prominence of the family involved. You are big enough not to be swayed by the fact that this defendant is a poor German carpenter. Justice demands that the still voice of your conscience be given full freedom to decide this case.

If the beginning of his remarks were thoughtful, what came next was explosive. Reilly accused three of Lindbergh's household staff of being involved in the crime. "Colonel Lindbergh was stabbed in the back by the disloyalty of his servants," he said.

He attacked the prosecution's eyewitnesses for being old, for being glory-hounds, for being wrong. He said there was not enough evidence to convict on a murder or kidnapping charge. "Don't send this man away because ransom money was found on him," he said. "That is a charge of extortion, not murder. Let New York prove that. . . .

"Circumstantial evidence is no evidence."

But his main contention was that his client had been set up. The four nail holes had been put there by Bornmann, he said, who had swapped out the original Rail 16. The ladder "was a plant, and nobody went up that ladder that night, if it was ever up against the house." The police wrote Condon's phone number on Hauptmann's closet door. They stole his Stanley chisels, including the ¾-inch one.

"It is the most outstanding example of police crookedness in my career," he said.

As Arthur Koehler sat on the windowsill in the courtroom, he knew he would not be spared. Reilly wagged his finger at him and spared him no quarter, calling him a fake and "a lumber cruiser."

"I don't see how he can sleep nights after giving testimony like that with a man on trial for his life," Reilly thundered.

Do you suppose the board used in the ladder was ever taken out of any attic floor? Examine it carefully. It doesn't bear a mark from any hammer. But Mr. Koehler comes in and here we are again with expert evidence as opposed to horse sense and he would have you believe that the carpenter, Hauptmann, building a ladder for kidnap purposes, with a lumber yard around the corner, with lumber in his basement, crawled up into the attic and tears out a board for the ladder.

Here we have billions and billions of feet of lumber down in South Carolina and Koehler has the nerve to come in here and say there are no two alike, like fingerprints I suppose.

"I'll stake DeBisschop, the lumberman from old Connecticut, against Koehler any time," he shouted.

That's the good old common theory of hearsay against expert evidence. Can you believe that, with billions of feet of lumber being put out each year, that there could never be two boards alike? DeBisschop took a board 47 years old and one 8 years old and showed you they were alike.

So Koehler, testifying for glory, vanity, preferment, advancement, goes back on the stand and says that DeBisschop's two boards were also the same. He was afraid otherwise to go back to face the laughter of his fellows in Washington.

Reilly went on for hours, finally wrapping up simply by saying, "I believe this man is innocent."

With that, Wilentz would offer the closing summation for the state, a three-hour wrap-up that included a vigorous defense of all Reilly had attacked, including Koehler. He dared anyone to "find a blemish on the reputation" of the Madison scientist.

"Arthur Koehler," Wilentz said, "who has spent his life on this sort of thing, must have been ambitious for advancement. The man who one and a half years before Hauptmann was arrested traced the lumber to a Bronx lumber yard.

"What is there in life for Koehler? He's at the top of the heap in government service. But he's got to be assassinated in this scheme to free Hauptmann."

Koehler thought he was masterful. "Just imagine him at his best," he wrote Ethelyn. "Not too emotional, but sincere enough to strike the table with his fist once in a while."

No sooner had Wilentz completed his closing summary when a New Jersey pastor, Reverend Vincent Godfrey Burns, cried out, "A man confessed this crime to me in my church." He was immediately hustled out of the courtroom. That night, the picture of the New Jersey State troopers pulling him was on the front pages of newspapers around the country.

Burns had told both Reilly and Wilentz in the past that a man who came to his church on Palm Sunday, March 20, 1932, told him he had kidnapped and murdered Charles A. Lindbergh Jr. Both Reilly and Wilentz had thought him mad. Trenchard ordered the jury to ignore what they had just heard.

"By a strange series of coincidences it seems that I was fated to play some part in the Lindbergh kidnapping case," Burns later wrote.

After all, he had studied under the minister who married the Lindberghs, gone to school with Bronx District Attorney Tom Foley, and served in a church built by John Condon's son-in-law. Coincidentally, Burns also had a direct connection with Koehler. His "dear friend" John Brown Cuno, who had served as the best man at Burns's wedding, worked with Koehler in the initial part of the investigation.

At 11:21 AM on Wednesday, February 13, after forty-two days of hearing testimony and being secluded from their family and friends, the jurors returned to their room to deliberate. They would vote five separate times to decide Hauptmann's fate.

"Bitter argument, tears, semi-hysteria and exhaustion following in rapid succession," reported the *International News*.

While the world waited, the courtroom was transformed into a waiting room, as newspaper writers, lawyers, and spectators were "talking, laughing, reading newspapers, eating sandwiches, drinking coffee. The floor was littered with piles of newspaper and torn pieces of paper," reported the Associated Press. "The air was full of smoke. The place was hot, stuffy, growing unbearable.

"The apathy was suddenly disrupted by the sheriff."

Since it had been built, the Hunterdon County Courthouse had rung a bell to announce to its community that a verdict had been reached. Held in an octagonal, gold-leafed cupola, the bell was located toward the front of the roof just behind the portico. Designed to call local politicians back to their meetings after lunch, it also rang when justice was ready to be dispensed.

On the night of February 13, Undersheriff A. K. "Barry" Barrowcliff was in charge of ringing that bell when the jury had reached a verdict.

"Barry," the sheriff shouted in the courtroom, startling those in attendance. "Barry!"

"Spectators jumped to their feet," the AP continued, "their eyes following the chubby little man as he pushed his way excitedly through the jam in the aisle."

Wilentz arrived, as did Schwarzkopf and Lamb. They closed the doors. Reilly stood at attention. The room was quiet.

And then, at 10:25 PM, they heard the bell. The whole town heard it. Damon Runyon wrote that it "sounds like a church bell tolling a funeral service. The sound carried far out over the Jersey uplands." Anna Hauptmann was listening for that sound at the Flemington home she was staying at before rushing back to her husband's side.

A rush went through a crowd, estimated at more than seven thousand people who'd gathered for the verdict. "A mob," Runyon called it that "begins yelling. The faces of the men and women milling before the colonial pillars of the ancient building appear ghastly in the brilliant glare of the flares" set up for the photographers in attendance.

Eleven hours, thirteen minutes, and five ballots later, the jury returned to the courtroom at 10:34 PM. They were grave faced.

"Let the defendant stand," Trenchard said.

"Members of the jury, have you agreed upon your verdict?" asked the court clerk.

"We have," they said collectively before Charles Walton, their foreman, spoke for them.

"Mr. Foreman, what say you? Do you find the defendant guilty or not guilty?"

"Guilty," Walton said, stammering and shaking. "We find the defendant, Bruno Richard Hauptmann, guilty of murder in the first degree."

Reilly insisted they be polled individually. Each one asked for their verdict. Each one responded, "Guilty of murder in the first degree."

"There is nothing left for me," Anna Hauptmann cried out.

Trenchard moved to sentence Hauptmann immediately.

"Bruno Richard Hauptmann, you have been convicted of murder in the first degree," he said. "The sentence of the court is that you, the said Bruno Richard Hauptmann, suffer death at the time and place and in the manner provided by law."

That manner would be the electric chair. He set an execution date for some time during the week of March 18, just four weeks later.

Reporters swarmed when court adjourned. Everyone associated with the case was asked their thoughts.

Koehler simply said, "I've been working on this case for two years. I am glad it is over. I wish it had not been necessary."

The jurors would be offered vaudeville opportunities to share their stories on stages around the country for significant amounts of money. They chose instead to share their thoughts with specific reporters and media outlets. Many of them said it was Arthur Koehler who sealed the prosecution's case.

"The most brilliant performances in the witness chair should be credited to the handwriting experts and the wood specialist," said Walton to the *Los Angeles Times* for an article featuring all of the jurors on "How Hauptmann Was Convicted." "Their testimony was a treat to the jury."

Juror number 12, Howard Biggs, who had sat next to Liscom Case and listened to his thoughts on the wood evidence throughout, said, "The testimony and evidence conclusively damning of Hauptmann—probably the deciding factor in the verdict we are to give—were the testimony and evidence presented by Koehler, the wood expert."

The media covering the trial knew Case would compliment Koehler. His body language showed it throughout the trial. Indeed, Case explained what he had told his fellow jurors during their deliberation.

"Arthur Koehler showed a wonderful knowledge of trees and wood," Case said. "He knew a stick of wood when he saw one and, more than two years before Hauptmann was even suspected, he traced that ladder to the Bronx.

The ladder was made of a variety of woods. Through forests, lumber camps, sawmills and freight yards, Mr. Koehler followed those sticks. . . .

I looked at all these exhibits with a lot of interest. It was in my line. In contrast with Koehler and his clear story, there was a defense witness named DeBisschop whose testimony might have befuddled us. He brought in a number of samples of wood he said were thirty years older than the ladder rail. They looked as though they had all been cut from the same stock. What Mr. DeBisschop was trying to prove was that all lumber looks alike. But Mr. Koehler's reasoning had given us a different impression. . . .

My summing up will be simple. Hauptmann was in court because he was caught with a lot of the ransom money. The handwriting evidence, presented by men we could see were honest and sincere, left us no doubt as to his connection with the ransom notes.

Then came the wood story. Wood in a Bronx lumber yard got into the ladder found at Col. Lindbergh's home in Hopewell.

Hauptmann had worked in that lumber yard. Hauptmann had bought wood from that lumber yard. Pieces of it turned up in the ladder. Wood in the ladder proved to have come from the attic of the house in which Hauptmann lived.

Can you blame us twelve jurors for our verdict?

In the not-too-distant future, the governor of New Jersey would do just that.

12

In the weeks and months after Bruno Hauptmann's conviction, praise for Arthur Koehler flowed in from all over America.

Agriculture Secretary Henry A. Wallace prepared a memo for President Franklin Delano Roosevelt alerting him about Koehler's "many months of resourceful work" that led to Hauptmann's conviction. Colonel Breckinridge, Lindbergh's personal attorney, wrote to Koehler, "With the successful termination of the Hauptmann trial there stands out in bold relief the dramatic consequences of your splendid work. I think you have written one of the most interesting chapters in the history of jurisprudence."

Attorney General Wilentz sent Forest Products Lab director Carlisle Winslow a letter calling Koehler "a delightful man, able and willing to work at all hours" and calling his testimony "one of the main factors that contributed to the victory for the State."

But what moved Koehler even more were the comments from his professional peers and from average Americans whose knowledge of wood and trees, he hoped, was greater as a result of his testimony and public discussion about it. Axel H. Oxholm, who ran the Forest Products Division at the Department of Commerce, congratulated him on the "splendid publicity which you secured for the Forest Products Laboratory, or perhaps I should say for the cause of forestry? Everyone interested in the Lindbergh case has also been given a course in wood technology by reading your testimony and this has been of inestimable value in creating an interest in forestry research."

H. S. Betts with the US Forest Service, who had examined the ladder just a couple of months after the kidnapping, sent Koehler a note telling him that "the average American knows more about wood than he has for some time," courtesy of his work.

H. P. Brown, a professor of wood technology at the New York State College of Forestry at Syracuse University, said it "was a splendid task to bring home to the public a knowledge of what wood technology really is."

Professor E. Fritz at the University of California–Berkeley College of Agriculture told Koehler he thought his work tracking Rails 12 and 13 was his "greatest piece of detective work" and added jokingly that, as Koehler's fame spread, "the rest of us poor wood technologists must be content to bask in your reflected light."

Samuel Record, a professor at the Yale University School of Forestry, said Koehler's research and testimony were "a masterpiece. I know of no one else with the requisite combination of training, experience, skill and determination. You certainly were the right man for the job. From now on no attorney can claim that 'There ain't no such animal as a wood expert.'

"We have got to bring that realization home to other folks. . . . The methods to be employed are those you have used with such telling force—a grasp of the problem, a realization of its possibilities and indefatigable following through."

If the correspondence coming into Koehler's office at the lab was any indication, "other folks" were indeed making that realization.

From Koehler's home state of Wisconsin came a letter from Alice Carroll, who explained, "There had always been a doubt in my mind as to just how guilty Hauptmann was, but after hearing your testimony I am fully convinced that he got all that was coming to him."

"One reads occasionally of an individual citizen rising to shoulder a great burden with ease and honor and dignity. So it is with you," wrote Henry J. Schwenk, who worked for the power company in St. Louis. "I write as one of the countless thousands of Americans who appreciate your effort in our behalf."

A *Saturday Evening Post* article called "Who Made That Ladder?" and featuring an interview with Koehler was read by more than three million Americans, leading to even more plaudits coming his way. The lengthy article, running over seven pages in the magazine, allowed him to wax poetic about his work and his passion for the outdoors as he described his efforts tracking Rails 12 and 13 in the Hauptmann case:

> I love the forests, and so I often think of those Americans who came first beyond the seaboard and kept alive by reading the all-important signs of deer or bear or hostile Indians, printed ever so faintly on the soft floor of the wilderness. But just the same, and with, indeed, precisely the same instincts, some among us who have come long after them must learn to read and understand the machines from which we eke a living, make shelters and defend ourselves.

If Koehler in court was more academic in his tone, the Koehler in the popular magazine was far more rhetorical. "I felt sure," he said, "that the ladder's maker who thought himself so rich in cunning did not know [that] I kept on working, day by day and often late at night. . . . Looking backward now, I do not see just how I mustered patience for the job that lay ahead. How to chart a pinwheel's flaming circles would seem, at first, as simple as the thing I had to do. . . .

"Remember, I never hunted Hauptmann. The fellow that I sought was just a man who made a ladder."

The article "was better reading than the best fictional detective story," wrote the manager of the Cleveland, Ohio, Lumber Institute.

"I believe [your work] more than any other evidence convicted Hauptmann," wrote W. O. Appelquist from Libby, Montana. And B. A. Porter from Memphis wrote, "Had I been on the Hauptmann jury and the State had rested on your testimony alone, my verdict would have been guilty."

The story "aroused a great deal of interest and comment even in this rather remote district," wrote T. C. Emberg from Manitoba, Canada. Other letters came in from Edinburgh, Scotland, and from a chemistry professor in Amsterdam.

However, there remained critics of Koehler and skeptics of Hauptmann's guilt.

One man from Milwaukee who signed his letter as a "Free Mason!!" said the idea that Hauptmann built the ladder was "a dam stupid lie! The German carpenter is innocent, but you got the $10,000" —responding, no doubt, to reports after the verdict that the wood investigation had cost $10,000. In fact, other expert witnesses were paid, but Koehler was not; he received nothing more than his government salary during the entire investigation. He wrote in pen at the bottom of this letter, "I did not!" and signed it with his initials, placing it in a file at the lab.

A. G. Kent from Tampa wrote, "There was another carpenter (a Nazarene) almost two thousand years ago, who was tried and framed and (altho innocent) the people cried out all the more— 'Crucify him, crucify him. . . . ' We feel sure that he was framed."

The most prominent critic of Koehler, however, would be New Jersey Governor Harold Hoffman. As Hauptmann's appeals continued to be denied at all levels throughout 1935, including by the US Supreme Court, Hoffman's belief that Hauptmann had had an accomplice grew.

Born in South Amboy, New Jersey, Harold Hoffman was writing a weekly newspaper column on fishing at the age of twelve. After high school, he became a police reporter and later sports editor of the *Perth Amboy Evening News* across the Raritan River from where he grew up.

He enlisted in the army during World War I as a private, gaining numerous promotions for his fighting north of Verdun in France. He would leave the service as a captain of infantry and return to his hometown for a career in banking before getting into politics. He was elected city treasurer, then mayor at age twenty-nine, and a year later he embarked on a campaign for Congress. After two successive terms there he returned to New Jersey to run the state Department of Motor Vehicles, cracking down on drunk driving and becoming one of the nation's most prominent advocates for highway safety.

At five-foot-seven and at least 210 pounds, Hoffman was described by reporters as a "jolly fat man." His frequent invitations to dinners around New Jersey led to even higher readings on the scales and higher ratings in the polls.

There was no question Hoffman was built for politics, it was in his DNA. The comedian Joe Laurie Jr., a friend of Hoffman's, once wrote, "At the age of two, he passed a lead quarter to the family doctor. When he was seven, a gang of burglars held him up and he came out with a fine set of burglar tools and two gold watches. It was then his folks knew he was going to be a politician. And when at the age of eight he started learning the 3-Rs, his version was 'This is Ours, that is Ours, everything is ours.' Then, his parents were sure he was going to be a Jersey politician."

Hoffman ran for governor in 1934, and in a year when Democrats swept through his state, he had been successful. He was sworn in days after the Hauptmann trial had begun, and his first official act as governor was to renew the term of Justice Trenchard, which was set to expire in the middle of January. But Hoffman's popularity waned in 1935 after he pushed through New Jersey's first sales tax in the middle of the Depression despite opposition from his political party. It didn't matter that the legislation called for the 2 percent rate to expire in 1938, the political damage had been done.

Hoffman's outspoken nature may have served him well in campaigns, but when it came to Hauptmann, the public didn't understand. The governor granted Hauptmann a stay in his execution date, originally set for the week of March 18, 1935, and then delayed further by the state's highest appellate court, because he believed Hauptmann hadn't acted alone and shouldn't be killed until everyone involved was brought to justice.

Hoffman asked J. Edgar Hoover and the Federal Bureau of Investigation to reopen the investigation. He hired a detective in the fall of 1935 from a neighboring county to investigate the case.

"I insist, and I believe that there are hundreds of thousands of people in this country who share my opinion," he later wrote in a series of articles for *Liberty Magazine*, "that the kidnap and murder of the Lindbergh baby could not possibly have been a 'one-man job.'" He continued,

> There were confederates, either on the inside or the outside; and
> no child is safe tonight as long as there is alive a single person

who had a hand in this crime and who is being permitted to 'get away with it.'

It was said that I was casting [aspersions] upon 'Jersey justice.' I deny that! I wanted 'Jersey justice' to become just what the name implies; I did not want it to be 'Jersey injustice.'

I wanted, and still want, to be sure that all the participants in the crime and punished with equal vigor. I am not yet satisfied that we have done this.

Hoffman met with the convict in his cell in October 1935, at which point Hauptmann offered a passionate defense of his innocence and an equally passionate condemnation of the prosecution's case. Hoffman later told readers of *Liberty* that Hauptmann was "particularly bitter in his denunciation of Arthur Koehler."

He did not seem to think that there was anything particularly brilliant or impressive in Koehler's tracing of a shipment of lumber, cut in a certain way, to a retail lumber yard in the Bronx. Many hundreds of thousands of feet of lumber cut with the same saws or knives would be produced by the same mill, he argued. Koehler himself had traced many shipments of the lumber to different cities in the country. Hauptmann claimed that if a suspect had been held in any one of those cities, say Buffalo, Easton, Richmond, it could have been said that the lumber which was milled and planed in the same South Carolina mills had been traced to a retail lumber yard in the suspect's neighborhood.

"Vy vould the jury believe Koehler?" he quoted Hauptmann as saying,

"vhen he testified dot two pieces of lumber vhich vere given him in the courtroom vere from the same board? then ve show with Mr. DeBisschop, a fine witness, dot dey come from different places; von almost new—five or six years old—and the other from an old building nearly forty-seven years standing before it vas torn down. But vhen Koehler say dot two other pieces of board, von on the ladder and von vot they lie vas part of my attic floor are from the same board, he is believed. Vy?

"'I know vy!'" Hoffman continued.

Hauptmann had a far-away look in his eyes, although his thoughts were probably only a few feet away, upon the cloth-covered electric chair. . . . "It is because, even though a piece is missing dot must be supplied by the mind, dey vant to believe this von thing vhich vill help take my life. Because vhen my life may depend upon a mistake of Koehler's, dot is not important.

"Oh, no!" he concluded bitterly. "The poor child haf been kidnapped and murdered, so somebody must die for it. For is the parent not the great flyer? And if somebody does not die for the death of the child, den alvays the police vill be monkeys. So I am the one who is picked out to die. . . .

"Can any von honestly believe," he asked, "dot I, vorking many times as a carpenter, vould for two years haf a plane dot vould not be sharpened and vhich vould haf today the same nicks as it would haf two years ago. Besides, even the same blade of the plane vould make different marks vhen used by different people. But Koehler, he proves dot dis plane today, by different people, makes exactly the same marks dot it made vhen supposed to haf been used by me two years ago. The ladder has been taken apart many times and handled by many people. It must be shown dot I vas not always in the Bronx, but at Hopewell—so some von, maybe the police, might run my plane on the ladder rails."

This idea of planted evidence, first introduced by Reilly during the trial, gained credibility with Hoffman. His suspicions were magnified by correspondence he received from "concerned citizens" who felt Hauptmann was innocent. People questioned Koehler's testimony on the planing, on the chisel, and on the matching of Rail 16 to the Hauptmann attic board.

"I cannot understand how Mr. Koehler could positively be certain of these facts which might be the means of condemning a man to death," wrote Hugo Herfurth, the president of a general contracting company in Washington, DC.

Roy Knabenshue, who worked for the National Park Service, called Koehler's work "ninety per cent speculative" and said it "cannot be proven that he is correct. The writer is a carpenter by trade, had experience in a planing mill and also owned and operated a planing mill for years and thinks that Mr. Koehler is wrong when he says that he can identify a piece of wood by a dull knife in the planer head. I think he is also wrong when he says he can positively identify the board from the attic as being a part of the ladder."

Maybe Hoffman's closest counsel on the matter, though, was Arch Loney, a Department of Interior worker who was convinced that Koehler was wrong. "Don't become discouraged by caustic reaction as a result of your reprieve of Hauptmann," Loney wrote to Hoffman. "The case is abundant with inconsistent testimony. . . . I can help you on the ladder angle."

Koehler, meanwhile, had returned to his Madison laboratory after the trial ended to a bouquet of roses as a "welcome from members of his section." He spoke about the case two nights later at a dinner held by the lab for all staff members. More than two hundred people attended the event.

Condon and others were traveling the country telling their stories, but Koehler told the *Milwaukee Sentinel* upon returning to Madison, "I know I'm not going on the vaudeville stage."

Everyone wanted to know what he thought of the conviction, whether there was reasonable doubt, whether Hauptmann should have been sentenced to life imprisonment or death. To a person, Koehler told them, "I'd rather not say." However, when asked whether Hauptmann was involved, he was not at all hesitant.

"I am surer that the board in that ladder came from Hauptmann's attic than I would be if I had actually seen someone take a board from the attic and make a ladder," Koehler told the *Milwaukee Sentinel*. "When you take the evidence of the wood itself, there's no possibility of mistake. There's more chance for an eyewitness to be wrong."

His fame landed him spots in *Who's Who in America* and in *American Magazine*'s feature on "America's Most Interesting People," where it was declared "he can track down a toothpick to the very forest it came from. . . . He can tell you if your favorite pipe's genuine brier, and where it came from: France, Scotland, or Timbuctoo."

He was invited to speak to Lions, Kiwanis, and Rotary Clubs around Wisconsin and the occasional out-of-town address as well, like the speech he gave to a crowd of more than five hundred people at the Baltimore Criminal Justice Commission in May 1935. Unlike others involved in the case, Koehler did not get rich as a result. As he told his brothers, he got "a lot of free meals—and the Laboratory got some publicity which is the chief reason for giving the talks."

His biggest financial reward came from the *Saturday Evening Post* article, for which he was paid $738.46. Besides that, his financial ledger shows he made $240.40 talking about his role in the case, including $10 for an appearance in front of the Elkhorn, Wisconsin, Kiwanis Club.

Koehler had a net savings of $2,043.67 in 1934 and $1,293.18 in 1935. The drop was attributed to a trip he and Ethelyn took to Europe from August 21 to October 11, 1935, in part so he could attend a conference in Amsterdam of the International Association of Wood Anatomists and serve as a delegate to the International Botanical Congress.

While Arthur and Ethelyn were in Europe, Ethelyn's brother, E. Cadwallader "Caddy" Smith, and his wife, Alice, stayed with the two younger Koehler children, seventeen-year-old Ruth and five-year-old George, and experienced a scary moment in the process. On September 30, George cried out in the middle of the night, claiming someone was in his room. His bedroom had a door that opened out onto a deck that was the roof of a ground-floor porch.

"Now that our responsibility is nearly over, guess I might as well tell of an experience we had a couple of weeks ago," Caddy wrote in a letter to Arthur and Ethelyn.

We knew it would worry you . . . so thot best not to tell of it before this. Well, two weeks ago Monday, Florence [the live-in maid] as usual went out on the 2nd floor deck to shake her dust mop. She specially noticed everything was O.K. then. The next morning the first thing she noticed was the storm door opening into George's room was open & swaying. She went right in George's room and found the inner door unlocked and his play house, which stood against the door, was shoved out at an angle about a foot.

Three times the eve before, after Geo was in bed, he cried out, and when Alice went to him he insisted he heard someone walking around, but Alice thot he was just imagining it. Well, we called the police & they sent two men out. They looked everything over & said there was no doubt an attempt had been made to get in. We spoke of the thought that had been in our minds constantly ever since we had the responsibility of the children, that some pro-Hauptmann . . . out of revenge to Arthur, would try and snatch George.

The police agreed it was no joke, so ever since we have kept George in very close, and at night the police squad car keeps up guard. I nailed all the doors & windows tight, moved Geo and Ruth into front room & I have slept with a heavy cane side of our bed. We probably will never know just what it was all about, but it has been pretty exciting.

The start of 1936 found Koehler working his way through "things two years old" that had been buried on his desk while he focused solely on his business out east. The new year also brought a three-month stay of execution for Hauptmann, granted by Hoffman in his continued effort to find coconspirators. With no further action, Hauptmann would be put to death in early April.

Koehler was still publicly discussing his work in the Hauptmann case, even though "Hoffman raised so many doubts," he wrote to his brothers, and he gave talks to large audiences in Minneapolis, New York, Kansas City, and Detroit.

When the Koehler's home phone rang on Tuesday night, March 24, the family had just finished dinner. It was Colonel Schwarzkopf calling. He needed his wood expert in Trenton the following night.

Koehler packed a bag and immediately left to spend the night in Chicago. The next morning he left Chicago on an airplane at eight and landed in Detroit an hour and a half later. He boarded another plane and arrived in Newark after lunch, "a half-hour early."

"The weather was fine," he wrote Ethelyn, describing his flying experience, which relatively few Americans had experienced in 1936, "except the last half hour was a little bumpy and cloudy in spots below us. We were up 10,000 feet most of the time. We went through and over southern Canada and right over Niagara Falls. There was snow on the ground east and west of Buffalo and the rivers were high. Detroit was our only stop. I had breakfast and lunch in the air."

He was met by Detective Bornmann and Lieutenant Keaten and taken to Schwarzkopf's home in Lawrenceville, New Jersey. Wilentz was there too. They were talking about Governor Hoffman's latest actions regarding the Hauptmann case.

Roughly two months earlier when he had issued the stay of execution, Hoffman had ordered the New Jersey State Police to renew their investigation of the Lindbergh baby case, specifically to find Hauptmann's accomplice.

"I am not satisfied that the execution of Hauptmann will be a complete punishment for the crime," he had written in a letter to Schwarzkopf that announced his decision. "The ultimate fate of Hauptmann is almost the least important feature of this case. There is evidence, ample evidence, that other persons participated in the crime and there is absolutely no reason why our law enforcement agencies should regard this case as closed. . . .

"As Governor I direct you, with every resource at your command, to continue a thorough and impartial search for the detection and apprehension of every person connected with this crime."

He laid out multiple questions about the case that he wanted answered, questions of John Condon, Charles Lindbergh, and the authorities. As a member of the New Jersey Board of Pardons, Hoffman had Hauptmann's fate in his hands. He'd already stayed the execution once and was now seeking advice to see if legally he could do it again.

Hoffman demanded regular reports from his New Jersey State Police commander on the investigation's progress. Both Schwarzkopf and Wilentz were seething privately, but publicly they declined comment.

In a note dripping with disdain, Schwarzkopf wrote both NYPD Commissioner Joseph Valentine and J. Edgar Hoover at the Federal Bureau of Investigation that "in an effort to cooperate with his Excellency to the fullest extent, I am inclosing herewith a true copy of the Governor's letter together with the addenda for your perusal and consideration.

"It is respectfully requested that you again cooperate with me and my department and assist us in a coordinated and cooperative effort to carry out the Governor's instructions to me."

Schwarzkopf had gathered his team together to discuss the status of the case after receiving Hoffman's instructions. They agreed they had convicted the right man and that the governor was in essence a publicity hound, seeking to overturn the rightful conviction by a jury of twelve conscientious citizens.

The first report Schwarzkopf sent to Hoffman detailed that meeting and the letters he had sent to his peers in New York and Washington. He provided no specific answers to Hoffman's questions, only a renewed declaration that Hauptmann was guilty. Schwarzkopf's letter was met with anger, as the governor insisted its contents had been leaked to the media before he had a chance to review it.

"I am not interested in receiving further weekly reports simply indicating that the usual conferences are being held," Hoffman wrote in a letter back Schwarzkopf. "If you feel that the Lindbergh case has been completely solved and that no persons other than Hauptmann, now under sentence of death, were involved, it is your duty to so advise me, and to give your answers to the questions I submitted in my [earlier] letter. . . .

"The Lindbergh matter is quite generally referred to as 'the most bungled case in police history,' and it is to your interest and to the interest of all members of your organization, as well as in the public interest to work sincerely and effectively to bring about its complete solution."

The next correspondence between the two men came on March 23, when Hoffman requested that Schwarzkopf provide him access to Rail 16 for inspection and Bornmann for questioning at ten the following morning at the State Police Training Center. He instructed Schwarzkopf to inform Attorney General Wilentz, but no one else. The governor wanted "no publicity."

So that Tuesday morning, March 24, Bornmann, Keaten, and Schwarzkopf found themselves in a room at the training center with Hoffman, his secretary, a stenographer, and a private investigator named Leon Hoage. The sixty-year-old Hoage specialized in solving robberies and insurance cases before offering his services in writing to Hoffman in connection with this case. On the governor's request, Hoage had visited Hauptmann's attic a week and a half before to do some measuring himself.

Empowered by the state's chief executive, Hoage asked numerous questions of Bornmann regarding the condition of the Lindbergh nursery when he was the first officer on the scene on the night of March 1, 1932. They wanted to know whom Bornmann had seen, where he had found the ladder, and "if there'd been marks of a man's knee in the dust on the inside window ledge of the nursery window."

Bornmann said he "could not recall clearly the conditions exactly as I had found them that night" but told the men he was answering to the best of his knowledge.

Then Hoffman asked that the ladder and the attic floor board be brought into the room. As Bornmann would later write in his report, the governor and Hogue peppered him with more "questions about the board and the conditions under which I had first found it, who was present, the date, etc."

The governor was not satisfied with Bornmann's answers. He said he wanted to see the attic in person, to see the board's original position in the floor. He told the group he would make accommodations with the prosecutors to ensure that Rail 16 and the attic board would be brought to Hauptmann's former home in the Bronx and that he would have a stenographer present to take notes. Hoffman wanted to make this visit the following day, but on Schwarzkopf's request they were delayed until Thursday, March 26.

Hauptmann's execution was set for only eight days later, April 3, adding a layer of intensity to the proceedings.

That's what led Schwarzkopf to call Koehler. If the governor was going to challenge the wood evidence from the trial, the prosecution's wood expert —or "Wood Wizard," as he had been called by some reporters—should be there to explain it and defend it. Wilentz, though, wasn't sure that was the best strategy.

"[He] didn't know that [Schwarzkopf] had ordered me to come and didn't like it at first," Koehler wrote to Ethelyn. "He wanted to see what the Governor would pull off in the attic and then get me to come if desirable, but he changed his mind before the day was over and they were all glad I was there."

One of Hoffman's questions concerned Abraham Samuelsohn, who told New Jersey authorities a week after Hauptmann was arrested in 1934 that the accused had given him a "piece of drawing paper with measurements on it" in February 1932 and hired him to buy the lumber. Samuelsohn said a woman was with Hauptmann and that a few days later the lumber in question was picked up by two other men.

The New York cabinet shop owner said at the time the men picked up the wood, he asked them what "they were going to use the lumber for, and they said for a certain purpose." He told Corporal Samuel Leon with the New Jersey State Police that "he could identify this lumber by the grooves on the long pieces." When he was brought to the Police Training School in late September 1934, his story about the grooves changed, and now he "stated that he only put it on one or two." Further, he said the lumber had been recut since he sold it.

Leon was skeptical of Samuelsohn when he wrote up the interviews in his 1934 official report:

Mr. Samuelsohn's identification of the ladder was very vague, and that the marks which he identifies same from, were put there evidently, by the person who cut the notches in the sides to insert the rung, and that the marks which Mr. Samuelsohn told the investigator, he could identify the lumber by, previous to seeing the ladder, was not on the lumber. It is the opinion of the investigator that Mr. Samuelsohn is trying to seek notoriety in connection with this case. However, several pieces of lumber, which he claims were of the same board which the above strip was made from was obtained and sent to Mr.

Koehler at the Training School to be compared with that of the lumber in the ladder.

There is no record of Koehler having checked those samples. However, he remained convinced, more so than if he'd seen it with his own eyes, that the attic board and Rail 16 came from the same piece of wood.

As Koehler, Wilentz, and the others speculated as to the governor's true intentions the following day, Fulton Oursler, the editor of *Liberty* magazine, received a phone call at his Massachusetts home from Hoffman's secretary, William Conklin. Conklin told the editor that "the governor was about to fire his big gun in the Hauptmann case and would be able to prove conclusively that Hauptmann had been framed. It was the governor's earnest desire that [Oursler] come to New York at once to be present as the only representative of the press to witness this demonstration."

He and his wife immediately packed their bags to drive to New York.

At roughly 9:45 AM, cars began pulling up to Hauptmann's old home in the Bronx. Oursler's taxi got him there first. Hauptmann's lawyer, Lloyd Fisher, and Hoffman's press agent, George Maines, pulled up next. The next car held Wilentz, Hunterdon County Prosecutor Hauck, Bornmann, and Koehler. Another police vehicle brought Keaten and Captain Russell Snook. The last vehicle to arrive bore New Jersey license number 1 and Hoffman, his secretary, Loney, Hoage, and Professor Louis Hazeltine, a chemist at the Stevens Institute of Technology.

"No one at this time, except Governor Hoffman and Lloyd Fisher, had any idea what this meeting was called for," Oursler would later write. "I asked Fisher what to expect and he said: 'This is a shot that will be heard around the world. We have unmistakable evidence that the state has framed Hauptmann and that the evidence of rail sixteen is of absolutely no value whatsoever.'"

The men all headed into the narrow closet, up the four shelves arranged into steps, and through the small opening into the attic. When Loney, the first man up, broke the second shelf, Oursler said, "the steps in Hauptmann's ladders seem to have the habit of

This is the view from Hauptmann's attic, looking down into the closet and the shelves arranged into steps. Koehler returned there to face criticism from New Jersey Gov. Harold Hoffman, who believed the 16th Rail evidence was planted. (Courtesy: Dr. Regis Miller/Forest Products Laboratory)

breaking." Hoffman scowled at him. Seeing the rather rotund chief executive hoist himself through the hole in the ceiling, Oursler wrote, was a spectacle of "agility and celerity."

When the crowd was gathered in the attic, all fourteen of them, the plan of action became clear. Oursler had been invited because, while he believed that Hauptmann was guilty, he also thought Hoffman was justified in seeking to have his questions answered.

Wilentz was angry. He had known Hoffman since childhood. They had grown up in the same area and so when he addressed him, he didn't call him "Governor" or "Sir" or "His Excellency." He called him Harold, and that morning he wanted to call him some other names as well.

"I consider this an outrageous proceeding," he said. "I am here only to protect state troopers against intimidation. If you think that son-of-a-bitch Hauptmann is innocent, why don't you turn him loose? You are encouraging him in his son-of-a-bitch attitude of not confessing. He knows Governor Hoffman is his friend and is relying on the governor to keep him from paying the penalty of his crime."

Meanwhile, Loney and Hoage acted, Oursler wrote, "with a self-conscious truculence as if they were Sherlock Holmes twins about to disclose the secret of a great mystery."

At its tallest point, the attic ceiling was only six feet high, and it was hot in there. Standing up also ran the risk of being poked in the eye or face by one of the exposed and protruding nails. So everybody was either hunched over and sweating or sitting on a beam with perspiration and dust gathering on their suits.

"Well, they tried to find all kinds of faults," Koehler would later write Ethelyn, "but Bornmann and I knocked them over one by one."

Hoffman, "like a good showman," Koehler wrote his wife, had Oursler stand next to him to witness everything. The goal was to conclusively demonstrate that the attic board and Rail 16 were never one and the same and/or that the police had planted the attic board and then sawed off part of it before attaching it to the ladder. They believed Koehler's testimony "was unreliable guesswork and untrue in fact," Oursler wrote.

First, with the ladder rail in position over the nail holes, Hoage insisted that because Rail 16 was thinner than the attic board, they could not have been one and the same. Koehler said he was accurate, but diminished the fact's importance.

"The difference was not great," Koehler would later write in his report.

I suggested that the thickness of the two boards be measured not at the edges, because both edges of the board from which the ladder rail was cut were trimmed off, but more nearly between the two edges and preferably near the adjoining ends of the two boards. When measured there the rail was just a shade thinner. All of these differences are insignificant when it is considered that the lumber was low grade and therefore poorly dressed and not dry when dressed because it obviously had shrunk considerably after it was nailed down in the attic.

Consequently, slight variations in thickness would be expected due to uneven shrinkage.

After an hour of debate, the men continued to disagree.

Oursler said that Koehler was "appalled at the aura of antagonism surrounding him" and that Loney was a "bulldozing man who called Koehler an ignorant four-flushing son-of-a-bitch to me."

Loney wanted to know why the ladder rail was heartwood and the attic board from which it had been cut was sapwood. Koehler told him both were sapwood and showed him some boards in the attic that were heartwood and thus darker in appearance.

"He did not seem to be convinced," Koehler wrote in his report.

Then, Hoffman and Hoage pointed out that only one of the twenty-seven boards in the attic had any nails driven into it from the surface. Both the attic board and Rail 16 had surface nail holes. Their intimation was "that the cops, not being good carpenters, had ignorantly nailed down this fake board known as [State's Exhibit S-226] and also driven the holes through rail sixteen through the top because they did not know any better."

Koehler told him "this board undoubtedly was the first one laid and it had to be fastened securely so that the others could be driven against it." He told the group it was common practice for carpenters to nail down the first board with surface nails while other boards would subsequently have nails in their sides, so they could attach.

Hoage asked Koehler if he knew how many nails there were in the other boards.

"Now wait a minute," he said. "Don't look."

At that, Wilentz, who was sitting quietly and listening after having confronted Hoffman earlier, flew "into a rage," Oursler wrote.

"I want to know for Christ's sake who the hell you think you are," he shouted at Hoage. "I'll be goddamned if you're going to talk to Koehler that way. Who do you think you are to give him rules not to look? Who gave you the right to lay down rules here? Who are you anyway and what are you doing here?"

"I was only trying to—," Hoage responded before Wilentz cut him off.

"I don't give a goddman what you were going to do. I said before this was an outrageous proceeding but you're not going to talk to Professor Koehler [sic] that way because he doesn't have to stand for it and I'm not going to let him stand for it."

Hoage sat down next to Oursler and said, "I don't want discord, but he can kiss my ass."

Then Loney took up the case, pointing out that there were thirteen boards on each side of the attic ridgepole, a literal centerpoint for the room. He contended the twenty-seventh board, the one that constituted S-226 and Rail 16 "had been added . . . for the purpose of framing Hauptmann."

Koehler said "there was no reason why a rough floor in an attic should be centered," and that, regardless, "floors were not laid both ways from the middle but beginning at one side" and continuing until they were finished.

Another hour of debate over symmetry or lack thereof ended with continued disagreement.

Then the governor's group turned its focus to Bornmann. Loney stated openly that it "would have been impossible for [Bornmann] to have pulled the board up . . . without breaking the tongue." Koehler stood up for his partner in the investigation by stating that "many of the boards in the floor had shrunk enough so that the tongue was completely exposed."

Hoffman then pulled out a piece of cardboard, about 5x7 inches, attached to a thin wooden handle to prove his next point: that the shallow saw cut through the edge of the adjacent board to S-226 did not correspond with the cut made through S-226.

"The evidence seemed very convincing to Governor Hoffman," Oursler wrote. "It was utterly unconvincing to me. In days of manual training, I could never keep a saw straight under any circumstances and anyone knows that no matter how tightly the saw is held, it will wiggle one way or another."

They had been in that attic for roughly three hours, having kept the windows closed until only recently in an effort to keep the conversation confined to those in the room. A crowd of reporters had by that time gathered around the home, creating a sense of déjà vu for many of those who'd been there a year and a half earlier when Hauptmann had been arrested.

Hoffman had saved what he felt was his most compelling evidence for last.

"I want to say that I have never known a more dramatic moment than when this demonstration was made," Oursler wrote. "It seemed to make all these other preceding lesser matters more important."

Koehler described it as the governor and his group pulling "their biggest rabbit out of their hat."

Hoffman asked everyone to sit down. They had all removed their coats and vests and loosened their ties by now. He pointed out the importance of the nail holes found in Rail 16 and how they attached perfectly with the attic board when the original nails were produced.

"Gentlemen," he said, "the jury did not see this. The jury heard about it. But I have these original nails in my possession here and I want to fit them into these nail holes."

Koehler had done this very experiment himself back in October 1934. He had described the chances of being able to perfectly fit those four nails into Rail 16 and the attic board as a one in ten trillion chance.

He had declared that this wasn't a coincidence, as "there simply is not such a chance in human experience."

Hoffman had brought a bunch of little white sticks, the width of soda straws and cut to the length of the nails, and began dropping them into the nail holes. They should have gone in 1¾ inches. That's not what happened.

"They went in only one half an inch and there they stuck," Oursler recalled. "You couldn't make them go any farther."

Koehler didn't understand. His notes from those October visits to Hauptmann's attic clearly stated, "all nail holes in joists are 1¾ inches deep." He turned to Wilentz with a confused look and told him, "I had measured the holes originally and they were deep enough, and I had it right in my notebook."

"The answer seemed self-evident," Oursler wrote.

> The thing was framed and the police had not taken the trouble to drive the nails all the way. All they wanted was holes that would match in order to convince the jury.
>
> I have never seen such consternation in my life. Wilentz was pale and so was Hauck. There was no answer that could be made. There the thing was! The nails did not go into the holes. And thereby was demolished all the evidence that linked the ladder with Hauptmann's attic. The temperature in that room, which had seemed 120 degrees, suddenly felt like zero. I felt a chill down my back.

Wilentz found his voice and said the defense, which had controlled the attic for the last number of months, could have tampered with the boards. Behind his back, Loney and Hoage called Koehler a "son-of-a-bitch with every other breath" and said he was a laughingstock in the lumber industry.

Hoffman insisted Bornmann join him in the middle bedroom on the home's second floor, where he told him to confess that he had "framed the whole affair."

"I want you to tell the truth about that board," the governor said. "Do you still say that it was nailed down solid when you found it?"

"I told the truth," Bornmann said. "The board was nailed solid with the nails flush when I first saw it."

"For God's sake," Wilentz interjected, "if there's anything wrong up there that I don't know about, tell the Governor and let's get it over with."

Bornmann said there was nothing wrong and that he knew everything.

"I told the truth," he insisted, "and I wouldn't change it for no son of a bitch."

Hoffman continued, time after time, to say there was no way the board could have been nailed down. Bornmann kept responding that he had told the truth, "nothing but the truth and that I could pull the switch right now on Hauptmann with a clear conscience."

"Do you think the board was framed?" Wilentz asked Hoffman.

"Positively," the governor said.

Koehler, however, wasn't convinced, later writing in his official report that he "felt confident that Det. Bornmann would not have 'framed' the whole matter, and that he could not have done it without my detecting it if he had wanted to."

More important to the moment, he thought the nail holes were simply plugged up with wood shavings, the result of nails going in and out numerous times since he'd discovered the evidence on October 9 and 10, 1934. Hauck then suggested that parts of the joists containing the nail holes be cut out and split open to see if the holes ever were deeper than they now appeared.

Alfonso Maclario, a carpenter who lived on the next block, was summoned, and Oursler described it as "a groaning, horrible sound as those joists were sawn off." Hoffman and Hoage picked three of the joists for examination, and Bornmann picked another three. The question was where to go for that exam.

Koehler suggested Yale. Oursler said "that looked like a stall" to him, and he suggested Columbia. The journalist said Koehler "reluctantly consented."

The convoy of vehicles, with six pairs of joists and twelve nail holes in all, drove to the Manhattan campus of Columbia University. They went to the Michael Pupin Physics Laboratories, named for the nineteenth-century Serbian and Montenegrin immigrant who became an instructor of mathematical physics, developing on campus such things as rapid X-ray photography, secondary X-ray radiation, and sonar-related technology.

The building would later that decade be associated with the splitting of the atom that led to the creation of a nuclear weapon. Other research was taking place there in 1935, including that by George Pegram, the dean of Columbia's physics department, who was investigating the newly discovered neutron phenomena.

The entire crew walked through the doors to the Renaissance-inspired building constructed almost a decade earlier and into Pegram's office.

"He was interested but a little frightened that Columbia's name would be drawn into it," Oursler believed.

Pegram took them into a large laboratory and supplied them with an "iron blade, a chisel and two hammers." Then, he appointed Associate Professor Lincoln T. Work, who had been at Columbia in chemical engineering since receiving his graduate degree there in 1921, as an "independent observer."

With that, Koehler and Loney, each with a hammer in hand, took aim at the joists. The results in all but one of the twelve holes would completely exonerate Koehler and Bornmann.

"The most charitable explanation, and the one everyone seemed disposed to accept, was that nails had been put in and out of those holes so often during the investigation that they had rubbed enough so that dust from the sides was packed at the bottom one and a half inches to two inches in depth," Oursler wrote. "This substance had to be removed, but the full mark—the full shell of the nail hole—was painfully apparent.

"There was no doubt that one was as Koehler had represented it. The big cannon cracker had fizzled. It just wasn't so."

Koehler would over the next couple of days investigate the plugged material under the microscope and find it conclusively to be wood fibers. He wrote up what had happened in case Wilentz needed his account for the Board of Pardons set to meet about Hauptmann. He listed thirteen reasons he did not believe the evidence could have been planted. He wrote to Ethelyn that while he "did not make any slanderous remarks about the Governor, it

Koehler, Hoffman, and others took the boards from the ladder to Columbia University for further examination. Upon being split open, Koehler was vindicated as the nail holes were simply plugged up. (Courtesy: Dr. Regis Miller/Forest Products Laboratory)

wasn't exactly complimentary to him." He continued to his wife, "Well, what could he expect if he tries to make me out to be a liar." The whole experience was rather dramatic, he told his wife, as "Bornmann and I were both close to arrest some say but I would like to see [Hoffman] try it."

Koehler concluded his official report on March 30 by writing, "After this recent visit to Hauptmann's attic I am more than ever convinced that rail #16 came out of Hauptmann's attic."

Hoffman was not, saying what was found was "not conclusive." He accused the prosecutors of acting as "personal attorneys" for Bornmann and said he was "wondering at the sudden and jealous protection" of the ladder and floor boards from the attic.

Further, he said, "the whole case reeks with unfairness, passion and prejudice. I believe other persons were connected with the crime and that State police are making no honest effort to find them."

Still, he did not issue a second stay of execution. He had said he would not do so unless the attorney general consented, and that would not happen. Wilentz was quoted by reporters after the attic confrontation as saying Hoffman's detective work was "improper."

So on the night of April 3, 1936, the *Newark Evening News* reported,

> Bruno Richard Hauptmann, principal in the most celebrated criminal case in history, went to his death at State Prison last night in much the same manner as did the great majority of the 116 who have died in the same chair.
>
> The witnesses waited tensely in the small, brightly lighted execution chamber for fifteen minutes before the steel door to the death house opened. Flanked by prison guards and accompanied by his spiritual advisors, Hauptmann walked firmly and without hesitation to the chair. His eyes roved about the chamber and no detail seemed to escape his glance, his last on earth.
>
> Hauptmann uttered no last word. He remained mute from the time he entered the death chamber until the fatal current was applied. . . .
>
> It was exactly 47 minutes, 30 seconds, after 8 p.m., when he was pronounced dead.

A crowd outside the state prison erupted in cheers as a reporter shouted, "He's dying." When Hauptmann's body was removed in a hearse, it was closely followed by a car with a photographer on the roof trying to get pictures.

His spiritual advisors said his last few hours brought him peace. They reported that he remained consistent with his story about the case until the end, saying, "I repeat that I protest my innocence of the crime for which I am convicted."

Damon Runyon, back on the sports and Broadway beats, returned to New Jersey to finish the story he'd started at the beginning of 1935. The day after the execution he wrote a column entitled "Lest We Forget," designed to remind his readers about the evidence that had led to Hauptmann's conviction.

He walked his audience through the thousands of dollars of ransom money found in Hauptmann's garage, the defendant's handwriting samples that matched the ransom notes, the identifying testimony of Condon and Lindbergh, and, of course, the wood witness who had traced a rail from the kidnap ladder to a board in Hauptmann's attic and in the process captured Runyon's imagination.

"One Arthur Koehler, a woodsman who venerates wood, knows it from seed to flower and is one of the United States government's highly specialized experts. A pudgy, prosaic man, this Koehler, but what a story he told! He made new history in the science of criminology. They will be quoting him decades from now."

13

Thomas Maloney walked out of his home in Wilkes-Barre's Georgetown neighborhood to pick up the mail. It was Good Friday, April 10, 1936, just a week after the chaos in neighboring New Jersey had come to an end with the execution of Bruno Richard Hauptmann.

Maloney, a Catholic, was observing the holiday at home with his four-year-old son, Thomas Jr., and his sixteen-year-old daughter, Margaret, but he'd been home a lot lately. He had been laid off from his mining job a year earlier due to his efforts as president of the United Anthracite Mine Workers of Pennsylvania (UAMP), an organization set up to combat the perceived collusion between the United Mine Workers of America (UMW) and the coal companies.

The Wyoming Valley's history was written by the miners who extracted so much anthracite coal in the nineteenth century that Wilkes-Barre was nicknamed the Diamond City. In 1917, the region was producing 100 million tons of anthracite, but during the Great Depression, consumers went for cheaper energy sources like oil, electricity, and natural gas. By 1930, annual production had dropped 31 percent to 69 million tons.

The coal companies cut costs, which meant they cut shifts, and then they cut staff, usually the older miners who earned more. Anger grew, not just at the coal companies, who had also outsourced operations to nonunion companies, but at the union, which workers felt did not confront management appropriately.

Maloney, who was working for the Glen Alden Coal Company, had formed the rival union in 1933 and conducted numerous strikes over the next few years. When his union took on his employer, it lost an estimated $5 million, and Maloney lost his freedom when a judge ruled him in contempt of court after he defied an order to call off the strike. He had spent a month in jail, and when he got out, he was promptly fired.

The UMW was actively trying to resist its renegade counterpart, and Maloney didn't feel it was a battle he could win, so he dissolved his union. Now some of his members felt he too had sold out.

Inside the mailbox that day was a nicely wrapped package with the word *Sample* written on top. He sat at the kitchen table to open it with a penknife. Thomas Jr. and Margaret huddled close, eager to see if it was Easter candy. Their disappointment at seeing an expensive cigar box was counterbalanced by their father's happiness at the same sight.

He pried open the lid, tripping a tiny battery-operated circuit. The bomb inside detonated with a force so powerful it blew a hole through the back wall of his house. All three Maloneys were knocked unconscious. Father and son would eventually die from their injuries. Margaret Maloney would spend the next two months in the hospital.

Police had barely had time to respond to the Maloney's home when another nicely wrapped package was opened by Michael Gallagher, a sexton at Wilkes-Barre's St. Mary's Cemetery. He was killed and his son-in-law was critically injured.

Word got out immediately to the newspaper offices and radio stations. Extras and bulletins quickly spread the word not to open any packages delivered through the mail. Wilkes-Barre postal inspectors searched records and found six identical parcels were mailed in the city on Holy Thursday. One was caught at the post office before it could be delivered. Another one was intercepted by a letter carrier on his route.

That left two to be accounted for. One young man found a package delivered for his father and immediately doused it in water and called police. The final package, sent to a former sheriff, was opened, but the current short-circuited and the bomb did not explode.

Tips to the police from a cigar store clerk and witnesses who had seen a man around the mailbox on the date in question led authorities to arrest fifty-two-year-old Michael Fugmann, a former artilleryman in the German army who had deserted during World War I and after the war immigrated to Pennsylvania with his wife and child. He was a miner who had been part of Maloney's renegade union before it dissolved.

Fugmann insisted he had nothing to do with the bombs when he was questioned that summer. The evidence was circumstantial. The local police and the FBI noted that the cigar box was made of wood and samples had been recovered. The logical phone call to find help was to the man known nationwide as the Wood Wizard.

Koehler analyzed the wood samples and established that "the wood from four different bombs could be intermatched so as to show that they were made from the same pieces of wood."

Further, he'd discovered that

[t]wo pieces of wood from the defendant's home were of the same kind, method of manufacture (rotary-cut veneer), and one of them was of the same thickness as the partitions in the cigar-box bombs. The two pieces were of the same width as one of the reconstructed slats from which some of the bomb pieces were cut, and of the same length as two pieces which matched end to end from one of the bombs; they showed the same type of stapling at the ends, and then similar horizontal hand saw cuts at the ends which were not cut by a circular saw as did the pieces from the bombs.

When Koehler testified in the case that fall, Fugmann's lawyers moved to strike his testimony as conjecture, speculation not based on science. Like Justice Trenchard in neighboring New Jersey, the Pennsylvania court rejected that motion. Fugmann would be convicted and sentenced to die for his crimes.

"The evidence was not as positive as in the Hauptmann case," Koehler wrote his brothers, "but without [it] I doubt that he would have been convicted."

Koehler also was asked by the Federal Bureau of Investigation to help in the case of the abduction and murder of ten-year-old Charles Mattson in Tacoma, Washington. An earlier effort using a homemade ladder to kidnap a neighboring boy had been unsuccessful, but it led J. Edgar Hoover to contact Koehler for his help in the Mattson case. Koehler worked on tracing the ladder for three weeks before the authorities found out it had been taken from a vacant garage across the street from where it had been used in the unsuccessful kidnapping attempt. That case would never be solved. But Koehler's reputation would help solve other mysteries as the years progressed.

Wisconsin Deputy Fire Marshal William A. Greenwald credited Koehler with helping solve the arson of a vacant home in Sheboygan. Basswood chips were found in the basement of the house and also in an adjacent blacksmith shop. Koehler matched the samples, and Greenwald took that evidence into an interview with the homeowner. The newspaper headline the next day read, "Wood Chip Probe Brings Confession," with a picture of Koehler and the story of the arson solved.

The police chief in Fort Wayne, Indiana, sent him a piece of wood from a burglar alarm and a knife. The question was whether the knife had cut the wood. It left no marks on the sample, but Koehler found wood paint on the knife edge. That led to an indictment.

By and large, though, Koehler went back to his usual role as the federal government's chief wood identifier. He continued his work of going through thousands of samples each year, bolstering dreams and destroying grandiose visions in the process.

He helped a Wisconsin man prove that his old violin was a Stradivarius. As he peered through the microscope, Koehler "marveled at the exquisite finish of the wood, shading from orange to red, the secret of which Antonio Stradivari took with him to the grave," back in seventeenth century Italy. The musician would be very happy with that result.

Milwaukee Journal war correspondent Robert J. Doyle, who was with Wisconsin soldiers in the Trobriand Islands, off the eastern coast of Papua New Guinea, would end up with a less thrilling reply. The Wisconsin unit had seen "the ghostly skeleton of a ship strewn along the coral beach" and had visions of it having been sailed by Captain Cook or another famous explorer.

"The massive hand hewn keel, ribs and mast strewn along the beach stirred in the minds of the soldiers visions of treasure chests bulging with gold and precious gems hidden in some cavern by a one-eyed pirate when his ship was blown on a reef scores of years ago," Doyle wrote in the newspaper before sending samples to Koehler at the Madison laboratory.

Koehler's inspection proved that "ancient" wreckage had likely been there no more than a year. He identified the keel as a species of pine "of the botanical genus, *Agathis*," several species of which grew in the south Pacific. The mast was made of wood of the Dipterocrap family, which consisted of more than 380 species "confined almost exclusively to the Indo-Malayan region, but not including Australia or New Zealand."

The ribs of the ship confused Koehler, as they were made of balsa (*Ochroma lagopus*), which besides growing naturally only in the American tropics, was not a particularly strong wood, susceptible to decay. "The fact that the balsa wood does not show any advanced stage of decay indicates that the wreck could not have been there very long," Koehler wrote to Doyle.

Doyle would have to be satisfied with simply discovering a neat-looking ship. The final line of his article describing the experience and entitled "Wood Expert Wrecks Myth of Trobriands 'Pirate' Ship" read, "A great fellow, that Koehler. Don't try to pawn off the ship of some ancient mariner on him. He's too smart."

The scientist also dashed the hopes of New Orleans city leaders when a swimmer off Lake Pontchartrain stepped on a wooden shoe that had the date 1492 carved in its wood. Could that have been the first stop of Christopher Columbus as he discovered America?

They sent the shoe to Koehler and got a reality check.

The "shoe" wasn't really a shoe "but a hand-carved model of one." Further, "the wood was northern white pine, which grows much farther north than Columbus would have sailed."

Koehler enjoyed giving tours at the lab, sharing his knowledge and improving the general public's understanding and appreciation of wood. When groups got to his office, he liked to pull out of a cabinet two pine boards bowed like cowboy legs.

"These were straight when they were cut—then they bent," he'd say. "We had to find out why."

Across the room was an exhibition of southern pine mounted on the wall. "This shows what we learned. When this tree was young there weren't many others around it to shut out the sun and it grew fast—see these rings?" he'd point out. "Later on, other trees grew up around it; it had more shade so it grew slower—the outer rings testify to that.

"The resulting uneven quality of the wood resulted in the bowing, so now we can advise keeping southern pine forests more dense while the trees are young so they won't grow so fast."

But inevitably he would be asked by someone in a tour group about the Hauptmann case. It was both his and the Forest Product Laboratory's claim to fame among the general public.

After reading an article in the local paper saying that Governor Hoffman was doling out reward money to those who helped lead to the conviction of Hauptmann, Koehler asked whether he was entitled to a share. Even if he had been on better terms with Hoffman, who had all but called him a liar in the attic before the execution, he wouldn't have received any money, as government workers were prohibited from accepting that kind of payment.

The public's fascination with the kidnapping and the trial never faded, as books about the case came out and anniversaries of the kidnapping and trial passed. Koehler's work on the evidence continued to be praised by Hauptmann's own legal team.

Egbert Rosecrans, one of Hauptmann's lawyers, wrote down his thoughts on the trial after Hauptmann was executed and was effusive in his praise of Koehler: "Since not one person in thousands knew of the existence of one Arthur Koehler, wood technologist, it never occurred to Hauptmann that the wood in the ladder would be traced to the very lumber yard from which he bought it; nor that the now famous 'rail 16' would be proven conclusively once to have been part of a board from his attic."

Edward J. Reilly discussed Koehler with Edward D. Radin for his book *12 Against Crime,* published in 1950. "We would have won an acquittal if it hadn't been for that guy, Koehler," he said. "What a witness to ring in on us—somebody they plucked out of a forest. Do you know what he is? He's a, a xylotomist." Radin said Reilly sputtered indignantly at that last point, "almost making the word sound obscene."

As early as 1942, Koehler was discussing retirement; the six-day work weeks and a restriction on vacations during World War II taking their toll.

"My hobby still is to make things," he told a colleague at the lab. "I have a well-equipped workshop in my basement with power saws, planers, drill, etc., but unfortunately I have little time to use them." He had recently bought a book entitled *The Art of Leisure*, but as he told his brothers, "so far I have not had time to see what it is about."

He had done solid work during the war, applying his science to helping the armed forces best use their wood. His efforts led to stronger aircraft and ships, from gunstocks to textile shuttles, and to helping create artificial limbs for disabled soldiers. Another primary focus of his work during that time was determining how to preserve forests as the nation's supply of virgin timber decreased. Specifically, he studied how young trees could be grown to produce defect-free lumber needed for the future of the country.

Still, he wasn't sure how long the government wanted him to stay around. "Unless the Forest Service changes its mind, they are going to be very hard boild [sic] about letting employees stay on after they are 62 years old—partly to promote efficiency and partly to give the young ones a chance to work up faster," he wrote to his brothers in June 1943. "The law is that if a person wants to, he can stay on till he is 70 years of age provided he is not letting down in efficiency. That means I may have to quit in four years from now. By then I will be eligible for retirement on half salary (if they do not change it by then), and I think I won't mind."

He had identified California as the ideal place he and Ethelyn would spend their retirement years. His brother Alfred lived in Santa Barbara and loved it. As early as the late 1920s, Arthur was pining to live in California, writing to his brothers and parents in 1929 that he loved Berkeley as well. He reminisced fondly about Monterrey, where one could find the Monterey cypress and Monterey pine, and about a spot between Los Angeles and San Diego, the only place in the world where Torrey pines grow.

But instead of settling in any of those locations, in 1946 the Koehlers bought a five-bedroom home in central Los Angeles with a view to the west. They rented it out until Arthur was able to retire. "Los Angeles," he said in the news release announcing his departure from the lab, "has become an important center for the importation of woods from South America and the Orient. Most of these woods have never been tested and studied the way native United States species have at the Forest Products Laboratory and elsewhere. Consequently, there are lots of questions being raised about what they can be used for, what their properties are, and in fact what kind of wood they really are."

He would work through the war and set his retirement date for June 30, 1948. "In a way I am glad because I hope the strenuous life will be over (After we get settled in LA)," he wrote to his brothers and their families on March 14 of that year. "Of late I haven't had quite the gumption that I used to have. It may be partly due to anticipating retirement and partly to the fact that I have had no prolonged vacation for a number of years."

He had spent thirty-seven years with the Forest Products Laboratory, the last twenty-five in charge of the Division of Silvicultural Relations. At sixty-three, he was ready to head west.

His retirement would generate a three-page news release from the Forest Service, stating in part, "A little grayer—and possibly a little balder, too—than that day in February 1935, when his testimony in the Hauptmann trial catapulted him into the newspaper headlines, he is no less crisp and to the point about anything he does."

It was picked up in newspapers like the *Chicago Tribune*. Under the headline "Wood Expert Quits U.S. Post; Testified in Lindbergh Case," the publication described him as a "key witness" in the 1935 trial of Bruno Richard Hauptmann.

His peers were saddened at his decision to leave, pointing out that he remained in his prime.

"As the date of your retirement approaches, I become more and more impressed with the fact that the Laboratory will sustain a great loss in your departure," wrote George Hunt, who had taken over for Carlisle Winslow as the head of the lab in 1946. "You will gain freedom from the daily grind and the opportunity to see new country, new faces, and new tasks. We must carry on the old job without you. I think you have the better end of the bargain." He continued his praises,

> I have consistently preached that the Forest Products Laboratory is a living organism and no one or dozen of the staff is indispensable. No matter who dies, resigns or retires, the Laboratory goes right on. This is true, but not the whole story by any means. When we lose a man like yourself, who has carried important responsibilities for a long period of years and has been our leader in an important field of work, it will take us a long time to recover from the operation. To be sure, we will go right along, but anyone watching will be able to notice a distinct limp in our gait. It will be a long time, Arthur, before we cease to miss you.

He and Ethelyn arrived later that summer in Los Angeles. Their son, George, went with them to attend college. Arthur worked as a consultant to manufacturers, builders, and lumbermen, continuing to testify in a number of cases that required expert testimony about wood.

But Ethelyn was unable to enjoy the retirement they'd planned for years. Within seven months of their move to California, her health began to fail with Hodgkin's disease. She would be bedridden in the fall of 1949 and pass away in February 1950.

"It certainly is a sad situation," Koehler wrote to his brothers. "Here we were all ready to enjoy life together. There were many things that we planned to do, but fate decreed otherwise."

That summer, George would marry Margie Rennebohm, his high school sweetheart, and the three would live together in Arthur's home. By the following spring, Koehler had proposed to Margie's mother, Win, a widow who taught home economics at the high school level, and they would be married in the summer of 1951.

Arthur taught night classes in wood structure and properties at the University of California at Los Angeles before taking a temporary appointment at Yale University, in its School of Forestry,

After retiring from the Forest Products Laboratory, Koehler taught at UCLA, Yale University, and the University of British Columbia before settling down for good in Los Angeles. He continued to enjoy spending time outside, including feeding peanuts to the scrub jays who would visit his backyard. (Courtesy: George E. Koehler)

from 1951 to 1953. That school issued a four-page news release on the twentieth anniversary of the Lindbergh case promoting its newest faculty member.

"Koehler . . . is the famous wood technologist whose testimony about the kidnap ladder was so damaging to Hauptmann's defense case," the school news bureau wrote. "The Lindbergh trial popularized wood technology for crime detection—another in science's long list of contributions to police work. Two bullets can be checked under a microscope to determine if both were fired from the same gun. Tiny irregularities, not visible to the naked eye, will link a type written letter with the machine used. Koehler likes to compare his wood identification methods with these exact techniques."

After Yale, Arthur and Win returned to Los Angeles, buying a new, smaller home on the west side of Los Angeles, near the Westwood campus of UCLA. They bought one of the earliest "pop-up" camping trailers and traveled throughout the west to places like Yosemite, Big Sur, Yellowstone, and Seattle.

His desire to see more of the world led him to serve on the faculty at the University of British Columbia in Vancouver for one school year and where, his relatives were stunned to learn, he took dance lessons to prepare for the holiday parties held by the school.

The couple returned to Los Angeles for good in 1957. Over the next four years, they would volunteer at their church and take fifteen separate trips, to Colorado and other places throughout the West. Sunday dinner was spent with George's family, laughing with grandkids.

The Hauptmann trial would never be far from his thoughts. Shortly after its conclusion, he had built a miniature to-scale replica of the ladder and put together a presentation about the wood evidence, initially using lantern slides before converting to 35mm slides. He gave speeches on his role in the case as late as 1963, thirty years after he first examined the ladder.

"The Lindbergh case became part of his identity," his son, George, said, "but I never heard him promote this in an unseemly way. He was basically a private man, quiet, conscientious, exacting and scientific to a fault."

Now in his seventies, Arthur Koehler was slowing down. He had suffered a minor stroke in 1962, and by the summer of the following year, he was confined to bed for most of the day. That winter, he had a major stroke.

He spent his final years being cared for by Win and home nurses in attendance all day long. He still enjoyed spending time in his backyard looking at the flowers and giving peanuts to the scrub jays who'd visit.

Arthur Koehler died at home on July 16, 1967. He was eighty-two.

Upon his passing, every newspaper that wrote an obituary about Koehler—and there were many, including *The New York Times* and the *Los Angeles Times*—mentioned the Hauptmann trial in its opening sentence. Further, many of those articles described him as "the greatest scientist detective of modern times."

He could also have been called the father of forensic botany.

As his brother Walter wrote after his death, "Now his work is done, but his influence will be felt for a long, long time."

Epilogue

In 2011, the film *J. Edgar*, directed by Clint Eastwood and starring Leonardo DiCaprio in the title role as the legendary head of the FBI, debuted at a film festival in front of Hollywood's elite. The biopic focused on J. Edgar Hoover's career at America's most famous law enforcement agency and featured a segment on the FBI's role in the Lindbergh kidnapping and subsequent conviction of Bruno Hauptmann.

The cast included Academy Award winner Judi Dench and other prominent actors like Armie Hammer, Naomi Watts, and Josh Lucas. *Variety* reported that noteworthy character actor Stephen Root joined the cast to play Arthur Koehler, "an introverted man and wood specialist who helps J. Edgar Hoover piece together the mystery of the Lindbergh kidnapping case through an examination of the ladder used by the abductor."

The film should have been the cementing of Koehler's legacy. Except that it pronounced his name wrong, calling him Kohler, like the well-known kitchen and bath company, not Koehler (KAY-lurr). The movie character also never worked with Hoover or the FBI.

These errors were a dramatic difference from Koehler's status eighty years earlier, when his work riveted the nation. In fact, the Madison scientist had been mentioned in 2,653 articles in 284 newspapers in 40 states, according to the clipping service employed by the Forest Products Laboratory.

Just after the trial he was even featured in a fifteen-minute nationwide conversation that aired before NBC Radio's wildly popular *Let's Dance* program featuring the Benny Goodman

Orchestra and sponsored by the National Biscuit Company and its new product, Ritz Crackers.

At the time, Koehler's legacy seemed secure, but after Hauptmann was executed, dozens of books have come out about the crime, investigation, and trial, some criticizing Koehler, his methods, and his research, others labeling him a pioneer.

Dr. Regis Miller worked in the unit that Koehler ran at the Forest Products Laboratory during the 1960s and then from 1970 to 2005. "I think Koehler did a good job," he recently said. "Several people have looked at his work in detail. To my knowledge all of them concur that his work was based on good scientific reasoning and observation. . . . Today, we have better equipment, but I doubt we have different conclusions."

The elements of Koehler's involvement in the case that are still being debated today include his matching of Rail 16 with S-226 (the attic board), his work identifying Hauptmann's hand planer as the one that planed the ladder rungs and Rail 16, his tracing of Rails 12 and 13 using planer marks, and the testimony and evidence surrounding the ¾-inch chisel found at the kidnap scene.

The first of those is the one that generates the most praise. There are some who believe, as Edward Reilly asserted during his closing arguments at the trial, that S-226 was planted by the police and that the original Rail 16 was discarded. However, scientists studying the board and even those who believe the investigation and trial were fraught with errors agree that the matching of the two was Koehler's strongest work.

"His methods cannot be criticized," said Dr. Shirley Graham, who is a curator at the Missouri Botanical Gardens and who wrote a study on Koehler's work. "They were the highest scientific standards of the day. . . . He employed common sense and an ability to clarify what could have been confusing to the jury in demonstrating and explaining how one piece of wood differs from another so specifically. This piece of information alone unquestionably linked the floorboard in Hauptmann's attic to the ladder."

Dr. Lloyd Gardner, a professor at Rutgers University and the author of the most comprehensive and objective look at the case and trial, *The Case That Never Dies*, said that Koehler's "identification of the wood in the attic looks awfully good today. I am not sure if anyone could successfully challenge it."

That's what Kelvin Keraga, a senior project manager for the New York State Energy Research and Development Authority, sought to do a few years ago. He had read Scott Berg's Pulitzer Prize–winning biography, *Lindbergh*, and "wanted to know more."

He spent three years, with the assistance of wood scientists, lumber professionals, and historians, trying to figure out if Koehler's Rail 16 evidence was groundbreaking or inept. His report, *Testimony in Wood*, was featured on the television program *Forensic Files*.

Keraga's conclusion was that "trees are complex life forms, consisting of many specific characteristics. The carpentry processes used in transforming trees into boards add further individual characteristics. The intricate combination of all of these qualities in Rail 16, S-226, and the other attic boards precludes any possibility of a faked relationship, and demonstrates irrefutable evidence that Rail 16 was indeed part of Bruno Richard Hauptmann's attic floor prior to the kidnapping."

Michael Melsky, who works for the US Department of Justice as a prison counselor, is one of the world's foremost experts on the case. He is also one of the leading critics of the New Jersey State Police's investigation and Attorney General Wilentz's handling of the case and runs a website called the Lindbergh Kidnapping Discussion Board. He gives Koehler mixed reviews.

"When Pope said in court there 'was no such animal' as a 'Wood Expert. . .' [i]t could be said after the trial, there now WAS such an animal," Melsky wrote. "Koehler really worked his butt off and the skill required in order to do what he did was extraordinary. If he had just stayed within the boundaries of those investigations I believe anything he concluded would never have been challenged."

Koehler was an expert in wood identification, in matching wood through species and grain identification. The biggest criticism of Koehler surrounds his work in the investigation and testimony in the trial connected to tool mark identification.

Kevin Klein is a carpenter and an avid student of the case who constructed an exact replica of the ladder found at the Hopewell estate on March 1, 1932, for the PBS program *Nova*. His issues with Koehler concern the scientist's tracing of Rails 12 and 13 through planer marks.

"I believe [Koehler] furthered the science of criminal forensic investigation," he said. But he cautioned,

> By today's standards, however, Koehler would be called out for his lack of training and experience in forensic tool mark identification. His testimony, if admissible, would probably have been negated by a true tool mark examiner. Not that his conclusions were unfounded, he just overstated them.
>
> For example, how many variables are involved in producing a given planer mark on wood? What are the odds of a match given those variables? The honest answer in court and the one a tool mark examiner will give is that the marks are consistent since there really is no way to determine whether any other cutting tool in the world would match. Basically, the difference between 1935 and now, is that an expert on tool marks would generally agree with Koehler, but not his certainty.

The testimony surrounding the ¾-inch chisel found the night of the crime concerns both Gardner and Melsky. Koehler said in his original report that there was no way to determine what size chisel was used in the construction of the ladder, but he later testified that Hauptmann was missing a ¾-inch chisel from his tool set, intimating that they had to be one and the same.

"What is disturbing the most," Gardner wrote, "is the game he played at the trial when Wilentz asked him to walk by the jury box with the chisel after he had originally reported to the State Police that one could not tell what size chisel had been used."

In his book, Gardner said Koehler and Wilentz "had teamed up in a performance worthy of Blackstone the Magician—the most famous conjurer of the day." He stated that the chisel hyperbole does not indicate "he was wrong about the attic board. There are credibility issues here, nevertheless."

Keraga said there are two possible explanations for why his view changed on the identification of the chisel: either he simply missed it in his original examination, or he created the tool mark himself. He believes there is simply no evidence to suggest Koehler was deceptive, and the change of opinion was a simple error when he first studied the ladder.

Melsky took this a step further and said Koehler lied on the stand. The police report and Koehler's own report show that a ¾-inch cold chisel was found in the carpenter's chest. Melsky believes it was removed before the trial so as not to "confuse" the jury. Granted, it was not a wood chisel, but Melsky said, "Koehler was fully aware of what was found and where, so he's obviously completely on board with what's going on."

Melsky also challenged the evidence surrounding the tracking of Rails 12 and 13, stating that Koehler never found the exact match of planer marks in the samples from Dorn's lumberyard. He found the distinctive marks on the ladder rails and on a sample at the National Millwork and Lumber Company, but that sample also had another planer defect that did not show up on the ladder rails.

Finally, Koehler has been criticized often for asking for part of the reward. As a public servant, he wasn't supposed to put in for it, Gardner said.

Doing so "tarnished his efforts and plays into the hands of those who believe the police framed everything and that Hauptmann was completely innocent," said Melsky.

Koehler did not believe Hauptmann was innocent. But he remained circumspect until his death about whether he thought anyone else was involved. Either way, he felt confident he had done his part to advance the relationship between science and crime detection.

As he said in that February 1935 NBC Radio interview, "in all the years of my work, I have been consumed with the absolute reliability of the testimony of trees. They carry in themselves the record of their history. They show with absolute fidelity the progress of the years, storms, drought, floods, injuries and any human touch. A tree never lies. You cannot fake or make a tree."

Today few would dispute that assertion.

"He opened doors for a lot of forensic experts to come, not by telling them what to do, but by demonstrating how to figure out what to do with a strong knowledge base, with an inventive but objective mindset, and with hard work and discipline," Keraga said.

Interestingly, even with the advent and popularity of television programs like *CSI* and *NCIS* and others featuring scientist-detectives, scientists like Dr. Graham at the Missouri Botanical Gardens worry about whether there are future Arthur Koehlers being trained. She explained, "Today, very descriptive fields in plant science such as plant anatomy, morphology and taxonomy have taken a backseat to newer disciplines based on molecular information and increasingly on more sophisticated computer-based statistical programs of assessing data." Graham continued,

These data are not infrequently derived from studies of the past two centuries because insufficient numbers of new scientists are being [trained] in these descriptive fields. There is inadequate support in the universities for "classic" training and few positions available even after extensive postgraduate studies. I can think, for example, of very few practicing plant anatomists in this country today.

The legacy of Koehler's work is that there are still important roles for studies that generate the original data. To name a few, in fields of forensic science, or as data that demonstrates at an organismal level changes in climate through time, or for describing the still unknown plant species of the planet, or for working out the phylogeny of living organisms—the history of the various lineages of life forms.

Koehler's legacy was to show how basic descriptive science still has modern value and important applications.

Koehler himself believed he understood his impact and the impact of other scientists like him. He helped craft a paper called *Wood as Circumstantial Evidence* after the trial that addressed what he believed to be the nexus of science and detective work. In it, he wrote,

Surely the services of the chemist, the metallurgist, the wood technologist, the textile expert and other scientific specialties that our modern age has developed are needed in the fight on modern crime, in order to establish or complete the evidence and to extract the last shred of information from clues that every case affords.

It is true that evidence of a scientific and technical nature is apt to be of the kind called circumstantial. But circumstantial evidence—enough of it and of the proper kind—tends to become overwhelming. It tips the burden of disproof more and more heavily against the accused, until any possible story in reply short of a complete confession becomes fantastic. And a fair jury having ordinary reasoning faculties can be brought to see the point.

Not surprisingly, in retirement Koehler consulted with the producers of *Perry Mason* on a couple of their storylines. His popularization of forensic science continues to be emulated today in television programs like *CSI*, *Law and Order*, and *NCIS*.

It's a compelling legacy for the father of forensic botany, even if Hollywood does not know how to pronounce his name correctly.

Endnotes

Numerous authors have come before me in writing about the Lindbergh kidnapping and subsequent Hauptmann trial, but until now no one has had access to the hundreds of letters written by Arthur Koehler during the time he was involved in the case. They are currently maintained by his family and are not publicly available to researchers.

Many of the letters I have quoted in the book will eventually be kept in a file at the New Jersey State Police Museum, but the originals remain with the Koehler family. I have cited quotes from those letters and from publications within the text.

George Koehler has written about his family's history, and those publications were invaluable to me. *Two Cents Unaccounted For* (George E. Koehler, 1989) is a detailed look at Arthur Koehler's financial ledgers from 1900 to 1963; the original ledgers remain in George Koehler's possession. *The "Flying Dutchman" and other Family Letters of Arthur Koehler: Excerpts 1915-1963* (George E. Koehler, 2nd Edition, 1994) chronicles the letters Koehler wrote to his brothers and parents. The originals also remain in the family's possession.

The Koehler family history is chronicled in *Our Koehler Ancestry* (George E. Koehler, 2006), the only one of George E. Koehler's three books that is available to the public. It is in the holdings of the Wisconsin Historical Society Library and Archives.

Arthur Koehler was a prolific writer himself, exhaustively detailing his efforts on the investigation. A full copy of his official reports resides at both the Forest Products Laboratory Library in Madison and at the New Jersey State Police Museum. He also wrote twenty-nine pages detailing how he thought his testimony should go in court. That report and the actual court record of his testimony are found at the State Police Museum.

In addition, Koehler wrote many papers about his efforts that can be found at both locations. These include *Wood as Circumstantial Evidence* with T. J. Mosley, *History of Tracing North Carolina Pine in Rails 12 and 13*, *Some Unexpected Applications of Science in the Lindbergh Kidnap Case*, *Technique Used in Tracing the Lindbergh Kidnapping Ladder*, and *The Lumber, The Ladder and The Laboratory*. He also told his story to *The Saturday Evening Post* for a seven-page article in the April 20, 1935, issue.

Thousands of articles were written about Koehler's efforts in relation to the Lindbergh kidnapping and other facets of his work. I found the following ones most helpful: *Wood Technology and the Lindbergh Kidnap Case* (Forest Products Lab, 1971) by Donna Christensen; *Wood's Case Against Hauptmann* (*American Forests*, May 1935); *Arthur Koehler: Scientist-Investigator* (*Police*, September-October 1935) by Arthur S. Aubry Jr.; *As Wood Gave Witness* (*Wooden Barrel*, May 7, 1935) by Frederick A. Strenge; *Round the World with a Lens* (*Pen*, February 1947) by Alice Spencer Cook; *What Kind of Wood Is It?* (*Illustrated World*, February 1923) by Bartel B. Borchers; *CSI: Madison, Wooden Witness* (*Forest History Today*, Spring/Fall 2010) by Amanda Ross and *Wood Detective Solves 3000 Mysteries a Year* (*Popular Mechanics*, March 1937).

The transcript of Koehler's NBC Radio interview, *The Science of Wood Identification*, on February 16, 1935, also proved helpful. More information about the Forest Products Laboratory can be found in *Forest Products Laboratory, 1910-2010: Celebrating a Century of Accomplishments* (University of Wisconsin Press, 2010) compiled by John Koning.

Three books helped me understand much about the New Jersey State Police at the time of the case, and all three were written by the New Jersey State Police Museum archivist, Mark Falzini. His publication *Their Fifteen Minutes* (iUniverse, 2008) is a terrific guide to the characters involved in the case, from the troopers to many of the witnesses, and more. He subsequently published two pamphlets, *Trooper Togs: A History of the New Jersey State Police*

Uniform (2010) and *Headquarters: A Brief History of the Land and Buildings of the New Jersey State Police in West Trenton* (2011), both of which helped me set the scene where Arthur Koehler worked while in New Jersey.

The seminal work on Charles A. Lindbergh is the Pulitzer Prize-winning biography *Lindbergh* (Berkley, 1998), by A. Scott Berg. Delos A. Dudley's personal recollections, *My Lindbergh Papers: Personal Memories of a National Hero* (Delos A. Dudley, 1991), provided terrific information about Lindbergh's time at the University of Wisconsin-Madison. Anne Vandenburgh's *Lindbergh's Badger Days* (Goblin Fern Press, 2003) was also helpful.

The most comprehensive look at the kidnapping was written by Rutgers University Professor Dr. Lloyd C. Gardner, *The Case That Never Dies* (Rutgers University Press, 2004).

Other books about the case that provided additional background material included: *The Ghosts of Hopewell* (Southern Illinois University Press, 1999) by Jim Fisher; *Top Secret: FBI Files on the Lindbergh Baby Kidnapping* (New Century Books, 2001), edited by Thomas Fensch; *Kidnap* (Dial Press, 1961) by George Waller; *Scapegoat: The Lonesome Death of Bruno Richard Hauptmann* (Putnam, 1976) by Anthony Scaduto; *Lindbergh: The Crime* (Atlantic Monthly Press, 1994) by Noel Behn; *Hysteria* (Dorrance, 1975) by Andrew K. Dutch; *True Story of the Lindbergh Kidnapping* (Kroy Wen, 1932) by John Brant and Edith Renaud; *The Lindbergh Crime* (Blue Ribbon Books, 1935) by Sidney Whipple; *Science Versus Crime* (Bobbs-Merrill, 1935) by Henry Morton Robinson; *The Airman and the Carpenter: The Lindbergh Kidnapping and the Framing of Richard Hauptmann* (Viking, 1985) by Ludovic Kennedy; and *12 Against Crime* (Putnam, 1950) by Edward D. Radin.

I consulted Jimmy Breslin's *Damon Runyon: A Life* (Random House, 1991) for information about the famous journalist. Marv Balousek's *50 Wisconsin Crimes of the Century* (Badger Books, 1989) helped in researching the Wood County bombing case that provided Arthur Koehler with his first opportunity to testify in a criminal trial.

The Missouri History Museum Library and Research Center in St. Louis houses papers from J. J. Dorn. I accumulated more information about the former South Carolina businessman from the application to place his home on the National Register of Historic Places.

I better understood the science related to the case after reading two pieces of work: Kelvin Keraga's 2005 study of Koehler's work, *Testimony in Wood*, which was profiled on the television show *Forensic Files*; and Dr. Shirley A. Graham's *Anatomy of the Lindbergh Kidnapping*, a botanical look at Koehler's efforts first published in the *Journal of Forensic Science* in May 1997.

I gleaned overall wood knowledge from many of Koehler's trade papers, but his book *The Properties and Uses of Wood* (McGraw-Hill, 1924) was most helpful.

Research about what happened in the courtroom was aided by dozens of daily newspaper reports from 1935 and then by memories gathered by *The Princeton Recollector* in the spring of 1977. *Some Object Lessons on Publicity in Criminal Trials* is the famous report about what happened in the courtroom. It was written by Minnesota Supreme Court Justice Oscar Hallam in March 1940 for the American Bar Association and led to the banning of cameras from many courtrooms still today. Information about Ed Reilly was aided by *Owls Shouldn't Claw at Eagles* (*New York State Bar Association Journal*, June 2005) by William H. Manz.

Index

kidnapping of son and, 40, 58, 59
marriage to Charles, 39
pregnancy of, with second child, 40
as prosecution witness, 198
Lindbergh, Charles A., 313
as barnstormer, 33–34
Bruno, Harry, as press secretary of, 122
building of ice boat by, 32
college studies of, at Wisconsin, University of, Madison, 29, 30, 32
engagement to Morrow, Anne, 37, 39
enlistment in army, 34
fame of, xii, xiv, 36–37
Finn as member of security detail of, 122
flight of, across Atlantic Ocean, xii, xiv, 34–35
flying instruction for, 32–33, 34
friendship with Dudley, Delos, 29–30, 32, 33, 34
friendship with Plummer, Dick, 30
grand jury testimony of, 167
Harley-Davidson ride and, 30, 32
hiring of by Robertson Aircraft Corporation, 34
Hoffman's efforts to reopen case and, 274
honorary degree for, 37, *38*
interests of, in flying, *31*, 32–35
Koehler, Arthur, and, 37, 202
landing of, in Paris, 35–36
Madison apartment of, 29–30, 33

as marksman, 32
marriage to Morrow, Anne, 39
promotion of commercial aviation and, 36–37
return to U.S., 36
Sourland Mountain home of, 42
testimony of, 189–190, 214, 289
Lindbergh, Charles A., Jr.
birth of, 39
cause of death, 53, 74
finding of body, 52–53
kidnapping of, vii, xii, 39–40
murder of, 164, 166, 168
return of sleeping suit of, 52
Lindbergh, Evangeline, 34
move to Detroit, 33
move to Madison with son, 29
as teacher, 29, 33
Lindbergh house, 42
checking out of Gate house and Chicken house, 75
inspection of woodwork in, 74–75
use of Ponderosa pine in, 75–76
Lindbergh kidnapping
arrest of suspect, xii, 139, 140, 145, 146
circumstantial evidence in, xiv
crank letters as problem in, 47
familiarity of kidnapper with crime scene, 74
finding of thumb guard, 52
Finn in investigation of, 121–122
involvement of federal government in, 53
lack of evidence in, xiv, 40
Lamb, J. J. responsibility for, 64, 66

mother's handling of, 40, 58, 59
New Jersey State Police investigation of, 42–43
news of, for March, Iva, 58
nursery window in, *50*
offering of reward, 53
passage of Federal Kidnapping Act, 43
personnel assigned to, 61
physical evidence in, 43–44
public in punishing of suspect, 58–59
questioning of servants in, 44
ransom notes in, 40, 44, 52
thought on, as inside job, 42
tracing ransom money in, xii, 52, 123–131
wanted poster in, *45*
Lindbergh ladder
breaking of, during kidnapping, 43, 66
chain of custody for, 193
entrance of, into evidence at trial, 191–193
as homemade, xv, 47, 49, 66, 67, 73
poor quality of, 66–67, 68, 160
tracing of, to National Lumber and Millwork Corp, 146–147
use of, in kidnapping, 43–44
use of style of, 55–56
width of, 66
Lindbergh ladder investigation, 43
blade defect in, 111
chip marks in, 111
chisels in, 66, 73–74, 161, 182
clues in, *88*
cost of examining, 62
coverage of costs, 77, 79
cutter heads in, 87, 89

133, 153, 159, 183, 222, 233, 242, 244, 253
Nova, 306

O

Olney & Warren (NYC), Lindbergh investigation visit to, 76
O'Neill, Mrs. John, ransom money and, 127
Osborn, Albert S., as handwriting expert, 149
O'Sullivan, John J., on arrest of Hauptmann, 146
Oursler, Fulton, reopening of Hauptmann case and, 278, 280–282, 285
Oxholm, Axel H., 264

P

Padon, H. C., Koehler and Bornmann's visit with at the Yates-American Machine Company, 77
The Painted Pig, 39
Palace Café, ransom money and, 124
Park, Byron B., 4
Parker, Abram, 186
Paterson, J. E., Lumber Company (Mobile, AL), Lindbergh ladder investigation and, 92
Peacock, Robert, as Wilentz's assistant, 205
Pedrick, Mame, 177
Pegram, George, 286
Penn Station, ransom money and, 127
Pennsylvania and Reading Railroads, 82
Pennsylvania Lumbermen's Association, involvement of, in investigation, 77–78
People's Bank of McCormick, 99
Perkins, H. A., in ladder investigation, 95
Perrone, John, identification of Hauptmann by, 146

Perry Mason, 309
Pershing, John, in World War I, 84, 85
Pickering, Samuel F., as expert in chemical analysis, 142
Picric acid, in making pipe bomb, 2
Pill, Rosie, as member of jury, 195, 198, 229
Pinchot, Gifford, as U.S. Forest Service Chief, 17–18
Pipe bomb, picric acid in making, 2
Plummer, Dick, friendship with Lindbergh, 30
Ponderosa pine, 55, 72, 74, 75, 76, 82, 135–136, 153, 181, 222, 223, 225, 226, 234, 238
Pope, Frederick
    as assistant counsel for Hauptmann, 192, 206, 305
    cross examination and objections by, 205, 206–207, 211, 214–215, 219, 220, 222, 225–227, 243–246
    praise for Koehler, 252
Porter, B. A., 266
Production Machinery Sales Company (NYC), in Lindbergh ladder investigation, 76, 95
The Properties and Uses of Wood (Koehler), xi–xii, 20, 207
Pupin, Michael, Physics Laboratories, 285–286, *287*

Q

Queens County Lumber Company, Lindbergh ladder investigation and, 114, 115, 120

R

Radin, Edward D., 295–296

Ransom money
    Cemetery John and, 125
    delivery of, xiv, 190
    license plate number on, 130, 134–135
    location of, in Hauptmann garage, 144, 199
    recovery of, xii, 143–144, 151–152
    searching house for, 155
    serial numbers of bills in, 123–124
    spending of, 124–131
    tracking of, 123–131
Ransom notes, 40, 44, 52
    writing on, 199, 289
Rauch, Max
    reinterview of, 181
    testimony of, 200
Record, Samuel, 265
Reeve, Arthur B., 238
Reilly, Edward J., 210
    as defense attorney for Hauptmann, 179–181, 188–190, 250, 258–259, 295–296
    Koehler's testimony and, 236, 250
    on planted evidence, 270–271, 304
    reputation and nickname of, 180
    request for mistrial, 188
    verdict and, 260
Reilly, Peter, ransom money and, 124–125
Reilly, William J., Lindberg kidnapping investigation and, 134–135
Riemer, Svend, 178–179
Ritter, Mrs. George, 58
Roaring Rocks, 42
Robinson, George N., as grand jury foreman, 168
Rogers, Will, 35
    on fate of kidnapper, 59
Roosevelt, Franklin D., 264
    economic policy of, 123
    gold standard and, 123, 127
Roosevelt, Quentin, 35

About the Author

Adam Schrager is an investigative reporter and producer with WISC-TV, the CBS affiliate in Madison, Wisconsin. He has covered politics for more than twenty years, most recently at Wisconsin Public Television and at KUSA-TV in Denver. Previously, he worked at commercial television stations in La Crosse, Madison, and Milwaukee in the 1990s. Schrager is the author of *The Principled Politician*, a biography of former Colorado Governor Ralph Carr, whose stand on behalf of Japanese Americans after Pearl Harbor would cost him his political career. The book led state lawmakers to name the new state justice center after the former Colorado chief executive. His last book, *The Blueprint: How the Democrats Won Colorado (and Why Republicans Everywhere Should Care)*, co-authored with Rob Witwer, has been lauded by *The Wall Street Journal*, *The Washington Post*, and political figures on both sides of the political spectrum.

In his career, Schrager has won numerous journalism accolades, including more than twenty Emmy awards. He taught journalism at the University of Denver and at Marquette University and has conducted dozens of seminars on the impact of the media on politics. Schrager has an undergraduate degree in history from the University of Michigan and a graduate degree in broadcast journalism from Northwestern University.

He and his wife live with their three children in Madison, Wisconsin.